I0603099

Also by Stephen Oliver

Henwise (1975)
& interviews (1978)
Autumn Songs (1978)
Letter To James K. Baxter (1980)
Earthbound Mirrors (1984)
Guardians, Not Angels (1993)
Islands of Wilderness—A Romance (1996)
Unmanned (1999)
Election Year Blues (1999)
Night of Warehouses: Poems 1978-2000 (2001)
Deadly Pollen (2003)
Ballads, Satire & Salt—A Book of Diversions (2003)
Either Side The Horizon (2005)
Parable Of The Sea Sponge (2007)
Harmonic (2008)
Apocrypha (2010)
Intercolonial (2013)
Gone: Satirical Poems: New & Selected (2016)
Luxembourg (2018)
Heroides / 15 Sonnets (2020)
The Song Of Globule / 80 Sonnets (2020)

Recordings

Earthbound Mirrors, a selection, Stephen Oliver,
Ode Records (audio cassette) Auckland, Aotearoa/New Zealand 1984

KING HIT: CD ROM. Stephen Oliver reads a selection of his poetry to original music composed by Matt Ottley. Published and released through IP Digital, an imprint of IP (Interactive Publications) Brisbane, Australia 2007

UNPOSTED, AUTUMN LEAVES

A Memoir In Essays

Stephen Oliver

Introduction by Nicholas Birns

GP
GREYWACKE PRESS
Lat. 25°/50° South. Long. 145°/180° East

First published 2021

Greywacke Press
9 Lynch St
Hughes
ACT 2605
Australia
reid1801@bigpond.com
greywackepress@gmail.com

Oliver, Stephen 1950-
Title: *Unposted, Autumn Leaves: A Memoir In Essays*
ISBN 978-0-646-83311-8

Typesetting by John Denny, Puriri Press, Auckland
Cover design composed by Stephen Oliver
Cover photo: Petra Paignton: Tikitiki Road, Piopio, Waikato, NZ, March 15 2016

A catalogue record for this book is available from the National Library of Australia

Acknowledgements

Various essays under the banner of creative nonfiction first appeared in the following publications in a variant form and under these headings:

'An Analogue Fantasy' (revised), first published under the title: 'Seven Second Delay', *Landfall 152* (NZ) December 1984; 'Unfreedoms Of Expression' (revised version), *Antipodes: A Global Journal of Australian/New Zealand Literature*, (USA/Australia), December 2003; 'Dirty Bomb Poetic' under its original title 'The Poet As Fraud: A Composite' (revised version), *Antipodes*, June 2005; 'Voice Over: The Vocal Art Of Subterfuge' (revised version), *Antipodes*, December 2006; 'One Day In The Life of Vicki Viidikas', *Thylazine* (No. 5) March 2002; (revised version), *Antipodes*, June 2008; 'Chalk, Talk And Asphalt Days' [excerpt], *JAAM 15* (NZ) May 2001; (revised version), *Antipodes*, December 2009; 'A Big Fruity Guy', *Antipodes*, December 2011; 'A Nostalgia For Books', *Landfall 223* (NZ) 2012; 'A Small Matter Of Demolition', *Antipodes*, June 2014; 'O Brother Where Art Thou', *Asian Journal of Literature, Culture and Society* (Assumption University of Thailand, Bangkok), Vol. 8 No 2 October 2014; 'Gnosis, A Spark', *Antipodes*, December 2015; 'The Great University Break-In', *Phantom Billstickers Café Reader*, Vol. 9 Autumn 2016 (NZ); 'One Day In The Life Of Richard Ramos' [excerpt], *SoMa Literary Review* (San Francisco), June 2002 (revised version), *Antipodes*, Vol. 1.2, June-December 2018; 'Song Of The Immigrant', first published under the title 'Contempt: A Survey', section IV, *Deep South*, The English Department Ezine, Otago University, January 2002 (revised version), *Antipodes*, Vol. 1.2, June-December 2018.

Poems included here by the author are taken from previous collections as noted in the text, with the exception of 'Fig Tree'. The poem, 'An Alchemical Woman', an early example of inspired juvenilia, first appeared in the pamphlet, *Chance To Laugh*, Stephen Oliver, Superstar Productions Ltd, Wellington (copyright 1972), published 1971.

Patrick McCormack (since deceased), of Mornington, Dunedin, dug out a number of essays from the *NZ Tablet* archives, where he worked for many years as proof reader before the Catholic weekly folded. These essays, originally published in the 1890s/1920s, were written by my great-grandfather, Thomas McCormack [1841-1923], long-time resident of Dunedin and public figure of some standing in the civic affairs of that southern harbour town, from the closing decades of the 19th century and through into the early 1920s.

I am grateful to Tom Ryan SM who attended Marist Brothers, Tasman Street (1950-1953) and St. Patrick's College, Wellington (1954-1958) for correcting factual inconsistencies in the early essays on my schooling, and for providing statistics on Jonathan Hardy's athletic prowess during his schoolboy years at SPC.

I am especially grateful to Nicholas Birns, professor at New York University, for his generous *Introduction*. He is a leading scholar of Australian literature, and recently retired editor of *Antipodes: A Global Journal of Australian/New Zealand Literature*, the publication of the American Association for Australasian Literary Studies (AAALS).

My especial thanks to Damian McManus, Professor of Early Irish at Trinity College, Dublin, for his helpful advice on my use of Old Irish terminology, particularly as it relates to the ancient bardic system addressed in this book.

I also wish to thank Dr Nicholas Reid of Canberra (ANU) for his tireless support of my work over the years, and for his close editing of *Unposted, Autumn Leaves: A Memoir In Essays* which made the publication of this book possible.

I am particularly grateful to John Denny of Puriri Press, Auckland, publisher of my handset, letterpress chapbook, *Heroides/15 Sonnets* (2020), for his invaluable assistance in the formatting and layout of this book, without whose generosity this memoir would have been unlikely to see the light of day.

My thanks to the staff at the *National Library of New Zealand*, Wellington; the *Hocken Library*, Dunedin; the *Fisher Library*, University of Sydney; the *Mitchell Library*, Sydney, and the *State Libraries of NSW and Victoria*, Australia, where most of the primary research for this book was undertaken.

Contents

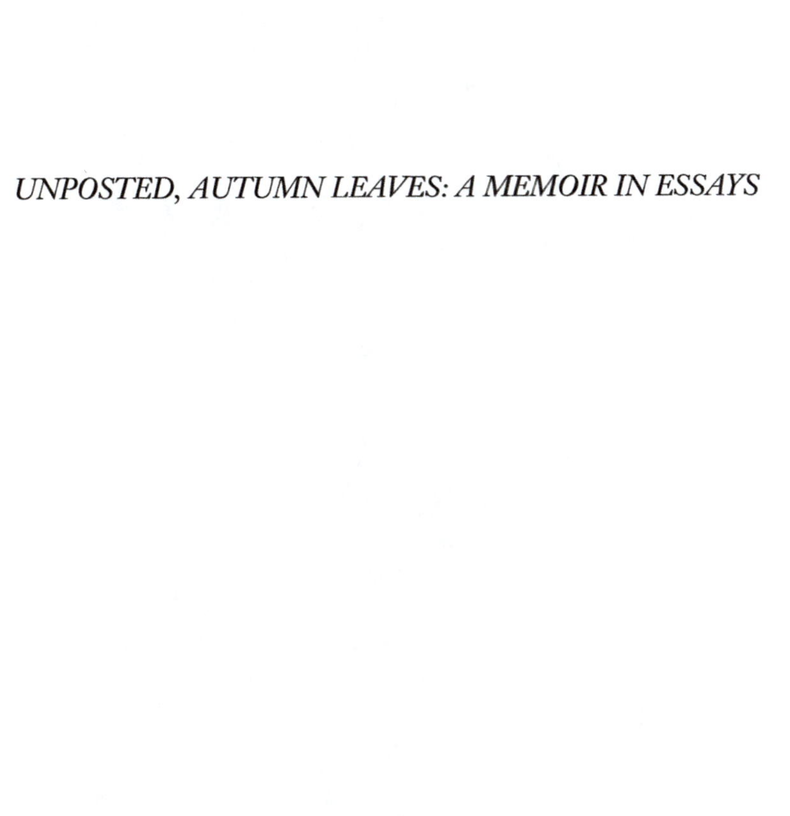

UNPOSTED, AUTUMN LEAVES: A MEMOIR IN ESSAYS

Stephen Oliver's Poetics of Childhood and Cultural Memory
An Introduction by Nicholas Birns

Stephen Oliver writes accessible prose, though haunted by something at once more obdurate more lyrical, and more rebarbative. He maintains an acrid, sardonic attitude towards the literary world, and is sceptical of national literary institutions. He writes autobiographically, but not transparently. He is a creative writer, but takes on much of the territory of nonfiction, whose work is filled with verifiable data and concrete memory. He is working in and for the twenty-first century, but his works are redolent of the tragedies, escapades, and renegade hopes of the twentieth. Stephen Oliver's memoir in essays is in some ways a counterpoint to Oliver's 2013 poetic epic *Intercolonial.* Yet it is a traditional autobiography in the traditional sense. Oliver mixes prose and verse, with the verse serving as illustration and/or commentary on the prose, in ways more reminiscent of Menippean satire. In other words, his work is catalysed by life writing (biography, autobiography, memoir) and its attendant genres but not constrained by them. Oliver, though a provocateur, does not mean to reshape the world. He chronicles his own maverick and innovative life in times that once seemed, despite all resistance, to be bending towards the maverick and innovative, then bent back—and even further back.

New Zealand literature has had a strong tradition of autobiography or autobiographical fiction. This has been represented by writers such as Sylvia Ashton-Warner, Katherine Mansfield, Janet Frame, and Frank Sargeson. These authors have all been dissident, often socially unpresentable or inassimilable personalities. Almost to make up for that marginality, they exuded a sense of intense subjectivity, of voices that insist on their own distinction, and that pour on the page with a sense of life so vivid and full. Stephen Oliver's memoir-in-essays, *Unposted, Autumn Leaves*, records the same sense of strangeness and indelible incisions of the curve of childhood memories towards adulthood. It is written by someone who, though creative and experimental, does not insist on his own uniqueness.

Oliver, while still remaining intensely personal in tone, deflects any core identity to all the specificity of reference in his works. There is specificity of place—Brooklyn-*west* and the crazy-quilt improvised governmental architecture of mid-to-late twentieth century Wellington is depicted with all the aura and atmosphere that so many American writers have found in another, very different Brooklyn—but also specificity of time. We learn of precise dates, we know the who, what, and where of events, in a way not just empirical or nervously pedantic, but which uses specificity as a check upon the ambitions of individual expression, which in any case, have moved beyond any one time or place: 'Beyond this clustered the small shopping strip, presided over by the Post Office opposite Brooklyn Library overlooking the bus terminus, and *Seymour's Bookshop* which finally shut down in 2000—the place must have been running for at least forty-five years, more an emporium stocked with stationary (HB pencils by the gross) and glossy magazines (*NZ Women's Weekly*, *Vogue*, etc), with thousands of 'useful' knick-knacks like white tallow candles, Christmas wrapping paper, and henna powder. The one shop that recalls this Aladdin's Cave remains Melbourne's *Jeffreys Books* in Glenferrie Road, Malvern. From Fawkner's cake shop rich baking odours wafted through the protective wire-mesh door, and I had a particular hankering for the rich cream buns (fourpence each though you *could* get credit), thick cream flecked with raspberry flavouring, crunchy with icing sugar, maybe a hint of sherbet. Jam tarts with a deep buttery biscuit base came in a close second.'

Place is vividly sketched. But it is understood to be open to the ravages of time, which means it both definitely exists yet is always in peril of ceasing to do so. Oliver is a countercultural writer. The Beat and Hippie eras, with their rebellion against conformity, define the aesthetic and vision out of which he works. This book chronicles a childhood in a slowed-down, settler colonial time, which interacts in a zig-zag way with a more general twentieth-century temporality, all the while bearing the marks of emerging from an insecure and provincial society. The earliest pages of this memoir, in revealing a New Zealand Catholic upbringing in the 1950s, show just what the counterculture was rebelling against: a sense of conformity, repression, duty-bound obedience. Yet Oliver reaches back to the past not just with the intensity of memory but the percipience of prophecy: 'This stretch of asphalt, which made up the central, or rather only playground, slightly elevated, fell away at either end. Somehow, as if guided by mysterious sonar, calibrated to precisely take her to the edge of the playground, she would unerringly turn-about in time, an inch from precipitate disaster. We willed her to lose her balance and topple headlong over the edge, but she never did. Sister Berenice was not a creature of the daylight. She was as sour as the bottled milk in alloy crates that was forced upon us by government regulation every day (the welfare state was in its full flowering—was this the realization of Julius Vogel's Utopian dream?) defiantly left out in the morning light long enough to go off. Daylight proved as disastrous to the sister's disposition as it did to the daily milk's freshness.'

Sister Berenice is not just a Catholic school disciplinarian. She is someone who incarnates the authority structures of her era, even if some of them, like that of the welfare state, are secular and left wing. The deft simile in which Sister Berenice's sourness is compared to the alloy crates of government-provided milk puts these two very different authorities into the temporal matrix of late modernity, as an era roughly having its *floruit* in the 1950s and early 1960s, in which people were taken care of, but were also subject to a levelling conformity that amounted to a significant loss of liberty. Oliver's Sonnet

48 in his 2020 volume *The Song of Globule* about the Sirius apartment complex in the Sydney neighbourhood of the Rocks, epitomizes both the late-modern mentality and the twenty-first century desire to erase it:

> Each apartment a tidy concrete box.
> Cosy, bigger than your average fridge—
> 'Demolish it!' I hear councillors yell! [1]

In a form that is only superficially different, Sister Berenice represents a conformist coercion whose only redeeming feature is that it will in some way take care of you, whether it is in terms of hierarchal religion or government regulation. The authority then will not only control, but also provide. This was increasingly experienced as oppressive (why the councillors want to tear down the Sirius apartment in the sonnet), and was so in twentieth-century history, until that century's later decades, when the free market came roaring back, associated with a rhetoric of creative ferment.

Oliver's parenthetical aside about the welfare state as the realization of Sir Julius Vogel's Utopian dream, though partially referring to the nearby suburb of Vogeltown, also opens up the floodgates of time, in that time is like a flood spilling out all kinds of eras willy-nilly. A nineteenth century New Zealand prime minister, who promised railway building and free market economics, Sir Julius Vogel was also a utopian novelist. Oliver's linking of his idealistic Victorian vision to the 20th century welfare state instances a certain disappointment and irony, a sarcastic let down. Yet neither Oliver nor most of his readers would reject the safety of the welfare state, absent in Vogel's day. Oliver portrays his New Zealand Catholic boyhood as oppressive, but in other ways protective. This becomes even more multi-layered as we know the future world of the young boy Oliver retrospectively depicts might with its resurgent economic liberalism, be indeed Vogel's free-market utopia brought back to life as dystopia, a nightmare that might make sour milk seem sweet.

Oliver thus writes about the past both with a sensate and palpable evocation and a sense of layered irony. Although as a poet his sensibilities are out of the sixties, out of what I term the 'very short twentieth century' of rebellion and nonconformity between the old and new hierarchies. Oliver can be lacerating when describing the bad behaviour and posturing of the sixties bard:

HEY BABE!

Anyway, no way
          so I said to Nicole
'Stay!' don't go (for the day)
          oh, what a night
let me take you down to the river
between your thighs
          babe, let my love flow
& do you see stars in your eyes (ha)
                                        still?
          (Yeah) so don't go
help me up by your love handles
          'cause love is in the air
& couscous on the menu
          so I said to Nicole
'Stay!' don't go (for the day)
          oh, what a night
but by then she had split.

This hilarious lyric, with its patchwork of rock song snippets and now-dated slang, portrays a countercultural bloke using bohemian lifestyles, and the then-exoticism of food such as 'couscous', merely as a route for easy sex. It will bring bemused recognition to anyone remotely on the scene at the time, who can all congratulate Nicole on getting out of there. But Oliver, while seeing through all the bad faith of the sixties and seventies, is still living the dream. The parody here would not be successful without the parodist—ironist, pasticheur—retaining a certain bardic lyricism. But Oliver is not patriarchal—as he shows in his willingness to stand up to loutish Camperdown bartenders, and it is here that the figure of Vicki Viidikas—female Beatnik, Australian rebel, and performer of a literary life at once successful and truncated—is so important to this book:

'Vicki Viidikas was just one more victim, a casualty of her generation. She may have knocked repeatedly on that door [Generation of '68] seeking acceptance, but by the time it was grudgingly opened an inch or two (even then in the poetic grand stakes, women were mostly relegated to the role of party objects), she had disappeared back onto the streets.

She was not one of those imitators of the American schools who became the very establishment they sought to change. Unlike many of her literary peers, she was not governed by cold-hearted careerist ambitions, nor by cowardice of spirit. Unlike many of her generation, she was not one of those who risked nothing in the frantic quest to gain everything. Nor was she crippled by petty rivalries and fear. Unlike a number of her colleagues, she was not dispossessed of that generosity of spirit, which reveals itself in a small, mean talent.'

Viidikas indeed becomes a vocational ideal for Oliver. She is somebody who neither sold out nor succumbed to bohemian excesses: and yet this combination of talent and integrity did not result in a long and worry-free life. Oliver's portrait of Viidikas—half-laudatory, half-elegiac—incarnates one of the leitmotifs of *Unposted, Autumn Leaves*, namely, the undesired and rogue power of literary neglect. Oliver is still little known beyond those who really follow the Antipodean poetry scene. Any reader of this book will want that neglect to be remedied. But we should not overlook the way neglect brings strength; to not be privileged by the literary marketplace gives one, if one is nonetheless a good writer, an extraordinary strength, and reservoir of absolute, crystal-clear integrity, that other more lauded writers would envy. No writer would perhaps deliberately choose neglect. Yet neglect, again, if one is a good writer, bestows such an adamant strength, a core of authenticity—rather than a writer being left instead with the necessity of positioning themselves and manoeuvring through dinner parties, conferences, and writing programs. This fostering of authenticity by neglect is even more intensified in the smaller, hothouse literary worlds of Australia and New Zealand.

The essay 'Dirty Bomb Poetic' with its apprehension of how 'middle-class expectations of measurable success' can find themselves embodied in a certain poetic careerism, must be seen in this light. The 'composite poet,' the central character of this essay who is the object of scorn and derision, is not truly gifted, but knows how to ape the mannerisms of the literary world, and adapts that savvy to his own generation. The neoclassical mode would have worked well for the 'composite poet' in the age of Hope and McAuley, but not in the wilder and woollier Generation of '68, and whereas earlier references to Shakespeare and Pope would have been *au fait*, now an awareness of Māoritanga (carefully avoiding any cultural appropriation) is what will help him. And it is a *him*, as, though Oliver recognizes that the poet is always an 'androgyne', it is in the country of masculinity that the 'greater number of poetasters, poseurs and confidence tricksters prevail'. Eventually, the composite poet becomes a 'dinosaur' and settled down comfortably to be a relegated part of the establishment he has now ineluctably joined: but he has had his innings.

Very few writers think they are part of the establishment. It would be easy to dismiss Oliver's castigation of the 'composite poet' as a grumbling ballasted by *ressentiment*, as the loser carping at the winners. But Oliver does not assume a universally prophetic stance, as the 'composite poet' is not just an Other, but partially himself, or what he knows he would have become if he had let himself lapse, and what potentially any writer can become: somebody who plays the game instead of truly facing themselves in the sometimes too-fiery cauldron of creativity.

The speaker is part of the counterculture he depicts, not allowing himself the convenient exteriority of the firebrand caustic. Even more strikingly, he recognizes that the snares that caught the 'composite poet' are a part of any writer's life. Though he is not against literature, Oliver has a key awareness of what Martin Seymour-Smith called *Kunstlerschuld*, artist-guilt: that art lies, betrays itself, cannot equal the hopes it raises. [2] It is for this reason the book ends with the life journey of the Sardinian immigrant Babbo: his migrating to Australia in the 1950s, his working as a manual laborer, and eventually achieving financial success in the new country. Babbo is not romanticized. He is stingy, right wing and patriarchal. (Oliver perceptibly remarks that in the 1970s feminism was largely for white privileged women.) But he is an example of how a meaningful life can be lived outside poetry. The Babbo episode shows an opening up to the other, a relinquishing of any prescriptive-prophetic stance, an awareness that even countercultures need their own countercultures.

Stephen Oliver is a *transtasman* poet. The term *transtasman* —one word, all lower case—means, in the first instance, he is a poet of both Australia and New Zealand, as the two nations are separated by the Tasman Sea. This is actually very rare, as Australian and New Zealand literary cultures have long looked past each other, first in terms of consolidating their own nationalism and national institutions, and then in hopes of greater acclaim in the great world beyond. Oliver is not just noteworthy, though, for contributing to the literary cultures of two nations which, despite popular supposition, are neither geographically or culturally that close to each other, but is noteworthy for continuing to manifest a dissident literary identity in both, from Brooklyn-*west*, in New Zealand, the

Wellington suburb where Oliver spent some of his youth, to Newtown, the grungy-hip suburb near Sydney University where Oliver spent some of his mature-bohemian years. (Perhaps Oliver is in this light as much a 'Neapolitan' poet as a transtasman one.)

Oliver does not wish to adhere to one set of literary identities or institutional matrices. (I guess a poet who did would be 'cis-Tasman'.) The transtasman does not exclude the cosmopolitan: we not only have Babbo's memories of Sardinia, but Oliver's own sojourn on Hydra, as significant to him as it was for a previous generation of bohemians from the Antipodes, George Johnston and Charmian Clift. It is important that Oliver uses transtasman alongside Australasian. Though including the suffix '-asia', Australasia, is a term defined by the 'Wallis Line' dividing Indonesia's 'Asian' west and 'Pacific' (Melanesian) east, and is laden with many racialized and contested connotations. Transtasman as a term focuses much more precisely on the Australia-New Zealand relationship.

This is not to say that Oliver's poetic is insensitive to the indigenous peoples of the South Pacific. Indeed—and here's the rub—much like his castigated counter-self-image of the 'composite poet', Oliver is aware of indigenous people, without trying to appropriate them. Yet the way the land of Australia and New Zealand was stolen by white people supports all the various senses of thievery—literary thievery, cultural thievery, experiential thievery—that lie behind the acts of literary bad faith committed by the denizens of Oliver's world. Importantly, Oliver's exploration of the *transtasman* is not just confined to his own life-trajectory, but reaches into the deep past, into ancestry, memory, and archetype: 'My great-grandfather, Thomas McCormack, was born in Dublin in 1841 practically at the beginning of the Great Irish Famine. He left his native land at the age of six (at the height of the famine) and arrived in Hobart, Tasmania, in 1847. Three years later, at the age of ten he relocated to Melbourne. Twenty-seven years later, Victoria went through a period of depression, and so in 1877 he thought he might try his luck in New Zealand and sailed for Dunedin aboard the steamship *S.S. Ringarooma.* I was not aware of the coincidence at the time, but when I arrived in Australia, I was the exactly the same age as Thomas McCormack, thirty-six years, when he first arrived in Dunedin all those years before. It seems that I had unconsciously retraced his steps, made my *right-hand circuit* as was the practice of the Irish ancients, when I ended up living in Melbourne some time later for three years.'

Oliver finds that his own migration is in a curious way a kind of homing, as his grandfather had previously engaged in the same sort of intentional criss-crossing of the Tasman as he did over a century later, seeking aboard, as example, the steamship *S.S. Ringarooma* economic opportunity, self-expression, justice. Oliver's speculative portrait of his ancestor as somebody of rogue masculinity full of a subversive energy winds his own story back through time, as does his detailed description of the Dunedin his forebear would have experienced, done with the same mixture of detail and reverie found in Oliver's own recollections of the Wellington of his boyhood. Oliver then goes back even further, into the Ireland of Thomas McCormack's own ancestors, its histories and legends, layers and legacies, to some extent tracing Oliver's account of his own childhood onto the imagined childhood of the human race. The effect is not unlike the Australian novelist Christopher Koch's diptych *Highways To A War* and *Out of Ireland*, where one protagonist, an Irish revolutionary and migrant, is the great-grandfather of the other; but Oliver's tableau is far wilder, and, in his ruminations on the backward extensions of the name 'Cormac', far wider, a vortex that limns Oliver's own heritage while tacitly acknowledging the parallel heritage of indigenous peoples on both sides of the Tasman. From the primordial Milesians to the Otago of his mother's family, Oliver delves into the pith and mystery of the cultural memory, evoking a mythic, imaginary reservoir of the numinous that is a direct rejoinder to the crass materialism of an economic-rationalist society.

Jennifer Lawn has said, paraphrasing Ian Wedde, that the generation born in the 1940s and 1950s in New Zealand prized anarchic creativity but lacked a sense of 'class betterment' [3]. Here we have, as it were, Sister Berenice and the composite poet in searing contrast. But *Unposted, Autumn Leaves* is not out to laud chaos and denounce order, but to look for the order within, and occasioned by, chaos. It is wild enough and animated by a sufficiently keen spirit to be aware of the constitutive limits of its own poetic expression.

Oliver's *transtasman* position means he has *Australasian* ambition. It also, though, does not just make him intermediate in space, but in time. I have often felt that, even if it is impossible for experimental or avant-garde writers to escape the givens of their life situations as entirely as they like, one of the virtues of an unorthodox or marginal self-positioning is that it can make you, as a writer, seem younger than you are, that the same features that make you not quite fit into your own generation can make you relevant to a younger cohort.

Stephen Oliver is a singular talent whose viewpoint is at once amusing, bracing, and heuristic. He is somebody steeped in the Western tradition, although in a very idiosyncratic and emotional way, all the while remaining alive to the contemporaneity of his own experience and that of others. He is aware of (and adept at) form but never hemmed in by any formalism. He is a poet more than capable of assuming all the bardic and inspirational stances of poetry, while also being a writer who knows that to let go of the reins of irony is to fall asleep in cognitive terms. Even more, though, Oliver's writing exemplifies a process of crossing global gaps without sealing them, going past national horizons without seeking enshrinement in a winners' circle. Oliver's intercolonial and transtasman aesthetic ethic is, for all its necessary individuality, at one with our own values in this respect.

It is important that Oliver does not capitalize *transtasman*. This is not an e. e. cummings avant-garde gesture, though it does have its roots in experimental poetics. It is a refusal to substantialise his poetic and cultural aesthetic, an avoidance of the stentorian and the authoritative. This is why Oliver is sinuously intercolonial and not categorically postcolonial, why he is countercultural yet maintains his countercultural identity by satirizing the counterculture. Amidst what Oliver calls the 'five-second grab' of contemporary opportunism, Oliver urges a lower-case subversion of accustomed givens. In the wake of this tragedy, an upper-case subversion can only preen: a lower-case subversion can take us, to use the nicknames bestowed on the local terrain of Brooklyn-*west* by Oliver and his childhood classmates, at least partially from the Valley of the Sorrows to Happy Valley. From sour milk to couscous, from Brooklyn-*west* to Newtown, Stephen Oliver at once shocks us with how seamy the literary life is and how inspirational it can truly be. Fuelled by the integrity of neglect, Oliver's crisscrossing of the Tasman demolishes many other barriers that have stood for so long, and that even Sister Berenice would want to see vanish.

Nicholas Birns
New York University

[1] *The Song of Globule/80 Sonnets*, Stephen Oliver, Greywacke Press, Canberra, 2020, p. 50.

[2] *Macmillan Guide to Modern World Literature*, Martin Seymour-Smith, Macmillan, 1985, p. 661.

[3] *Neoliberalism and Cultural Transition in New Zealand Literature, 1984-2008: Market Fictions*, Jennifer Lawn, Lexington, 2015, p. 176.

Chalk, Talk And Asphalt Days

'If a man spends his first twenty years in and about his birthplace, that is his country'.—Edward Thomas

I don't imagine the past, one's personal past, as flat terrain—*that* is very much the present with the past removed from it. It is like a family home under new ownership, the occupants having imposed their own fashions and will on a landscape that existed as tree and undulation, sacred corner and shadow, changed to a landscaped flat, green lawn. Every macrocarpa tree (Monterey cypress), mature giants that darkly swayed under the northerly gusts that whistled up the gully 'out the back' or on calm, still nights echoed with the call of the morepork, rooted out and cut down. Everything so much smaller, somehow reduced in scale; memory withdrawing from itself that recreates a varied terrain of recollection. Perhaps in the end why landscape is imbued with such personal, tribal significance, why memory is ultimately totemic. At least, that was my experience when I revisited the family home in Brooklyn-*west*, Wellington, long since passed into other hands and owners, after an absence of twenty-odd years.

My middle age afloat on the raft of childhood-memory, foundering. 'Never look back' a traveller once told me years earlier on the island of Hydra, though perhaps he was referring to my almost mystical infatuation with a German girl who, after a rather intense encounter, I felt could read my mind, or anticipate my thoughts. This had as much to do with the Aegean as anything else (see my poem, 'The Fig Tree' at the close of this essay), an experience I later found echoed in the words of the Greek poet, Odysseus Elytis: '... *he moved time / hours ahead whenever he embraced a woman*'. Yet at a certain time in one's life there is a yearning to do this, to look back, maybe a dangerous nostalgia, something which must be done, even if this involves the shaking down of a life to one's very foundations, anticipating loss and further loss.

I played out my school days and developed my respective literary appetites through Marist Brothers, Newtown, and latterly, St. Patrick's College, Cambridge Terrace, Wellington. The Marist Brothers were teachers and foreign missionaries by trade, while the priests belonged to the Society of Mary. My Catholic education had started with St. Bernard's Convent, Brooklyn, and the Sisters of Mercy. Those were the days in the mid-fifties when the nuns washed your mouth out with warm soapy water if you swore, or strapped your open palm with the leather strap, that same strap worn about their waists as part of the order's habit. Nor was it uncommon for school kids to have their knuckles rapped with the sharp edge of a heavy, wooden ruler.

The Convent School in Ohiro Valley, 'of the moonless nights' or Happy Valley as this southern corridor to Red Rocks, Island Bay, Worser and Princess bays was known locally—into the Valley of the Sorrows, from my home high up on Karepa Street, Brooklyn-*west*, and the long walk down the hill to run the gauntlet of the state school kids who taunted, 'Catholic dogs stink like frogs in their mother's bathing togs'. The school was dominated by Sister Berenice, an avowed practitioner of 'the strap'. At playtime or during the lunch hour she would patrol the school grounds mercilessly. She would pace back and forth the main stretch of playground where we were required to eat our lunch on the seating that ran along classrooms at the back of the school with its large glass windows, her eyes shut in prayerful concentration as her fingers chewed through the rosary on the large black wooden beads which hung from *that* strap. Who needed gothic, caped and cloaked cartoon characters when you were presented with a black grotesque like Sister Berenice! A creature sprung from the ramparts of Notre Dame.

This stretch of asphalt, which made up the central, or

rather only playground, slightly elevated, fell away at either end. Somehow, as if guided by mysterious sonar, calibrated to precisely take her to the edge—she would turnabout in time, an inch from precipitate disaster. We *willed* her to lose her balance and topple headlong over the edge, but she never did. Sister Berenice was not a creature of the light. She was as sour as the bottled milk in alloy crates forced upon us by government regulation every day (the welfare state was in its full flowering, the realization of Julius Vogel's *Utopian* dream), defiantly left out in the morning light long enough to go off. Daylight proved as disastrous to the sister's disposition as it did to the daily milk's freshness.

The one lay teacher I remember, wistfully (she was perhaps a nineteen- or twenty-year-old), was the beautiful Miss McClelland, with Celtic dark locks and milky-white complexion, who was on a par with the nuns in this one respect—that she had no ability to teach us anything other than the ABC written in chalk with each letter illustrated, *A is for apple*, etc. A Catholic school in those days was notorious for the hiring of untrained, inexperienced lay teachers as they were then called, and to whom they paid a bare pittance. This was the beginning of my *mis-education*. The teaching standards did not match the skills of the disciplinarian. I fell in love with Miss McClelland for all her haughty unapproachability. The more so because she repeatedly picked on me, asking questions I had no hope of ever answering, paralyzed as I was with embarrassment before the rest of the class. Invariably, I was rebuked as I looked (usually heavenward) for some means of escape ('No Mr Oliver, the answers are *not* written on the ceiling!'). I withered. I have been trying to seduce her image ever since.

Some days, I got to walk Pauline Bonish home and even carry her books. Pauline was blonde and pretty and lived alone with her single mother in a '40's style white apartment block overlooking the Brooklyn chemist shop and fire station above the beige trams grinding up and down Brooklyn Road from the city, along Ohiro Valley Road, swinging into Cleveland Street (past *Pickett's Corner*), to where the lines abruptly ceased near the Post Office. The trams could be driven from either end but required the switching of poles to begin the return journey. The driver would alight, pull manfully upon the spooled and sprung black cable, manoeuvre the pole with its swivel runner back onto the overhead wire. This seemed to demand a great deal of speedy physical labour and the occasional expletive—an endless source of amusement to boys who felt they too were strong enough to pull on that cable and disconnect the pole if the tram slowed just long enough to allow ambush. Pauline could even suggest to a six- or seven-year-old boy, that just around the corner there existed another way of looking at girls (such was her power). A vague sense of unarrived-at desire crouched, coiled like a promise. She had the gift of making you see into the future.

We got one weekly visit from the parish priest (the church stood directly across Taft Street from the school), to the inevitable sycophantic flapping and flurry of nuns. This priest told tales of black magic, voodoo and invisible barriers blocking missionaries from entering native villages in the tropics. The devil was loosed upon the world. We could not get enough of it, and each week, like a matinee, had to wait for the next terrifying instalment of Good *v* Evil. We especially enjoyed the adventures of the *Curé of Ars* (perhaps a precursor of virtual reality), who reputedly could be in two places at once, a trick that every boy wished he possessed. Those days of St. Bernard's church (initially known as St. Anthony's), with its one sycamore tree by the porch entrance, and the mystery of its spinning 'helicopter' seedlings in autumn.

The first time I saw a man die was in that old tongue and groove wooden church. One of the parishioners erupted into a rasping and uncontrollable coughing fit, then collapsed in the pew heavily. Someone from the congregation tiptoed up to the priest and tapped him on the shoulder; he stopped the service, which left me thinking that this unprecedented hiatus was something terribly fragile. The mass was still being said in Latin, and the priest performed the greater part of the service with his back to the congregation as though guarding whatever alchemical concoctions of the spirit that were taking place there from the vulgar stare of the rabble, and the stricken man was carried bodily out over our heads by a few good men to the church porch where the priest administered last rites. He came back, announced that the man had died, and offered up the mass for the salvation of the dead man's soul. One for the church. In the hymns that concluded the service, the notorious 'silver songster' boomed still louder and held his notes even longer, beyond the last demure fading notes of the congregation, confidently off-key. But it was the deathly sound of that deep, rasping cough, a gasping for air that stayed with me long after the quiet ministrations of the priest had concluded, and the slow creak of the swing doors that gave onto the porch from the aisle, allowing a glimpse of that prostrate form.

We learnt to read with *Janet & John* books and to this day I do not recall what happened to Janet, or John, or whether they made it to the top of the hill, and what they did when they got there. We learnt most things by rote. You progressed through a series of numbered and illustrated books and these seemed to go on forever. One oddity of schoolroom etiquette I recall as being rather innovative: if you wished to be excused from the room to go to the 'toilet' (a genteelism my mother insisted—the correct term was 'lavatory'), you placed a coloured strand of wool, threaded through a wooden-spool, painted a bright orange or blue or red, around your neck. This device was hung on the door handle of the one main exit from the room. If the spool was absent, then the 'toilet' was in use and a child was out of the room. If not then it hung from the door handle like a *declaration of banishment* and you were free to excuse yourself, but only after asking permission from the teacher. This method of accountability had the effect of making you feel claustrophobic, rushed, and somehow furtively guilty. Not quite the 'Welsh Not' but no less humiliating. [1] Looking back, I realize now that this was the first and last time I ever shared a school room with *female* school children. Growing up through the Catholic school system would come to mean blanket segregation. Gregarious freedoms were easily condoned in the world of pre-puberty.

The nuns would put on a 'special occasion', that is, something that broke the monotonous routine of classroom instruction and would build up our expectations days in advance. We would be given a rare movie screening, and only those who were 'very good' would be permitted to attend. This did not mean an Audie Murphy western nor the sunny smile and equally sunny voice of a freckled Doris Day (that came a few years later at the *Brooklyn Vogue*, reinstated as the *Penthouse* movie theatre with restaurant after years as a 'closed' production house for television commercials), but a religious flick in shaky black and white. This screening coincided with having my mouth washed out with warm soapy water. The movie was about the three shepherd girls at the Cova da Iria, in Fátima, Portugal, who in 1917 saw a vision of the Virgin Mary. Stony hillsides and sheep and clouds and a bright suffusing light, more to do with burning carbon rods in the old projectors and flickering beams than anything divinely intended by the director. Children, open mouthed but not scared, staring up in awe to some far away vanishing point.

Then suddenly, I don't think we ever got to see the Virgin Mary; each of the three girls acquired, I swear—a spray of flowers over the chest (heart) to denote, I suppose, that they had received the Holy Vision from Our Lady of Fátima. There were no special effects to assist us toward an unconditional state of grace. Even to my untrained eye I could see what looked like a wooden tray (something similar to a matchstick girl's), clumsily attached to each little girl's chest and balancing a precarious bunch of flowers—in a wobbly vase! Was this 'the vision?' I didn't buy it, and I believe made a loud facetious noise to that effect. The following day I was administered a soapy warm tonic by Sister Berenice. I may have complained to my parents, and my father (a confirmed atheist, my mother was the strong Catholic), might have had a word with the sisters, but here memory fades like a faltering vision. The following is taken from my poetry collection, *Unmanned* (1999):

MYTH & MARIOLATRY [2]

At a small village not
far from Manila, in the house
of armaments and munitions,
in a house of grenades
and ammunition, the plaster
statue of the Virgin Mary as
humble as a trademark,
stands splashed in carmine
tears like some peasant
shot on a quiet morning bearing
water from the creek.
The hovels strewn about
the hills are so many broken
boxes. The sun is spinning
clockwise for hope. One
cloud out of nowhere & then a
drape of blue that might
be the sky. The gathering of
people is more impressive
than a food drop. They come
at the appointed hour when
the boy who serves as
runner to the 'Beautiful Lady'
arrives, breathless, with
the Word. Occasionally,
the statue weeps paint-fresh
tears. They will leave

once faith is gathered in
abundance like so many wild
flowers from the near mountain
meadow. Here, under a glass
blown moon, a cool wind shall
leave this place sacred.

The iris of memory opens upon one other major crisis. I deliberately and energetically ran into a closed circle of boys at full tilt and was pushed over onto a sharp piece of tin and for my trouble slashed open my left-hand palm (a self-imposed stigma perhaps?) for which I received 13 stitches done very badly by the local Brooklyn GP who accused me of *'carrying on like a two-bob watch'*. The scarring is as vivid and white today as it ever was. This experience served to remind me that I did not belong or conform to groups, especially groups of men; certainly, a dangerous attitude to develop in later life as far as job security and career orientation went.

Predictably I looked forward to the leisurely walk home (school ended in the afternoons around 3.30, sometimes earlier on Fridays), and back along Ohiro Road. 'Ohiro' was the original spelling before the change to the politically correct 'Owhiro' some decades later. I hoped to avoid the state school boys always ready for a bit of name-calling and a fight. Past the Brooklyn shopping centre off to the right, with 'Percy the Barber', famous for his *short back and sides* haircut, executed with Calvinistic severity and doused in Bay Rum. I paused at Fawkner's cake shop, a squat, free standing white-washed building with a green canvas awning and front-window display of confectionary situated a few yards from the old fire station on Cleveland Street.

Beyond this clustered the small shopping strip, presided over by the Post Office opposite Brooklyn Library overlooking the bus terminus, and *Seymour's Bookshop* which finally shut down in 2000—the place must have been running for at least forty-five years, more an emporium stocked with stationary (HB pencils by the gross) and glossy magazines (*NZ Women's Weekly*, *Vogue*, etc), with thousands of 'useful' knick-knacks like white tallow candles, Christmas wrapping paper, and henna powder. The one shop that recalls this Aladdin's Cave remains Melbourne's *Jeffreys Books* in Glenferrie Road, Malvern. From Fawkner's cake shop rich baking odours wafted through the protective wire-mesh door, and I had a particular hankering for the rich cream buns (fourpence each though you *could* get credit), thick cream flecked with raspberry flavouring, crunchy with icing sugar, maybe a hint of sherbet. Jam tarts with a deep buttery biscuit base came in a close second.

Then homeward bound again up Helen Street, past the cul-de-sac of Sugarloaf Road, at the end of which the World War One memorial soldier on his plinth rose high on the hill, facing toward the Tasman Sea. Apuka Street at the top forked left and continued in a loop behind Brooklyn-*west*, and right—down the short end of Karepa Street. The left fork skirted the grassy-topped reservoir, past *Fitchett's Farm*, gorse patch, toi toi with its waving war plumes, yellow broom and manuka with scrub thickest in the gullies, weathered brown grass on the higher slopes, rolling away further west beyond *Hawkins Hill* to the pine tree belt that thickened on the horizon—decimated by the Wahine Storm in 1968. Otherwise, the hills appeared empty of activity aside from the odd rabbit, a scattering of cows, and a solitary horse or two. The stone-battered tin sign, 'Trespassers Will Be Prosecuted,' wired to the gate, meant that we kept off the dirt road, out of view winding its way up toward the higher reaches of Fitchett's Farm and the 'forbidden zone', the dam and city water supply hidden beyond the pine belt and closely patrolled by mysterious men you never got to see close up in Land Rovers tracking yellow clay fire-breaks.

We played amongst the World War Two concrete bunkers (old gun emplacements usually filled with green, slimy water), facing south to the Tasman Sea for the attack which never came, or in the old abandoned quarry about midway up the farm road. Incidentally, the quarry is gone now, under the creeping development of the *Kowhai Park* sub-division sprawling over the high-backed hills, up to the fenced off native bush reserve and reservoir, presided over by one giant wind turbine, already a city icon. Could this be Wellington's answer to the Christ The Redeemer Statue set high above Rio de Janeiro? I prayed that one day this mechanical giant would shunt the whole mess off into the Tasman. I lived down the short end of Karepa Street, city and harbour spread beneath me, the Rimutaka Ranges ringing Wellington, snow-capped right into early summer beyond the Te Awa Kairangi/Hutt River and foothills. Yet I grew up at an elevation higher than Mt. Victoria which dominated our eastward facing view whose flanks rose in a sweep from the harbour city, in those early days not yet trepanned with a hill top road.

The very road you lived in constituted your world—it seemed to go on forever; the New Zealand Broadcasting Corporation (NZBC) still ran its morning serials, 'Portia Faces Life', 'Philip Temple' and 'Dr Paul,' produced by Australia's Grundy Organization. The 2ZB mid-morning show presented that unstoppable gabbler, Aunt Daisy, '*Oh, Good morning! Good morning! Good morning!*,' introduced by her equally famous theme song, '*Daisy, Daisy, give me your answer do*'. On a Monday night at 7.30 I listened to 'Life With Dexter' or later, in 'Night Beat' 'Randy Stone' calling '*Copy Boy!*'

There were other radio serials, too, like 'Horatio Hornblower' and various westerns ('Hopalong Cassidy' and 'the lost Dutchman's Gold Mine'), and spooky science fiction stories. These were usually broadcast on a Sunday morning, along with the sentimental (weren't they all?) story of the girl united with her lost horse—and the song she sang, 'Palomino'—and the perennials like Denis Norden and the team in 'My Word', and 'Round the Horne' with Kenneth Horne which my mother enjoyed. Soon enough came the divinely inspired idiocy of

'The Goon Show' and the suburban subterfuge of 'Hancock's Half Hour' which in turn gave birth to the '60s 'Beyond the Fringe' with Dudley Moore and the doomed Peter Cook, whose distortedly Dickensian humour had its final flowering in the surreal antics of 'Monty Python' with John Cleese and crew. Thankfully, I had a television-free childhood, a reprieve that extended into my early teens.

It could be that where memory fades, anxiety and personal neuroses, the pain of exile from our own personal Eden takes over, so that the pictures in the head which make up the years and constitute our piecemeal lives give way to instinct-driven atmospherics and sensations of loss, and that the *state of childhood* in space and time had, as it turns out, nothing to do with memory yet remains a constant and never-ending present. In reality, this is sustained, but to a lesser degree. Sensation and discovery shot through with colour, an unending though chthonian awareness, so that your surroundings were as much a part of you, as you were of your sensations. A borderless hyper-reality. Time only comes into existence as a measurable commodity, as an objective reality, when you have something to recollect, and the attempt to recapture that lost emotional and physical terrain is peculiar to you *alone*. If waiting mutates to fear in our adult years, it could be that we are facing in the wrong direction; oblivion is behind and not ahead of us. We live our lives cursed with the promise of belonging and nothing, not marriage, home-life, the accumulative itinerary of personal achievement, nor even the consolation prize of death can replicate that long-lost state. Happiness, or some sort of corresponding equilibrium, may well turn out to be atavistic, after all.

My world expanded and rippled out soon enough. Marist Brothers, Newtown, meant a longer walk down Brooklyn Road, over Bidwill Street (an oak grove at the very top overlooking the rise that turned off to Bell Road with its grass-topped reservoir, was a great place to lay an ambush, especially in autumn with the ground strewn with acorns), and into Adelaide Road, Newtown. It was at this primary school that I first met Geoff Cochrane, the poet, though I have little recollection of it, not having as yet defined a common ground of interest or reaction. Our boyhood friendship established itself later on at St. Patrick's College. We were still in the process of orientating our personalities, identifying the dangers, *who* and *what* to avoid—the balancing act of the personality, building the mechanism of provisional survival in a circular world.

The Marist Brothers had preordained that sport and scholastic rivalry were the best ways to achieve this, essential ingredients to solid character building, a programme of tuition heavily enforced with the unbridled use of the bamboo cane. An old fashioned, liberal education. Classes were divided into *houses* similar to a medieval guild system, and each house had its own silk and tasselled banner (similar in texture to the vestments of a priest), embroidered with an identifying colour and boasting a saint's name. My house was *Xavier* and we hoisted a gold and green banner.

This activity involved some sort of point-scoring system based upon monies sought for long-term building projects. Parents were expected to give generously and thereby contribute to the success of their child's house. This further instilled into us that competition bred good fortune. Of course, donations were welcome, no matter how small the amount. The results were posted on a display-board exhibiting the name of each house over a *painted thermometer* with the respective colour rising and falling according to the houses' weekly fortunes. Usually, such ostentatious ceremony was reserved for visiting celebrities and other significant occasions like Sport's Day. We carried out parade ground exercises once or twice a week; the ranks we formed into were based on the Roman phalanx, perhaps a contradiction, though we were undoubtedly God's little soldiers. These performances were staged a couple of times during the year, mostly for the benefit of the parents and the brothers.

When the South African Springbok team came to visit our primary school we were regimented according to our respective 'houses' and marshalled into serried and colourful ranks in the upper playground for inspection. I think one of the South African rugby players was called Piet Botha, a giant of a man, who played lock. The city hotels could not furnish a bed big enough to accommodate him. The *Evening Post* and the *Dominion* ran a front-page story at the time with a photo of Botha (1965 Springboks) supine and spread out with Lilliputian disregard across two king size beds. I think the All Blacks won the test series that year—the same year the legendary great fullback, Don Clarke, famed for his kicking boot, retired. Innocent enough days before civil reaction to apartheid gathered across all levels of society, and subsequent political boycott kicked in at the end of the '60s.

Ultimately though, this sporadic activity would coalesce into vicious protest and riots in the streets of Wellington with crowds facing off against a helmeted and baton-wielding police force. Riots were orchestrated throughout New Zealand's main cities. Cry the beleaguered country. Famously, a few years later in 1981, at another Springbok/All Blacks encounter, some guy in a *Cessna* buzzed Eden Park, Auckland, and flour-bombed the players when the game was in full swing. South Africa was eventually banned from international competition, left out in the cold for twenty years until the final dismantling of apartheid under Nelson Mandela.

The principal, Brother Paulinus, was built like a slab of granite. Short, square shouldered, chisel jawed, broad chested, swarthy and pockmarked. A man of volcanic temper exacerbated by his bad hip and pronounced limp. Yet he could move at great speed when in pursuit of his quarry. He would appear out of nowhere and was upon you in an instant, scowling—his voice pitched in ground-shaking anger. A terrifying sight to see him bear down upon some boy and cuff him heavily with a solid back-hander. I always thought he looked like the movie star, Jeff Chandler. Brother Paulinus's masculinity carried with it an indefinable nobility beyond his erratic behaviour, and inspired fearful respect amongst the boys.

Brother Paulinus was the *Camp Commandant* and a veritable martinet. Fortunately, he never taught or seriously bothered me in the course of the next four years, though he did impart at my mother's request some emphatic and *manly* advise about standing on my own two feet, and not letting myself be 'led around by the nose', referring to my dependency on a boy I had known from pre-school days, and who proved to be entirely manipulative. His advice, concluded with a roar, eventually proved effective, and I broke away from the unhealthy influence of this early playmate (he, too, lived in Karepa Street), a dependency that had evolved out of insecurity and habit, not real friendship; simply wanting to be accepted. This had as much to do with escape from my eldest, and shortest, brother's constant and vicious bullying—a frustration that arose in part from his inability to meet his father's expectations of becoming a chemist. He had no aptitude for passing exams, especially in the positive sciences, and performed poorly. Nevertheless, he earned my father's anger and denunciation.

My attempted escape into an alternate dependence had as much to do with entrenched family warfare (there were six of us) as with anything else. Regrettably, our next-door neighbour, the Lemons, a 'High Brethren', quiet and entirely civil family, on our left and on a slightly lower level, referred to us as 'the feuding Olivers' much to my mother's profound disappointment. On our right, and at a higher level, lived the Cassidys, a solid working-class family. We could always tell when Mr Cassidy arrived home from his day's work, usually about 5.30 pm; we tracked his smoker's cough as he wearily climbed in long strides the long flight of concrete steps that led up to the house. He always spoke out the corner of his mouth, one of the most laconic men I had ever met, and who greeted you with a lop-sided, cowboy grin.

Only now do I understand my mother's angry disappointment when, years later, I missed out on being conscripted into the army and subsequent service in Vietnam around 1969 in the final year of compulsory conscription before it was abolished. I missed out by one day, and my mother threatened to write in for a recount. The discipline would do me good, or so she thought. I would have found ways to avoid it as a conscientious objector (We Shall Not Cease) had it come to that. Rebellion was in the air. Whether by accident or design, my marriage service in December 1971 (a youthful, and brief involvement) was conducted through a Quaker ceremony in Palmerston North. The 'friends' as they were known, were of course, pacifists; and at that point, I knew I was safe from any further *threat* of compulsory involvement in someone else's war.

There was one defining incident when Brother Paulinus did on one occasion deeply embarrass me. Often, kids were dispatched as 'runners' between classrooms to deliver messages on behalf of the teachers. I was sent to Paulinus's classroom on an errand. Having delivered the message, I turned to go, and was told to stop. Standing up before a classroom of staring boys was one of my deepest fears. 'Take off your shoes,' he commanded. I took off my shoes but it was the humiliation of having holes in my socks that galled me. 'Walk a few steps forward,' he commanded. I did. 'Turn around and walk back slowly toward me. Now turn your foot side on to me and press your foot down at hard as you can'. Time slowed and my senses numbed. 'You have *flat feet!*,' he triumphantly announced to me, *and* the entire class. 'Did you *know* that?' I was not aware of this fact, nor had my family picked up on it. Revelation! *I had flat feet.* To put it mildly, I was stunned, paralyzed with embarrassment. He informed me that this resulted from wearing sandshoes. Such footwear gave little or no support to the arch, he informed me, and so my arches had terminally collapsed. His interpretation proved correct. I don't think he meant to be vindictive, simply—that he had made a discovery and declared it without due concern for my sensitivity or shyness. 'You will never be drafted into the army,' he concluded. He called a spade a spade.

Nonetheless, I felt somehow betrayed, aware that he and my mother had struck up a friendship—they seemed to have a genuine affection for each other. I remember seeing them returning from a bush walk together, engrossed in each other's company, at the yearly school picnic held on this occasion at Wainuiomata, a suburb of Lower Hutt. I felt distinctly uncertain about their obvious camaraderie, though this suggested to me something of a more humane 'off-duty' attitude at work within the otherwise fixed coordinates of school, parent and child. Catholic and companionable, yes, but what could it possibly mean if anything; for me, a safe passage through school, perhaps? Somewhere in the background a car radio blared the beginnings of a new generation, Bill Haley's 'Rock around the clock'. Meanwhile, far away in England, John Osborne tinkered with his stage play, 'Look Back in Anger'.

I thought then, how could Paulinus do this to me, given his confirmed friendship with my mother? Another lesson came home to roost; never bank on someone else's good will, or expect to borrow favours against another's friendship. I soon learnt through those chalk, talk and asphalt days to bury disappointment like a toxic substance, only to wonder why it should surface again much later as anger, or a closely cultivated rejection in that as yet untravelled country beyond puberty. The overbearing Paulinus was a pragmatist by disposition and impatient by nature.

There was no question that he acted at times as the vicious disciplinarian, administering the cane to a boy for some minor offence with unnecessary and overbearing strength. I was vaguely aware, too, that he was not liked by my father, and this was cause for contention between himself and my mother.

It must be admitted, natural-born innocent that she was, with an inherent sense of dignity and breeding, she truly enjoyed the society of the brothers, and latterly the priests. Natural enough when you consider she had come from a strong, Irish Catholic family background, and this equipped her not only with an unshakeable pride (take *faith* as read), but a sense of 'rightness' in the company she chose to dwell in, artificial and mannered as it may have been.

In the end, I think my father was defeated by that cultural and emotional divide that existed between them; not even the stoic silence and heroic suffering of the Presbyterian temperament could bridge that lonely gulf. In fact, it was an obvious cause for alienation—convention in those days meant they stuck at it. I imagine this had much to do with my father's plummet into alcoholism and subsequent death at the age of fifty-three. A tough call for an atheist, or 'dialectical materialist' as he called himself. A man of high ideal and scientific brilliance, he was a leading chemist and one-time Principal of the Pharmacy College in Cambridge Terrace, yet was destroyed when his idealism and belief in people were negated through a number of botched business dealings. He was no businessman. I offer this address to my father taken from *Intercolonial* (2013), [3] my epic poem in the original italic as published:

> **O**ur father *who fell down the porch steps often our father*
> *fell down red concrete steps our father lost his balance liquored*
> *up he was lost his balance and bumped his head our father*
> *did that heaps he did drunken fell and bumped his head now he*
>
> *is dead our father who made our life hell is not in heaven*
> *still maybe falling into the after-nothingness he believed in our*
> *father is still falling for ever and ever our father the bright*
> *young man who matriculated at fourteen star in the ascendant*
>
> *our father the communist our father bio-chemist and scientist*
> *finally destroyed by the men he trusted our father idealist*
> *Principal of the Pharmacy College Cambridge Terrace Wellington*
> *we watched him sicken and fail and drink himself to death*

dead at fifty-three he was our father forfeited his life to despair
and the family always flammable blew itself apart like some
laboratory experiment gone horribly wrong in the heart's alembic
none of us escaped strangers at last to each other our father

from the King Country the Presbyterian dictum honest day's work
honest day's pay men of the land pragmatic and practical our
father prematurely aged whose father said of his son at his funeral
he should never have left the country our father who art dead.

Trusts betrayed and patents stolen by a shark car dealer, and one or two bogus 'socialist' mates. Principal among these was a hulking Russian ex-wrestler, every inch of his 6'5" frame opportunistic. One way or another, these likely 'assassins' all had pretensions to culture and played this as a bargaining chip. What noble egalitarian principles these pariahs possessed! How quickly they disappeared when my father, pathetic as he became, had nothing more to give or was incapable of doing so. In fact, I never really knew him, having come fourth down the list of six children, and would have been too young to have any memory of him in his heyday. All I saw was a shambling wreck and a man aged well beyond his fifty odd years. You would think that life in the final analysis is just too short to indulge in the complexities of self-destruction. If anything, that belongs to the romantic tradition of the *death-wish* and is more a fantasy attributed to youth. A life negatively spiralling out of control is a deadly, serious business sucking the whole family down with it. We each of us coped with his decline in our different and varying ways, each of us a stranger to the other.

Right to end of my tenure at the Marist Brothers primary school in Newtown, Brother Paulinus' masculine charisma continued simultaneously to fascinate and repel me, and still I found no other way to interpret him. I could be nothing other than ambivalent toward this man who assumed, in the end, the mantle of anti-hero. Further on down the hierarchy, various of our other teachers contributed to our sense of, if not the 'sanctity of knowledge', then the absurdity of personal eccentricities; for each of them appeared to be quite disconnected from the other, as though they hardly knew or talked with each other, and were rarely seen to publicly interact. You wondered what dramas were being played out in the one building standing silently apart from the school in which they all slept and ate. A cause for endless speculation, and a secret life to which we were not privy. Each of them sold us into an eternal tunnel vision with the varying force or weakness of their personalities.

We were in thrall to our insecurities and abashed by our inability to effectively rebel. There could be only temperamental and futile displays of rejection at this time, and these were quickly quelled. It would be a couple of years into secondary school before we could form true allegiances and focus our perceptions beyond the immediacy of involuntary reaction. We knew then that the brothers were hardly of the same calibre as the priests who occupied one of the inner circles of heaven. God's enforcers or something (we as children were, as mentioned, God's little soldiers), while *these* 'brothers' didn't quite make the grade, and were merely journeymen if anything, though as we came to understand much later, many were confused young men caught between career choices. Or biding their time. There was something of the officious and controlling bureaucrat associated with this character-type. Autocratic social workers in uniform. Many of the younger brotherhood left for more lucrative forms of employment, or marriage. We pretty much took what was handed out to us—how could we do otherwise? Films like 'The Ruling Class' and 'If' were as yet some five years (an aeon) distant.

FIG TREE

Remembering Christina from Baden-Baden on Hydra

Nothing seemed significant about it;
but this appeared to me over and over again,
there set in a recess on the hillside off the track
leading up from the harbour cafes and shops on Hydra—
one fig tree, early winter, late November, 1979.

I hold this as memory I carried
with me from an arched, Venetian stone bridge over
some small stream or ravine along the coast,
to where she resided; either coming back, or going
over that ancient bridge, late in the evening, with the
German girl, she clutching a bottle of Demestica,
as she stumbled, nearly tripped—

who read my mind as I read hers
later on into the night. 'Now you have everything you
want,' she whispered to me.

The hum at the back of the head making of it an
amphitheatre for voices, echoes, oracles. I again recall
that fig tree, standing there by the track, on the
island of Hydra, the memory of my night with her,
yearningly recent, reverberating within me as I passed
the fig tree to where I had stayed amongst
the white washed villas high up on that mountainous
island—

witness to how my senses had
vibrated like the strings of a finely tuned lute at the
back of my head in one stilled, sensual moment,
as I paused, and passed on by.

[1] The Welsh Not' (W.N.) *was a wooden plaque strung on a leather cord. A legacy of British oppression in Wales during the 18th century when Welsh school children were banned from speaking Gaelic. If caught speaking it in school they were required to wear this device around their necks. The last child left wearing this at the end of the school day would be viciously caned by the usually inept schoolmaster.*

[2] *Unmanned* , Stephen Oliver, HeadworX Publishers, Wellington, 1999.

[3] *Intercolonial*, Stephen Oliver, Puriri Press, Auckland, 2013.

He invariably arrived at school in the mornings on a cream scooter and clad in a black duffle coat. This was, after all, the era of the beatnik, the jazz and folk club, the coffee house. The most popular venues, right through into the late '60s, were the *Monde Marie* and *Chez Paree* located diagonally across from each other on Majoribanks Street at the end of Courtenay Place. The *bodgies* and *widgies* of the milk bars *(Oh, oh Susie darlin, I love you so oh oh...)*, and the V-8 boys with 'DA' brylcreem hairstyles ('duck's arse'), were in the process of disappearing back into the suburbs from whence they came as conventionally married couples and bus commuting office workers.

Jonathan Hardy was out to impress from the start. I was at that time in 'Standard Three' (newly arrived), and he was appointed one of our teachers. Primary schools, if you didn't jump-start first with an intermediate school which offered no more than a two-year tenure (the point of an 'intermediate' remains a mystery to this day), ran from standards *one* through *four*. Secondary school loomed large like a dark fortress in our minds, an inescapable and at the same time a seemingly unachievable goal. Slowly and relentlessly we moved closer to the adult world and the clenched fist of authority. The inevitability of this was presented as a threat, and if we didn't buckle down *now*, it was unlikely we would ever shape up for the hard years that lay ahead. Mr Hardy wore a distinctive silver ring, inset with a large oval greenstone on his index finger. He would boast to the class that with his ring hand *tightened* into a fist (he demonstrated, showing the ring off to good effect), he had dispatched several 'yobs', hooligans who had the misfortune to confront him (oddly, these attacks always took place over a weekend, so we got to hear the tales on a Monday), and left on each of their chins (there were several of them) the imprint of that greenstone ring. Something like 'the phantom' I supposed. And yes, we were impressed.

I don't recall him ever teaching us anything useful in the conventional sense. He liked to practise his 'vocal techniques' and 'accents' before the class. He read us aloud two classics. Robert Louis Stevenson's *Kidnapped* and Bram Stoker's *Dracula*. It was the last which gave me nightmares. As I lay in bed at night, and watched the wardrobe door creak open and the blackness expand and spill out, or listened to the wind roughing up the large macrocarpa tree outside my window, I would see shadows crawling and coalescing upon the wall and blood-red eyes, the flap of a cape or was that a bat falling from the cloud-wrecked sky? I very soon developed the habit of going to sleep with my back to the wall and facing the bedroom door which didn't help much as the window was directly above and behind me.

It might well have been complaints to my mother which prompted 'the boys', my brothers, to come up with the ingenious figure of *Brambleface*, an horrific bogeyman that purportedly lived in *their* bedroom (I shared with my youngest brother and was 'banned' from entering theirs), who stole children from their parents, especially if they were 'sooks'. And I, apparently, was a sook. They showed me Brambleface once, and that was enough. They had managed to pack up one of the lower bunk beds into the bulky form of a 'body' with a pair of sandshoes sticking out the end. I wanted to be convinced and that did the trick.

Inevitably, Mr Hardy fell foul of Brother Paulinus. A boy was sent on an errand from Paulinus's class room to ours requesting of Mr Hardy a box of matches. He thought it rather amusing to send the boy back with an empty box. Suddenly, the door flew open and in stormed Paulinus who thundered at Mr Hardy about infantile behaviour and practical jokes, etc, and then departed in long, limping strides to the crashing of the door behind him. This ploy on Mr Hardy's part was designed to create a conspiracy between himself and the class, against Paulinus, and proved largely successful. He had the audacity to contest the *autocrat*, and he kept his head! Inevitably, he would not get to keep his job; was he fired, or did he just not bother to turn up one morning?

The pantomime was still a popular form of family entertainment in Wellington (television had not yet arrived), put on a couple of times a year at the old Majestic Theatre diagonally opposite Perrett's Corner, backing onto Boulcott Street via a fire exit. Jonathan Hardy was the lead player in this brash burlesque, performing as the heavily mascaraed and villainous king out to condemn and thwart the young hero lovers. There were I think, crowd dances, and much frantic running about by costumed figures in the mock-medieval style, and something to do with a 'cow' (one performer either end of a cow-costume managing head, legs and hind quarters), which involved dropping *cans of condensed milk* on cue as punch-line to some awful sight gag, unsurprisingly, prompting much raucous laughter. The show was high camp if nothing else. We preferred Mario Lanza in full vocal flight at the Saturday afternoon flicks any day. Early days though for the ambitious drama student, and villainous indeed he turned out to be. He would choose students to administer the caning of other boys. He would sit back and watch. The disciplinarian as voyeur. Those to be caned were the usual 'losers', the neatly dressed mummy's boys, or the ethnic urchin sort (east European) who might be called *Ivanisevic* or something similarly Slavic.

The mummy's boy reddened and blubbered. The eastern European didn't so much as flinch a facial muscle and took it, staring straight ahead, unblinkingly; and because he didn't visibly weaken was given another dose. Hardy in his role pointing a shaky finger and saying in a well-practised, hoary voice, 'give the boy six hard ones.' The boy in question was required to bend over one of the front desks, so the class was treated to a real-life drama, and the various facial contortions of the victim. Sweeney (the nominated wielder of the cane and class thug), gave it all he had and swung into the boy with obvious relish and gusto.

There were one or two others chosen for the task, and I recall one boy, a victim by the name of Prendergast, screaming in pain. There were one or two other incidents—the school swimming pool had of course to be monitored by a teacher at all times, and we usually swam during the lunch break because that was the longest period we had. One boy found himself in difficulty in the deep end and was in the process of panicking, well on the way to drowning. Mr. Hardy, already in his swimming trunks, in a leisurely manner *breast-stroked* toward the floundering boy, quite unhurried in order to heighten the drama, and fished him out in due time. Again, amongst the boys he was the undisputed hero of the day, though, within the hermetic circle of the brotherhood, negative criticism was mounting against the redoubtable Mr Hardy.

Then one Monday morning he wasn't there. The sinecure was over. He had not given notice and just didn't bother to turn up. Jonathan Hardy had as far as anybody knew completely disappeared. He had done a runner. Curiously, Hardy, who had attended St. Patrick's College (town), was celebrated for his physical prowess in athletics[1] which, considering his short, stocky stature and tendency toward rotundity, might be considered somewhat freakish. Regardless, everyone thought Paulinus was behind it. He had vanished. Exeunt Jonathan Hardy. He was to re-surface some years later in the 1976 Australian movie (the Australian cinema industry was at the peak of its renaissance in the '70s) written, produced and directed by Fred Schepisi called *The Devil's Playground.* This was an edgy and dark movie set in a Marist (or Christian) Brothers' school compellingly centred on the frustrated sexual fantasies of the brothers (writhing, underwater, slow motion sequences) and, naturally, the crisis of faith which attended such aberrations. A homoerotic interpretation of the crucifixion, a 'breaking of the covenant'; demonic possession.

As an attempt at European-styled sophistication, the film worked passably; though it missed in that such 'sophistication' is in reality rather 'tired' and 'decadent'—qualities which inject a peculiarly sardonic and underplayed atmospheric boredom. Unfortunately, in this part of the world, we don't possess the heraldic *ennui* of a baroque European history necessary to achieve such an effect. It comes down to innate style rather than self-conscious *pastiche*. The Schepisi film betrayed its 'new world' innocence in being too frantic, an abrasive quirk promulgated, for example, in the Australian TV 'cop' series, 'Wildside' (1997-1999). When in doubt get down and get blokey—*yell, mate!* The film didn't, thankfully, fall into the kitsch excesses of a Ken Russell production. It was probably a 'version' of these experiences as a 'teacher' listed on his CV which secured Hardy a supporting role in the movie.

Several years later nearby an old converted boarding house I had named *Poets' Palace*, where I lived at the time in France Street, now known as Mercury Lane, off K'Rd, Auckland (the 'palace' played host to any number of emerging writers and artists), I spotted Jonathan Hardy. The year would have been around 1984. I hadn't physically seen him for twenty-seven years or so. Middle aged now, short and compact, the same distinguishing bushy, black eyebrows that fascinated us as children. The boarding house was situated right next door to the Mercury Theatre. The old kauri weatherboard guesthouse *vis a vis* 'Poets' Palace' was demolished in the late '80s. The elusive Mr Hardy apparently had been brought over from Australia under contract to the Mercury Theatre to work a couple of seasons as director on a low budget, undistinguished musical. A basic journeyman's commission, so 'off Broadway' in fact that you could measure it in latitudes. He seemed particularly discomfited as well he might when I hailed him in the street (actually, it was from off my balcony overlooking France Street), and introduced myself as one of his long lost, and I imagine, hopefully buried pupils. Unfortunately for him, those forgotten years were not altogether forgotten.

He had done measurably well for himself in theatre and to some extent film, though never quite repeating the success he found in *The Devil's Playground.* So, when I ran into Mr Hardy back in the '80s at a *McDonald's* up from the Mercury Theatre on K'Rd (it was evening) he was with a young male companion, but was understandably cagey and, really, who could blame him? I was the last person in the (his) world he wanted to know. We didn't have much to say to each other beyond a few passing and guarded platitudes. Did he, in fact, have something to hide? His manner certainly seemed to suggest it. The somewhat smarmy vanity was undeniably in evidence though the youthful posturing had largely been replaced by a well-crafted cunning. Maybe recalling the images of those boys bending over a desk, squirming in pain and in plain view, was a little too much to bear? Somehow, I doubt it. But there he was, caught in the snare of memory, and there I was, gazing back at him. Satisfaction enough, I thought, in having reminded him of those 'innocent' days back in Wellington at Marist Brothers, Tasman Street.

Hardy was a regarded as a valuable player at Downstage Theatre (situated opposite the *Taj Mahal* edifice squat on its traffic island between Kent and Cambridge terraces, Wellington), when it was first set up in 1966-7. About the same time James K. Baxter was involved with the *Globe Theatre*, Dunedin, under the helmsmanship of Patrick Carey. The Downstage Theatre was originally owned by one Harry Seresin who ran the *Walkabout* Coffee Bar downstairs; various actors and writers of the day suggested combining this with a stage, and so Wellington's first innovative theatre was born. It was similar, I suppose, to the early days of the *Nimrod* in Sydney and *La Mama* in Melbourne, along with the burlesque sexual high jinks of the 'Australian Performing Group' (popularly located at *La Mama* in Melbourne, as a spin off), producing experimental work around about the same time. The various 'players' behind the setting up of this enterprise were Tim Eliott, the actor, Peter Bland, the poet and playwright, in conjunction with Martyn Sanderson (who gave the theatre its name) and Harry Seresin. Other key contributors along the way were the playwrights, Bruce Mason of 'The End of the Golden Weather' and 'The Pohutukawa Tree' fame, and the late Warren Dibble (1931-2014).

Warren Dibble, the 1969 recipient of the *Burns Fellowship* (originally set up by the University of Otago in Dunedin), had already written extensively for radio and stage. Warren was the first to incorporate the use of video on stage in a New Zealand stage production. His play, 'a cartoon for theatre' *Operation Pigstick*, was first produced in 1966 under Tim Eliott at Downstage where Jonathan Hardy played one of several interchangeable roles. This was his most important play of the period, he told me. 'A furious gesture at New Zealand's involvement in Vietnam', as the theatre reviewer and enthusiast, Peter Harcourt noted. [2] Other players in this production were Jennifer Dakers, Ken Blackburn and Peter Mackenzie. The review in the *Dominion* heralded this work as a 'brilliant piece of political satire' and 'amongst the best political satire produced in this country'.

The review goes on to praise Hardy's characterization, 'Jonathan Hardy playing the part of the American Senator on a visit to the battle front gives a superb but frightening performance. His main speech sent cold shivers down my spine as he expounded at a fantastic rate on the merits of the Great Society and screamed "*the only way to combat communism is with bombunism*". Warren said in this regard that he was making 'napalm jokes long before *Apocalypse Now*'. In September 1969, two further Dibble plays, *Lines to M* and *Lord Dismiss Us*, ran at Downstage, and at the end of that same year Warren Dibble finally moved to Sydney. Hardy played in other light musical entertainments popular at the time like *O What A Lovely War*, where he appeared as a demented drill-sergeant.

He clearly had his successes in those heady days. Hardy was latterly remembered by Warren as 'A big fruity guy with a lot of theatrical energy'. The late and 'outlandish' Brian Bell, a Wellington eccentric (already notorious in the generally staid '50s), has been quoted on Jonathan Hardy, thus: *'I suspect he thought others saw him as a Greek God, I saw only an extroverted flasher'.*

BALLAD OF THE TAJ MAHAL [3]

A restaurant with fountain and water-clock
comprised one plan for a shutdown toilet block—
domed like a mosque, chained, under padlock;
enshrined as the Taj Mahal.

Years long and rusty this privy stood disused,
many a gland, they say, was here defused;
such gentlemen taken short were not amused—
preyed on at the Taj Mahal.

Came here the councillors plans to invent,
they prayed that success would be heaven sent;
but know their bowels were as thrifty as lent,
squatting in the Taj Mahal.

The saturated walls soon gave short shrift
to new laid plans when the precincts were sniffed—
many shed a tear over schemes gone adrift,
to jazz up the Taj Mahal.

A smart Greek suggested a drive-in car wash,
so why go down-market when you can go posh?
It's all one to derros—they don't give a toss,
pissing on the Taj Mahal.

Oh, the writing, it's certain, was on the wall,
though not all such sentiments were shared by all—
still, drains will gurgle after heavy rainfall,
in troughs by the Taj Mahal.

If the walls of Jericho fell to the trumpet;
know that these will stand or fall on their merit,
no matter what gay boy sets out to mourn it—
        lost days at the Taj Mahal.

Some dream of precious stones from far away,
some of amethyst, or onyx with pearl inlay,
some of greenstone from down Hokitika way;
        to brighten the Taj Mahal.

If fire engines scream, and the traffic roars by,
and walls have ears, though you cannot guess why—
take a glass of Chablis beneath a domed sky,
        to salute the Taj Mahal.

Afterword

The following is taken from the *Notes* section which relates to this ballad in my poetry collection, *GONE, Satirical Poems: New & Selected* (2016) : 'The public toilet block known as the "Taj Mahal" designed by architects of the Wellington City Engineering Office was built in 1928. The building's design is not without a certain, architectural humour; its curved north and south end walls, each capped with a dome, resemble that of a "mosque". This quasi-imperial style is listed on the *Heritage Inventory* as "Inter War Free Classical". The edifice functioned as a WCC public toilet for forty years and finally closed in 1966. Fortunately, a strong public outcry saved the building from demolition. For about a decade it was used as storage space for nearby *Downstage Theatre.* In 1978, after extensive renovations, the *Taj Mahal* reopened as an art gallery and patisserie and became, latterly, a restaurant. Environmental artists, Terry Archer and David Waterman, were commissioned to paint a fresco (Muldoon's visage peers troll-like from the puffy clouds), on the northern dome ceiling by the owner, Cynthia Cass, who bought the property in 1980. The building remains a significant cultural landmark, though continues to serve as a "public bar" under shifting ownership and name.'

Jonathan Hardy (1940-2012). His obituary appeared in the *Sydney Morning Herald*, on September 3, 2012 which lists his many accolades as an actor on both sides of the Tasman in theatre, film and television; he latterly gained a certain quirky fame as the voice behind the puppet character, Rygel XVI, in the Australian sci fi TV series *Farscape* (1999-2003) which flopped in Australia but gained cult status in the States. Indeed, I was a fan! I quote an excerpt from Jonathan Hardy's obituary:

'After attending the New Zealand Players' Drama School, Hardy was a gold-medal student at the London Academy of Music and Dramatic Arts, better known as LAMDA, which led to contracts with the Royal Shakespeare Company and the (British) National Theatre. By 1971 he had moved to Australia, making his film debut as advertising executive Groove Courtenay in Beresford's breakthrough film *The Adventures of Barry McKenzie* ... Johnathan Hardy was an archetypal character actor, a common presence in Australian movies, television and theatre for 40 years. He appeared in many movies and scripted others. His screenplay for *Breaker Morant*, co-written with director Bruce Beresford, earned an Oscar nomination.'

[1] The archivist of the Marist Fathers in NZ provided the following information on JH that appeared in the athletics sections of the SPC school magazine, *The Patrician*, for 1958:

Annual College Championships: J.D.Hardy 1st.in Senior Long Jump 21ft.1,3/4ins. First in 220yards:22.9sec. 1st. in 50yards. 5.6sec. ALL NEW

RECORDS. And J.D.Hardy (sp) 1st. 100yards, 11.1 sec. 3rd equal. 220yds. Discus J.D.Hardy 1st. 98ft.4ins.

PRIZES: Senior. Gilbert Cup J.D.Hardy., Keogh Cup (Jumps & Hurdles) R.T.Murphy, J.D.Hardy & G.M.Hoskins. (Throwing) Mahony Cup J.D.Hardy.

Old Boys Cup Meeting: Long Jump 1st. J.Hardy,19ft.6ins. 100yds 1st.J.Hardy,11.3 sec: 220yds. Ist.J.Hardy,22.9sec., Discus, 3rd J.Hardy. (Silvertream won the Cup).

McEvedy Shield: 1st 100yds 11.1sec., J.D.Hardy (sp), 220yds. 3rd equal. J.D.Hardy(sp) C.Hunkin (H).

[2] *A Dramatic Appearance: New Zealand Theatre 1920-1970*, Peter Harcourt, Methuen, 1978.

[3] *GONE, Satirical Poems: New & Selected*, Stephen Oliver, illustrations by Matt Ottley, Canberra, Greywacke Press, 2016:

'O Brother Where Art Thou?'

My early schooldays as a student at Marist Brothers Newtown, Wellington (a kind of transit camp Catholic schoolboys were subjected to, before progressing inevitably onto St. Patrick's College), were troubling enough. A number of these brothers had an effect and influence measured in varying degrees according to the force and imposition of their personalities, rather than any ability to impart knowledge or learning. Except of course, for Miss Dobson, but more of her in a moment. There was Brother Henry who took a particular interest in me expressed in flattery more than anything else, though what physical looks I may have had, or whether my eyes were a green or blue colour, I could not see as having any relevance to my education. Maybe this was a lesson in acquiring self-confidence. Brother Henry, in his 'civilian days' had worked as an ambulance driver. He, too, fell foul of the head honcho, Brother Paulinus, and I liked him because he didn't kowtow to the Paulinus bullying technique. He stood his ground fearlessly and was hated by the formidable Brother Paulinus. Brother Henry would in the end leave the order, marry and raise a family. When in doubt, procreate.

There was one particular lay teacher, an Englishman named Pringle, a swinish, sadistic individual who got great satisfaction from literally flogging boys with the cane for minor misdemeanours. Often, at the slightest provocation, he would schedule these occasions to take place in the lay teacher's office as lunch time entertainment for one or two other teacher-spectators, particularly, for the emerging thespian, the now late Mr Jonathan Hardy. They worked this routine in tandem like a dirty little secret. One middle-aged brother took a singular delight in dandling boys on his knee in the classroom. Boys would talk of how he would stroke the boys' thighs, but I don't think much came of it. Brother Roberts took us for history (though it was not uncommon for teachers to interchange subjects such was the general application of knowledge), and he was a no-nonsense individual with slicked back black hair and horn-rimmed spectacles with a rectangle shorn out from the hairline. Whether this ever grew back I can't recall. It made him look rather vampire-like. You knew this man possessed incontestable strength both of manner and physique. A distant figure. Notwithstanding, they all robustly caned the living bejesus out of us in turn. Even Brother Felix, the Fijian, who giggled like a drag queen and took to calling me 'orotund'. But for the most part, Brother Felix was a gentle and harmlessly coquettish individual; though he displayed a more temperamental anger when caning boys (across the finger tips) that was strangely un-masculine, accompanied by much nose twitching.

Peripherally, Brother John (he didn't teach me), always appeared quietly tortured in a vainglorious way and was, apparently, renowned as a fine middle-distance runner. He took inordinate pride in his 'stylish' running technique—rather mincing, I thought, though the mothers liked it. On sports day we could observe him in action when it came to the Brother racing Brother *heats*. Brother Henry proved to be a speedy 100-yard contender and invariably won, in fact, he beat Brother John who didn't take defeat well though his silky black hair (that flick of the front lock) remained in place. He too eventually disappeared from the order, and was rumoured at the time to have had either a tantrum or a tearful breakdown at school. He was what my mother would have termed, 'a sensitive young man, without a vocation'.

Even then I was not the most academically attuned pupil—and was never destined to be—and possessed little self-confidence. My reading ability was barely average. Miss Dobson was the only true teacher I had during those primary school years, and she took a special interest in my case, both in and out of school. I had on occasion to visit her home, and was more than willing to, for additional instruction in reading techniques. 'Remedial reading' was the official term. Under her patient care and understanding, devoid of any of the egotistical palaver associated with the other teachers, I made huge advances in learning and thoroughly enjoyed the process.

There was no negative criticism here, simply a real and sincere concern for the well-being of a student. As a result of her instruction I eventually won an end of year school prize (sneered at by my eldest brother) for 'the most improved in the class'. The award so dedicated and inscribed was a book titled *Black Beauty*. In any day or age, Miss Dobson, who had taught for many years, would be regarded and celebrated as a true teacher. She harboured no careerist ambitions nor private agendas. Her only interest lay in helping and getting the best out of her students without the slightest hint of dishonesty or coercion. She never once had recourse to physical and psychological abuse to get 'quick' results. She gave me confidence—so I believed in myself.

The only other woman on staff was the music teacher, Miss O'Shea. She had a severe neurological disorder that may have been cerebral palsy in part. But on the other hand, it may have been something akin to *Tourette Syndrome*. Twitching, and little muscular convulsions of the neck and arms, even cursing! Angst ridden facial contortions. Whatever nervous disorder afflicted her, she was what one used to call 'highly strung' but she was a brilliant music teacher and created one of the finest school choirs in the history of Marist Brothers, Newtown. I was in that choir and we were the toast of the town. Neurotic though she was (she appeared tremulously in awe of Br. Paulinus), Miss O'Shea's one driving ambition was to create the best possible boys' choir in the city, and she did it. All through her tantrums and tears, Brother Paulinus acted as her personal guardian and would not tolerate any form of misbehaviour on behalf of the boys. This was the only occasion I saw him act tenderly or protectively toward anyone.

We were to commit ourselves wholly, body and soul, just like Miss O'Shea, and so we did.

The choir following months of practice gloriously paid off at the end of year festival before we 'broke up' for the longed-for Christmas holidays which ran for about eight weeks. We sang in multiple harmonies though there was a male lead called Stephen Keith who did long solos in the best *Vienna Boys' Choir* tradition, and that was what she was aiming for. A few of the numbers were the standard Catholic hits like 'The Song of St. Bernadette', 'Ave Maria', good old standards like, 'Silent Night' and a song with lyrics that went, '*Set mid a scene of courtly pomp, dim in the mists of long ago, courtiers perform their stately dance, with measured step and slow...*' and oddly, 'The White Horse Inn' (Harry Secombe's signature tune, though he was more famously known as *Neddie* of 'The Goon Show'.) This was Miss O'Shea's night-of-nights and her great triumph. This too, was the only time she wore lipstick and makeup (badly) and something like a white starchy dress with a floral pattern of roses. She looked mummified. We had two years of her instruction and then she suddenly left, mid-term, unannounced, and without warning. It didn't take long for the choir to deteriorate under the temporary replacement, baton-cum-cane of Brother Paulinus with his usual frustration, impatience and anger. There was no one else to replace her, certainly not of her calibre, though a disgruntled Brother Felix eventually took over.

I learnt that Miss O'Shea had taken off to the UK and then completely disappeared. She was in fact, subsequently reported missing—discovered some months later, wondering the streets of London, incoherently babbling to herself, head shaven bald as a Buddhist monk. Where she had been, and what she had done during her Agatha Christie spell of amnesia, no one knew, least of all Miss O'Shea. She had suffered a psychotic episode—maybe she was bi-polar—a complete nervous breakdown. The woman was perfectionist extraordinaire and ultimately could not sustain the expectations or high standards she set herself. I never discovered what became of the woman after her failed bid for greater musical success in the UK. She did return to New Zealand, but to what fate I do not know, though she never returned to Marist Brothers, in Tasman Street, Newtown.

In that wedge of hill and gully between Ohiro and Brooklyn roads, on the western slopes steeply falling away to Aro Street and the city beneath, lay *Central Park*, with its network of root-bound dirt tracks, its canopies of towering pine, eucalypt and macrocarpa, the upper slopes planted in rhododendrons, coral-pink, and azaleas ribbon-red skirting Brooklyn Road, extended haphazardly down over the hill and opened out onto a flat space with a few battered swings, suspended chains from bars with hoops, a lop-sided carousel, constructed out of heavy planked timber, a faded green, with metal bars to hold onto, and a square weather-board council building painted a dirty white with wire-meshed, opaque windows.

The Central Park Tennis Courts on Brooklyn Road (diagonally opposite the sub-station), used to be the venue for international celebrity matches, or was up until the late '60s. *Charlton 'Chuck' Heston* may have been one of those who sauntered onto the courts resplendent in his white cottons, though he did play with John Souter against Peter Snell and Robert Clarke on Mercer Street, Central Wellington in 1966. Central Park Tennis Courts is also where the exhibition basketball team, the *Harlem Globetrotters* came to strut their stuff. On the other, lower level of the park, a white, narrow wooden bridge on high concrete pillars and arch connected the dirt tracks of the wilderness onto gravel paths alongside dull shrubbery beds that led down to the ineffectual wall fountain (slimed grotto) that dribbled from a little basin into a semi-circular collecting pool beneath it.

Here, the big metal gates of the main entrance exited onto the bottom of Brooklyn Road, around Nairn Street (with its row of run down, identical houses on the rise known as the 'three sisters'—there used to be five until the mid '50s), Brooklyn Road finally joining onto upper Willis Street that continued down into the CBD. Central Park offered me a suspension in time within its moody confines, especially under the two buzzing pylons on rising knolls that contributed to the wild, abandoned aspect. I walked up and down through this largely forgotten and unruly section of the town belt all through my secondary school days. Wellington and the harbour with Matiu (or Somes) Island, a faded brown in the middle distance, spread before me in the mornings and behind me in the afternoons, as I trudged back up into the Brooklyn Hills.

A Small Matter Of Demolition

St. Patrick's College (Wellington) occupied the corner block facing onto Cambridge Terrace, opposite the Basin Reserve and bounded by Buckle and Tory streets. The main building, a forbidding grey pile, we knew as *Colditz Castle*. The lower grounds in front of the 'castle' comprised a half-acre grassy expanse with a couple of football posts, the area completely cordoned off from the road on two sides by a fifteen-foot wire fence (winter lingered down here in muddy patches a little longer). On the upper level, and behind the main building off Tory Street stood a concrete building similar in size to an aircraft hangar that served as an Assembly Hall for the entire schoolboy population.

Assembly took place every morning with roll call and each boy answered loudly *'Yes, father!'* when his name was called out by the discipline master. And that person was Fr. Silverwood, a goofy looking priest with a perennial and lethal smile we called 'Bottles' because of his odd pear shape. We all lived in fear of this man because his seemingly mild manner and quirky grin belied his uncompromising exertions with the cane, and the strength with which he applied it. He was all the more fearful because his expression never changed. That smile remained. 'Bottles' could make even the most hardened six former weep.

The Assistant Discipline Master was Father Terry O'Neill. His technique was to fix the entire Assembly with an uniquely fierce blue-eyed glare and he invariably stared us down into silence. His other distinctive feature—ears that predominantly stuck out some distance from his head. He was a *short back and sides* man, with a low parting and well-oiled black hair. Black Irish. The ferocity lay in the hypnotic and laser stare. This was followed by the morning's dressing down and dire warnings, recriminations, observed petty misdemeanours and minor breaches of school protocol, the various boys singled out for individual treatment, and those (alas!) who were called to visit the discipline master in his room where the caning took place at lunch time; then the morning collective prayer, and we were dismissed, marching in single file and in an orderly manner, out past the main driveway entrance and the practice nets for cricket, and off to our respective classes, in disciplined silence, at least until out of sight.

This functional building backed onto the only other large grassy area in the school's grounds. Various pre-fabricated outhouses had been banged up as school rooms and identified by a 'letter' D Block, for instance. This gave the place a herded, transit camp atmosphere. But of course, you would prefer to be in one of these lightweight structures in the event of the earthquakes that happened often enough, than being caught in the old building which we quite correctly regarded as a danger and more than likely condemned as an earthquake hazard. Earthquake prone Wellington had not yet started on its building boom with most of the inner city being dismantled and rebuilt according to the latest building codes.

In the middle of this open area, and facing the west wing of the main building, stood a dilapidated tongue and groove that served as the school library. This backed onto the main scullery and kitchen area that provided for priest and lay teacher alike. The Buckle Street entrance (the soup kitchen run by the Sisters Home of Compassion was in the same street close by) took you directly onto a small asphalt tennis court preserved in the main for recreational activities of the priests, past the science block of dull modernist design with school rooms situated beneath the labs. A covered-way led down past the tuck shop and into the back entrance of the main building, through a narrow foyer, where the weekly grades for every student were posted behind a glass billboard, and into the very bowels of the building.

Heavy oaken glass-panelled doors swung round beneath the grand stairway and into an expansive hallway hung on the left as you entered with dark oils commemorating the various rectors and founding fathers from, it appeared, the beginnings of time. The lower, purgatorial regions. Directly opposite were the staff rooms for the lay teachers. The hallway terminated with the administration and rector's offices, an area generally out of bounds to the student unless otherwise summoned. The Rector in residence when I entered secondary school in 1963 was Fr. 'Jock' Mannix, a mild mannered yet rather distant figure who did not seem altogether aware, or did not wish to appear so, that he was either a rector, or in charge of a school full of unruly boys. 'Jock' had often been observed remonstrating *sotto voce* at 'inanimate objects'.

Fr. Minto arrived at St. Pat's ('town') in 1964, sent down from the august precincts of the boarding school, St. Patrick's College, Silverstream, in the Hutt Valley, and made Rector in 1965. He was one of the new breed. This priest's attitude by comparison was perfunctory and his attitude decidedly careerist. From the ground floor and the centre of the building, the grand stairway with its thick banisters led up two floors into the dim regions where the priests had their individual 'cells'. These wide hallways with creaking and uneven, polished linoleum floors (a honeyed glow) existed in a state of perpetual, dusty twilight, as though this place were one of the forgotten ante-chambers of heavenly judgement, suspended forever in or out of time. Our very own *Gormenghast*.

No direct sunlight had penetrated into the depths of this building since the day of its completion back in the 1880s. Naturally, fund raising activities for ongoing building projects were a constant feature of school life. The priests relied as much on donations from corporations with a strong Catholic bias, or wealthy Irish Catholic families with construction interests—and businesses like the Flynns, responsible for various medium high-rise apartments around Wellington—as they did on regular term fees. For a couple of years after I left St. Patrick's, I continued to receive packets of raffle tickets, printed in blue ink, the school's colours, which I promptly threw into the garbage bin. To the school's credit, in needy cases school fees were waived where families suffered financial hardship and couldn't pay up.

This was the preserve of the English public-school system. *Competition and manliness* were the cornerstones of our education. Ours was not a Jesuit education (those storm troopers of Roman Catholicism) but a poor imitation of the same, set down in the colonies during the first days of settlement. Most of the 'provinces' were made up initially of the working classes, until such time as they could make enough money to move a notch or two up the social ladder. But not St. Patrick's town; here you had the Italians (the *Tesorieros* and *Grecos*) from Island Bay, the Poles and assorted east Europeans, a few Lebanese, and the Anglo-Celts, many from poor working-class families with about a third middle class representation. School prefects were 'cloned priests,' chosen as role models on the basis of academic and sporting excellence.

There were one or two Māori students, in particular, a boy with the surname of *Love* (his father was a 'wealthy' wharfie, the unions still had real clout in those days), and only two south pacific Islanders; a quiet boy who had suffered from polio and walked with difficulty, and another, a huge Samoan called *Otto Dun*. This man-boy took his caning (at Marist Brothers, Tasman Street), across the palms in front of the class in a bored and indifferent manner, in fact, you could almost say, relaxed—which in turn propelled the teacher to double his efforts with exasperation and fury. No teacher ever got the better of Otto Dun, either at Marist Brothers or, latterly, St. Patrick's. There was the rare example of the boy who was not Catholic, but nevertheless admitted to St. Patrick's. Such a boy was undoubtedly enrolled because his parents had a great deal of money, and the school committee worked relentlessly for additional funding and sponsorship. One assumes the parents were looking for a relatively inexpensive, private

Catholic school not particularly distinguished by its scholastic or even sporting record. Fatefully, this proved to be the case with my family after my father spiralled out of control and into terminal alcoholism.

Most of the *wealthy* families sent their boys on to St. Patrick's College Silverstream in the Hutt Valley north of Wellington. Our school colours were blue chevron on a grey jersey, or for dress occasions, a royal blue blazer with school monogram blazoned on the breast pocket, a white shirt set off with a blue and white striped tie and long grey trousers. Their colours were the same in most every respect except of a correspondingly paler hue. The Silverstream boys, gallingly, too often beat us in sport, *rugby especially*. 'Town' did hold its own academically against 'Stream'. Geoff (a fellow poet I hung out with) and I weren't into sport on any level and avoided it at all costs. This is probably how we came to conspire together at St. Patrick's as outsiders and thereby discovered a mutual interest in reading and literature. This occurred in the middle years of our secondary school tenure, and early on in the fifth form. The 'losers' who avoided rugby and cricket were at least required to do *something*, and these 'rejects' usually ended up with the harriers. I managed to get out of that too by pleading poverty and getting a job after school in a local butcher's shop on the Buckle Street end of Kent Terrace facing the Basin Reserve. The butcher, a socialist pal of my father's, would sprinkle a 'special' powder over the meat that intensified its redness making it look fresher. The work area floor had a layering of sawdust. This got soiled. One of my tasks was to sweep this up and replace it. My next job during my senior years was with a small tailor's company on Tory Street that specialized in the production of men's tweed jackets. My tenure at college was ending and I dreamed of escape.

The recollection of rugby practice on those late, cold winter afternoons at Hataitai Park or Wakefield Park back in the Marist Brothers days, seemed to me even then a pointless waste of energy, and an exercise in unnecessary discomfort. I played rugby without distinction. As far as competition went and the business of winning, I never really got the hang of it, and the physical effort alone involved in this activity didn't make much sense to me, if the end result was simply to get more points on the board than your opponent. But this was meant to be good character building stuff, and the Protestant spirit of Calvin stalked through the land in seven league boots all the way from Invercargill and 'Outward Bound', a reality which I was always being threatened with by my parents. OB was a sort of fitness camp based on army principles, a discipline and training regimen, which meant getting up at 6 am and going on long marches with a full pack before breakfast six days a week. A sort of boot camp for recalcitrant boys. Both the Catholic sense of manliness and the Calvinistic ethic of hard work, denial and an austere life, somehow overlapped in the collective consciousness of the New Zealand psyche, and entered into the school system of all denominations. An atmosphere ripe for rampant masturbation. Competition was the name of the game and this equalled success and prestige. We were being prepared for the world though *whose* world and *when* remained obscure.

Somewhere on the horizon loomed the glassy high-rise ghosts of the corporate conglomerates and stock broker's hounds of globalization, a dystopia for the new millennium that had not yet been set loose under the new technologies ushered in by the digital age; *Company America* gambolling toward us through Disneyland via Hollywood, Microsoft and the World Trade Organization. Global citizenship. A global civil society requiring one to brave a new world in which large corporations plunder the resources and cheap labour of third world countries when they should be obligated by international law, and as part of their investment charter, to set up hospitals, schools, universities, housing infra-structures in locations like Malaysia, S.E. Asia and obscure South American countries, etc.

Once you artificially displace the horizon you obliterate any sense of both your personal and historical past. There were still eccentric characters to be seen, though the *Rawleigh Man* driving the country roads (Vincent O'Sullivan had written a rather overly mannered poem called, 'Don't Knock the Rawleigh Man'), and the *Bon Brush* salesmen out of the '50s, were beginning to become a legend; but for the moment, the 'man of the land' suggested at least, some standing in the community. (Silhouette against skyline, one foot on tree stump, rolling a *smoke*—frozen in the thousand-mile stare—later, satirized in Vincent O'Sullivan's *Butcher Poems* sequence). The deer cullers, the pig hunters, and the 'good keen men' of the King Country. Characters made to populate such social-humorist books like the 'Gus Tomlins' stories of Frank Sheldon Anthony [1891-1927] collected in *Me and Gus* and, latterly, the popular Barry Crump novels celebrating the day-to-day absurdities of the everyday bloke with his dry, knockabout humour. *A Good Keen Man* and *Bastards I Have Met*. Days when you could get a different job every week and move about the country with ease. Workmen's huts dotted the landscape. Otherwise, we were destined to be 'men alone'. I'm sure that most of these archetypes came into being, or evolved from the early settlers and individual explorers (or 'exploiters') of the landscape. The beautifully wrought descriptions of the botanist, John Carne Bidwill (1815-1853) for instance, in his *Rambles in New Zealand*, reaching out into the 'interior' suggest that life may have been short, but at least it was intensely interesting.

No matter how you looked at it, there was no easy passage, as we were to find out. In the first couple of years from forms three to four students were subjected to compulsory army training in schools. This ran over a couple of weeks in summer in which we practised at army drill, and the priests mysteriously became transfigured into an assortment of commanding Officers, Btn Commanders, Btn. Adjutants, R.S.M.s, R.Q.S.M.s,

O.C.s, Coy. Commanders, C.S.M.s, Platoon Commanders and Sergeants (a veritable cross-dressing fiasco, or a crossing over into the civvy world) in snappy regulation dress, while we were outfitted in heavy khaki uniforms with the texture of sandpaper. The various corporals, sergeants and platoon commanders through to battalion commanders, came from the ranks of the school prefects, excellent training for the future world of the CEO, officious, competitive bullies in the making. We were given old Lee-Enfield rifles (sans firing pins) and taught how to march and wheel by the right and left with regular parade ground monotony until our inner thighs were chafed raw. For two weeks the usual classroom tuition was suspended while we played at soldiers, and the priests played at being non-commissioned officers. At this time, in the last days of the National Party regime under Prime Minister Keith Holyoake (the long-standing member for Pahiatua in the Wairarapa District of the lower North Island), all males in secondary schools were subjected to military training for two weeks of every year, and compulsory conscription was still in force for those males eighteen years and over, a system based on ballot.

Army training in schools was thankfully abolished after my third year around 1966, and national, compulsory conscription in 1969. In that last year (my first out of school) I missed out on being drafted into the army and serving in Vietnam in the ballot by one day! All those born on the 4th of December in my year were conscripted. I was born on the 5th. My mother was so annoyed by this that she quite seriously considered writing in for a 'recount' if such a thing were possible. James K. Baxter had already published his political poem, *A Bucket Of Blood For A Dollar* that first appeared in broadsheet form from John Summers Bookshop, Christchurch, in 1965. There were other poems like *The Gunner's Lament*, about a Māori gunner who lay dying 'In a paddy field north of Saigon,' published in the same year in Wellington in cyclostyled form. A stanza or two from this poem will adequately serve to illustrate the well-established opposition to the New Zealand National Party's alliance with American foreign policy and its involvement in Vietnam:

> 'I fried a village,' said Uncle Sam,
> 'with the new phosphorus bomb
> The day a Yankee Army nurse
> Was killed by the Viet Cong;

By 1967-8 street marches against America's involvement in South East Asia were well under way throughout the main cities of New Zealand, anticipating the apartheid riots of the early eighties, and Baxter had followed up on his earlier poem with '*a death song for mr mouldybroke*'. The psychic landscape had altered forever and time had picked up momentum throughout the South Pacific. The world was increasingly becoming a public arena. The first essay I published as an eighteen year-old was titled 'A Dimension of Student Revolt' appearing a year or two after I had written it in a Catholic academic journal called *Dialectic* in 1971.

The abstract conceits expressed in this piece on 'selfness' owe much to my reading of Pierre Teilhard de Chardin and to related literary and mystical theories on 'detachment'. These were developed later into the 'anti-ego' stance with which I came to characterise the over-hyped '60s artistic phenomenon; see my essay, 'The Poet as Fraud: A Composite'. (Antipodes, June 2005), retitled here as 'Dirty Bomb Poetic'.

It was almost as though the Southern Hemisphere now turned counter-clockwise, and worked on an opposing thread to that of the northern hemisphere; you could hear the profound, yet unstoppable grating of the psychic, tectonic plates. Baxter's poem concludes:

'I'm a simple chap,' said Holyoake,
'Politics frighten me;
But whether it's frozen meat or men
We send across the sea,
We want good prices for our veal—
what can you guarantee?'
'Just name your price,' said Uncle Sam,
'And leave the rest to me.'

Nineteen sixty-three was the year John F. Kennedy was shot dead. The following year I started third form at St. Patrick's College. The portents did not augur well for my academic success. 'New boys' were 'streamed' in those days; this was the infamous Otis Intelligence Test, an American invention, long since discredited, and abandoned in the late '80s. We had to sit a number of tests and were assessed principally on our mathematical ability and streamed or graded into levels from low to high stream. I had absolutely no aptitude for numbers let alone maths. For the first couple of weeks fortune seemed to smile upon me. I was placed in the higher level with the bright kids who studied Latin, French, Physics, and Chemistry. Of course, I felt totally out of my depth. It was not long before the priests discovered that a horrible mistake had been made. There were two new 'Olivers' at this time (unrelated) in the school.

My older Brother, Bill, had already been a student at St. Pat's for three years by the time I arrived in 1963, and my youngest brother, Michael, was five years away. The two eldest brothers, Laurence and Gary (deceased) had been packed off to 'Tech', the co-ed *Wellington Technical College* (now known as Wellington High School) not far off Adelaide Road and Newtown. My father's Marxist/socialist principles won for the two eldest. I was called before the Rector, Fr. Mannix, and duly informed of this mistake in my class allocation, though he was more interested in drawing my attention to an invisible point on the horizon from his window which I failed to see, than dealing with the more mundane matters of my destroyed self-confidence. I was then placed in one of the lower streams, and told that if I worked hard, I might be transferred into one of the higher streams. If I worked hard. Ah, the promise of failure! I then took my place with the lower working-class kids from the poorer families of Newtown and Island Bay suburbs, a varied ethnic mix; already the Italian contingent was well on the way to advanced puberty. You knew it by the black hairy legs and that rank, sweaty odour peculiar to those for whom masturbation is as familiar as school yard bullying.

It wouldn't be long before the Tesoriero boys set up a gambling racket placing bets for class mates (the Lebanese and Greeks were enthusiastic punters) at the local TAB and raking off a healthy percentage on the takings. Every Monday morning we checked the 'glass billboard' at the entrance foyer of the main building for our weekly grades. Once or twice I was singled out and named in morning assembly as one who had achieved distinction on a regular basis and I was congratulated. Forlornly, I remained condemned to inhabit that infernal, lower Dantesque circle. The priests didn't see fit to transfer me to a higher stream or class even though I had requested it. At least, this remained the case for the first couple of years. My subjects were: English, History, Geography, Commercial Practice and Christian (XTD) Doctrine—a step down from the French and Latin lessons of the first couple of weeks.

I progressively did well in English and could hold my own against all comers and levels of academic achievement as the years progressed. History too, and oddly, XTD. I liked the freedom of abstract thought and philosophic conjecture. I usually gained a first in my class on this subject. *That* and English, and occasionally, I got a second in History. Doing well in XTD was a curiosity as far as my father was concerned, a declared atheist. He baited me with questions like, 'Can God make a stone so big he can't lift it?', or 'Can God make a square circle? To which you would reply, 'Of course he can't, there's no such thing!'

This answer was hardly satisfactory, and the response came, 'Well, if he can't do these things then God cannot do everything and [*ergo*], God isn't God and doesn't exist'. The family rosary orchestrated by my mother maybe once a week in the evening during my childhood years (soon abandoned with the advent of puberty) apparently had little effect upon my father's decidedly intellectual and rational approach to life. My playing into this circular argument proved at least one thing though I was not fully aware of it at the time—and that was I understood even less than I was prepared to admit.

In any event, mine was a general education. *Cleverness*, at least as far as I was concerned, belonged to formulaic talents, or so I would later come to believe regarding many of the contemporary literary lights feted by publishers and popular literary cliques of the '70s. The essence of my education came through reading, or more particularly, through the discovery that I was interested in reading, and that such pleasure was an open-ended thing, and could not be (by either act of government or individual edict) denied me. How important it was to realise and to treasure this knowledge in an otherwise mediocre society as the true nature of freedom. The fragility of such knowledge became my sacrament and Holy Grail.

A Nostalgia For Books

One of the first books that truly entranced me was Joshua Slocum's *Sailing Alone Around The World.* It was an advance on those novels for kids after the *William* Books and others, where tweedy English gentlemen or ex-colonels fell off bikes into hedgerows and yet played eccentric hero to some rebellious boy's dreams. Such material fed a quaint and romantically painted biscuit-tin view of the world with comforting, soft green rolling hills and oak and elm groves with babbling crystal (and manageable) streams that echoed magically with the rumble of horses hooves ridden by medieval knights or outlaws like Robin Hood. But then there were always the deserts and mesas of Utah or Arizona, the Rockies and conifers and chaparral, mountain or plainsmen inhabiting the world of Zane Grey—and I continued regardless to think that Grey was great (that Old West *purple* nostalgia), all the more so when I discovered that he had been responsible for opening up big game and marlin fishing in New Zealand, and that he was a regular visitor to Lake Taupo in the early '20s.

He set the example for later generations of American he-men, like the film star, Lee Marvin, to make regular visits to places like the Great Barrier Reef off Queensland and indulge in wrestling the black marlin. Adventure as philosophy. Somehow, this made the American all the more complete; the man was real, he was a true-life hero, a pre-puberty version of Hemingway and the South African poet, Roy Campbell. The following stanza is taken from my poetry collection, *Either Side The Horizon*, (2005):

77. OCCUPATIONS [1]

All roads lead to Boot Hill; all roads lead
to the charnel house; all roads lead to the bone
yard; down cemetery road literary guns from

> the legendary past went herding a cumulus cloud:
> Zane Grey, Hemingway and Roy Campbell.

In the first instance, the world may be a bubble, but as long as it lasts, lasts forever; that is, for as long as the reduced perspective within the child's world contains the vastness of his round imagination, and the world for him remains a much bigger place, and adventure lies somewhere beyond the end of the road in which he grew up.

I attended St. Patrick's College (long since demolished) on Cambridge Terrace, Wellington, from 1964-1968. Fr. Smith usually vented his frustration by informing us that given our lack of attention we had better *'Apply for our gold-plated broom and shovel now!'* and be done with it, that the future held little hope for us as far as getting on in the world went. As our XTD teacher he walked us through the usual Catholic one-stop salvation shop with a not unengaging disquisition. I enjoyed the debates or at least my right of reply. He seemed to find favour with a few of the more independent-minded boys, in particular, Geoff Cochrane, that is when Geoff took it upon himself to turn up at school. Some years later, we asked Fr. Smith to deliver the funeral service and sermon for our mutual friend, Philip Kennedy, who died as a result of (drunkenly) leaping into a bush and falling down a steep slope.

Foolishly, this was a game we had invented between us, finding a suitable bush and hurling ourselves into it, the sort of activity which usually followed post-pub (the infamous Duke Hotel), or party activity around Mt Victoria or Aro Street. The funeral oration delivered by Fr. Smith spoke of the difficulties of survival in a changing world, youth culture as he saw it, and how one had to guard against *'The forces of negation'*. I thought the remarks unadorned and quite dignified. Geoff, I understand, was not wholly satisfied at the time with Fr. Smith's approach and perhaps expected something a little more theatrical and pointed. But what more could one expect? Death is, after all, the ultimate declaration of anonymity.

Theatrics as a style belonged in abundance and without apology to Fr. Peter Salamonsen, known to his fellow priests as, 'The Swede'. He was the 'Hollywood' of priests with his outrageously thick and wavy, combed back, auburn hair with looks not unlike Roger Moore, or the young Clint Eastwood. A tallish, strutting man of slim build. He was very much the peacock but done with a self-deprecating humour. There was no denying his flamboyance. Fr. Salamonsen didn't particularly like the bully-boy type, and generally favoured the good-looking or admiring boys in the class; needless to say, mothers adored him. He could erupt with sudden, focused violence, especially when a boy showed indifference, or refused to be compliantly impressed with the person of Fr. Salamonsen.

I saw him on one notable occasion in our geography class fire a blackboard chalk duster (a rectangular piece of wood with a piece of felt glued to the bottom of it) at the back of a boy's head, after he had instructed that boy to walk down the aisle back to his desk. Whatever the offence, it was a minor misdemeanour. The first time he missed. The boy was instructed to pick up the duster, and return it to the priest. The boy had to repeat the same act of 'dead man walking' back to his desk. This time Fr. Salamonsen didn't miss with the duster. There was a resounding *thwack!* and the boy paused, but didn't lose his cool. Because of this, the same act was repeated. The boy slowly buckled, broke down out of sheer pain. Fr. Salamonsen subsequently left the priesthood in the late '70s, married, fathered a daughter, and completed a doctorate in history later in life. For me, he would always be the cinematic hero—the dignified gunslinger turned cattleman who finally wins the heart of the beautiful senorita, and thence retires to his spacious ranch of the sweeping vistas.

If there was any other priest he got on with, it was Fr. Fred Bliss, and yes, almost too coincidentally, he was the school's

Spiritual Director. If you had any problems of a personal nature he was the man to see, though we were reminded that any priest could be approached. There was nothing of the disciplinarian about him, and his manner suggested an effeminate aspect that he kept well under control. He was certainly likeable enough. I even took up the offer of a private visit to his room and in the process of discussing my teenage angst that may have had something to do with the difficulties of my family situation and my future prospects, undertook to make confession *entre nous* there and then. I was asked to kneel on a purple cushion with gold tassels before him, or rather to his side.

When I mentioned masturbation (he asked) it wasn't just a case of whether I had, it was a matter of how many times. I would have thought that one occasion would have sufficed for all, and didn't think the occurrence was quantitative in any way. Perhaps he was acting not out of concern for my spiritual well-being but out of mere voyeurism? How my average stacked up against other boys I shall never know. In any event, he did prophecy that I would 'never' lose my belief in God but in all likelihood would lose my faith. A sort of damned if you do and damned if you don't scenario. A fail-safe doubt instilled for future reckoning, I supposed. Regardless of these peccadilloes the man retained for me an altogether non-threatening charm; and I always thought he looked rather uncomfortable decked out as a captain or colonel on the school parade ground during those two weeks of army drill. He seemed to be lost in his uniform. His army swagger was more of a mince. Fr. Bliss went on to become the Rector of Silverstream College, then Provincial (official leader of the Marist Fathers NZ province for a set term), and latterly on to Rome where he ended up teaching theology after gaining a doctorate there. He returned to New Zealand in 2014 and took up his retirement in Napier.

His comrade in arms, Fr. Salamonsen, revelled in the experience, officer's baton gripped with his left hand and tucked elegantly under the arm-pit and a *Stuyvesant* cigarette, which he relished, held jauntily between the (nicotine stained) long fingers of his right hand, half raised as though about to bless the troops, everything performed with his trademark flourish. Even the 'sacred conditions' of saying mass didn't escape his crowd-pleasing antics; a wave of the handkerchief (you expected a bouquet of flowers to suddenly materialize), loud nose-blowing as though by way of an announcement, and then back to the serious business of the consecration—*again*, that back turned to the congregation, and you were left thinking that you were observing the deadly ministrations of some gaudy, gold-backed beetle, and thence to the raising of the host, executed with slow motion deliberation before the captive congregation during the yearly retreat.

I ceased going to mass long before they modified the service from Latin to English and changed some of the basic stage directions. For us, this was 'time out' from normal school lessons, scheduled for one week every year, when priests were priests and not authoritarian and soutane-clad teachers, all normal classes suspended, while our spiritual welfare was purportedly attended to, and the priests cast about as though on a recruitment drive for those boys who might have had a bare *inkling* of a vocation. We always hoped that the priests might say something interesting in their sermons, and occasionally they did strike a chord. Regrettably though, much of the sermonizing was party policy stuff. But for most of us this was simply *a life* before we did something else.

Each of the priests was located within the given hierarchy of popularity amongst the boys and found his place through a natural process of selection. Fr. Bill Durning, for instance, who didn't teach me. There was a well-established clan of Durning priests sprinkled up and down the country. Baxter dedicated *Jerusalem Sonnets* to a Colin Durning, though this kin (Bill) was a poor cousin, intellectually). He was one of the 'main men' amongst those hotshot older boys with the macho attitude. Fr. Durning was a public and heavy smoker (he surreptitiously shared smokes with the 'in' group) and always seemed to be in a hurry, *somewhere*. You could say he was one of 'the lads'. Fr. Scambary (Sports master), on the other hand, was given minimal teaching duties as far as I could see and was put in charge of general sporting activities and rugby training. He may have had something to do with either the first or second XV. The boys across the board generally liked him because he presented no threat and seemed set apart from the whole priestly spectacle. It was not uncommon to smell booze on his breath, and you noted that he was snubbed by a number of the other priests.

He informed me once that it was a sure sign that the boy who gobbled down his food came from a large family. It was a matter of getting one's share at the trough, he suggested, or inevitably being relegated to the lower ranks in the pecking order of things. The lions first, then the hyenas, and lastly the vultures and buzzards. An invaluable observation, and one I considered a measurable contribution to my education. The cunning and the feeding frenzy that came with ambition and success I could, thankfully, never get a handle on, and it took some time for me to realise why I was, on many occasions, treated with cold suspicion by people whose principal skill lay in disguising their trenchant lack of originality, in favour of passing fashion. In this, one became a threat, real or imagined. *What is his agenda?* For the most part, it seemed to me that such people projected their own greed and failed to realise that they were competing against their own murky reflections. He came into his own when stirring the boys onto greater athletic achievement. Fr. Scambary was, thankfully, no overbearing scholar.

One of the more benign incumbents was a little round priest called Fr. Roach, SM., S.T.D., Hist. Eccl. Lic. who to everyone's surprise ended up going to the SM 'General House' in Rome and the Holy See to do work researching the history of the Society of Mary. He had done a doctorate in church history earlier in Rome plus one in theology (if one can be forgiven the pun, he had bigger fish to fry). Fr. Roach was an authority on church canonical law—this was a big career move that took the priestly fraternity happily by surprise. He was a man with very shiny oiled hair (the perfect burgher) and a freshly minted tidiness. Another outsider, though of a different stamp, who came into the school for one full year in 1969 (I left in 1968) was Fr. John Weir who had leapt upon the Baxter band-wagon early on and ended up writing a couple of books, in fact publishing his Master's thesis on Baxter. This apparently qualified him to edit the first edition of Baxter's collected poems [Oxford University Press, 1979] plus a few of previously uncollected works in the mid '70s. He went on to edit other works of Baxter including, latterly, his collected letters in two volumes—*James K. Baxter: Letters of a Poet* (2019) which contain, much to my surprise, a letter from Baxter to me regarding two of my earliest poems (thankfully, lost) I had posted to him shortly after the second year of his tenure as Burns Fellow in 1967. His letter is addressed to me 9 April 1968. He closes his missive with this advice, 'The slogan for the poet, as well as I can guess it, is—"Every man his own psychiatrist." At least, that has been the way I have interpreted the old Greek Saying: "Know thyself."'

Fr. Weir was a man not overly concerned with the tedious business of teaching boys and had a rather preoccupied and removed manner. I had returned and shown him a few of my early poems once during his brief tenure and found him somewhat taciturn and unhelpful. So too was Fr. Frank Mc-kay, who lectured in English Literature at Victoria University, a year or two later when I showed him a few of my poems, and who appeared puzzled by the fact that I didn't write about 'love' in any really declared, or emotive form. Curiously, while he was torturing himself over my lack of sentimental emotionalism, in sashayed a sexy blonde student who, tossing her hair (and hips) informed Frank that the sensual nature of the book she was returning to him didn't do anything for her at all! And promptly turned about and left. The man appeared to be wracked with repressed carnality.

Fr. Weir had bigger game in mind, and because he was regarded with distinction and seen as something of a poet himself by the order, was afforded plenty of time to pursue his publishing and literary interests. He was given minimal teaching duties during his short tenure at St. Patrick's and developed the remarkable gift of invisibility. He was rumoured to be living somewhere on the premises, hidden deep within the rarely visited labyrinthine ways of the main building amongst 'so many corridors so many lurches'. The late night tapping of the typewriter, *they said*, burning the midnight oil, *they said*, and indeed, a midnight traveller might well ask, cupping the candle flame along the draughty corridors within that Gothic pile—*Is there anybody there?* But John Weir's ambitions lay not mouldering, but elsewhere.

You would be forgiven for mistaking the school library for either some old smoke house or railway shack with its sun-bleached, wavy tongue and groove, the three or four bowed wooden steps at its narrow single door entrance—the building was little more than one rectangular outhouse. The only book I recall borrowing was Chesterton's *Orthodoxy* and I particularly enjoyed his playful and witty denunciation of G.B. Shaw's puritanism. Those were the post-Edwardian days when the great literary minds sparred with scintillating engagement over concrete *ideas* and philosophies of life, civil, moral and political, with a stylistic charm now lost to contemporary *litterateurs*—who seem content enough to absolve themselves in a lukewarm mix of popular literary and mechanical theory, the abstract debunking of text in favour of semiotics, and fashionable cool, this last condition designed to disguise a barely ordinary talent and complete dearth of intellectual humour. Wit is nowhere to be found.

A final flowering may be glimpsed in the 'silvery, Latin prose' of Cyril Connolly from the '20s through to the '40s, particularly in his collection of essays, *The Condemned Playground.* There were intimations of such wit being carried through in the poems of Philip Larkin (Auden is the last great poet of the 20th century to possess it fully), a dedicated admirer of Connolly, but whereas Connolly carried his barb with playful humour and genuine *joie de vivre*, Larkin possessed nothing, or not enough, of the true innocent—becoming merely sardonic with a schoolboy's pornographic snigger, bitter into the bargain. Wit demands a certain ease of expression, a leisurely disposition, not a contrived or merely patient one; Larkin failed because he tightened up and torqued down on what might have otherwise been wit, into that peculiarly English, public school boy *sneer* that finally became a muffled hatred and ultimately, sterile silence. He and Kingsley Amis enjoyed an exchange of titillating letters through their long friendship where they practised at being wits but merely exhibited the snide, almost masturbatory side of English priggishness amounting to what only can be described as an inverted brand of 'classless snobbery'. The destroyed romantic become the pornographer.

We live in a time where manipulation and cunning generally supersede honesty, talent and purpose, and those without style who display a paucity of wit usually win the day. It is not so much there being not enough creative talent around, far from it; at the outset there is always a sufficient number within each generation, and spiritual survival depends on the existence of at least a few torch bearers. The problem lies with the public's inability to recognize these qualities, either within themselves or elsewhere, because the greater part of the populace is governed by blanket consumerism, globalization fed through the optic fibre cable and the contrivance of the internet into the body corporate. Ours is the functional age of the *Realpolitik.*

The danger lies in the risk of being absorbed into the world of visual display and in electronic or digital saturation. Creative endeavour is reduced to an assembly-line product, and the media excels in promoting the lowest common denominator based upon the dictates of advertising and the demands of weekly circulation figures. Our daily newspapers, which once contained arts and book review sections, now offer coloured lifestyle inserts, indistinguishable from the sales catalogues which accompany them. Such are the death throes of print journalism, products of a disposable society made ever more disposable through the facility and ease of computers—and the legions of graphic design 'artists', baseball-capped hipsters with all the creative spirit of an amusement arcade street punk. Robotic minds with the intellectual facility of technicians.

We have heard much of this before, but what is new is that we have forgotten most of it, and under such pressing technical overload, not even repetition is a valid method of retention and learning any more. Looking back, if the 20th century can be distinguished for anything other than its innumerable and sometimes great technological achievements, it can be remembered as the century in which we killed off collective cultural memory; a century in which the last remaining spark of the world's indigenous and stone-age peoples was finally extinguished, and the remnants were banished to the zones of suicide and alcoholism, and with it our only living access back into primal memories; a century distinguished by its jumble sale of technologies and its non-culture of *storage & retrieval* where documentation has replaced memory; a century of universal amnesia and unprecedented noise, a century in which the clocks rotated hours within the space of a minute, a spinning out and a dislocation of gravity, lost in an inky, inner space where time exists only as more time; a century to be recalled as the black hole at the very centre of nothingness, where even the very existence of historical and spiritual truth was doubted.

Survival, if ever it were a noble thing, has been reduced

to distrust and expediency buried deep and hidden within the cult of personality. Arguably, the manifold techniques of deception have triumphed over vision. We confuse knowledge with information, and I continuously implore whatever ancient gods who still call upon wisdom, who preside over the humanizing covenant of vision, to beat a hasty retreat back into the deserts, and to the mountainous caverns beyond. Maybe those ancient gods are yet amongst us, as suggested in Heinrich Heine's essay, 'Gods In Exile'?

But here we are back in the age of filing cards and the mid '60s. Archie Naylor was the man who ran the library, an English teacher (a layman with the untidy air of the time-honoured and valuable retainer), of many years standing within the Catholic school system. He was very much favoured by Geoff Cochrane who I believe, latterly, recalled Mr Naylor as 'a balanced man'. Perhaps he was, though from what I gather Archie Naylor had suffered severe shell shock during World War Two. (During our army manoeuvres he held the rank of *O.C.A. Coy* alongside Fr. Bliss, *O.C.B. Coy*). This gave Archie a distinction beyond his rather prosaic teaching techniques, and certain pronounced physical mannerisms. He didn't suffer from any affliction like *Tourette Syndrome* but he did, similarly, twitch and stutter. 'Mustard gas' we surmised, even though he was a Second World War vet. But this lent a certain 'dramatic nobility' to the shambolic tragedy that was Mr Archie Naylor.

Archie Naylor, English teacher/careers advisor, had the unnerving habit of hitching up his pants abruptly and with apparent aggression at intermittent intervals. Whether this was shell-shock, trauma or shyness, I couldn't say. His eye twitching seemed to suggest a transmission of some kind, a sort of encoded communication by which he was imparting to us an invaluable intelligence, but which we as agents of higher learning failed to decipher. He was the true teacher in the old tradition, agreeably removed, without frills or fireworks, maybe not the most inspiring figure nor even the most ambitious, but he was one you could wholly trust. That was measurably the virtue by which student and teacher could gauge a degree of reciprocity; an exchange could be made, and something learnt.

Directly across from the library was the open grassy patch I spoke of, located alongside the assembly building. This higher ground was open to the city on two sides, a space pleasantly removed from the busy traffic of priests and the general swim of school activity in the open asphalt areas between the prefabricated classrooms. A number of us with similar interests and attitudes would congregate here during the lunch hour. This is where Geoff and I first intersected and it was here at a quiet remove we discussed our burgeoning literary interests, which initially revolved around Dylan Thomas—though I think we were more intrigued by his bohemian life style and hell raising than any of the self-conscious, verbal contortions of his poetics.

We had heard him read his works and the poems of others on the Caedmon record label, the one with the woodcut image of Dylan on the sleeve where he reads other poets: W. H. Auden, Thomas Hardy, Edward Thomas, Henry Reed, his delightful, 'The Naming Of Parts' poem, and his pastiche of T. S. Eliot. The record remains a collector's item; and we were, like a generation of writers before us, 'hooked' by that *actorly* and sonorous Welsh voice. He would prove to be a deciding and near fatal influence upon Geoff in the following years, within the context of *drunken persona* adopted and emulated than for the primal cadences of Thomas's poems.

We were moving into the sartorial zone of cloth ties and coloured shirts, corduroy and tweed jackets. Geoff, for the first few years after we left school (he left a year before I finally decided to throw it in), was to be seen in an old beige duffle coat in winter and a chocolate brown corduroy jacket in any weather. I preferred my black and capacious duffle coat with the deer-antler toggles and green tweed jacket, complete with standard issue desert boots or suede shoes. This sort of dress afforded plenty of roomy inner pockets in which to stash sheaves of freshly written poems by which we hoped to impress each other.

Geoff was fairly consistent with the cloth tie in a variety of shapes, sizes and, occasionally, paisley hues. We had discovered through reading any number of colourful biographies of Dylan Thomas that he happily purloined other people's ties and coloured shirts. It was a matter of dressing down rather than presenting ourselves as outrageous exponents of counter-cultural fashion. As far as group movements went, literary, hippy or otherwise, I was very much of the 'tradition and the individual talent' school; in those early days, we were a couple of co-conspirators in search of a style.

No one invited us to join the 'Generation of '68'. It seemed to us that this was a 'movement' more to do with self-serving minor talents and shrewd entrepreneurs who had leapt upon the bandwagon of American '60s folk poetry from the Black Mountain School, the NYC '50s school of O'Hara, whose torch was passed onto Ashbery in the '60s (and then through to Olson, Creeley and Duncan) and rolled onward, like a Democratic Campaign, to wash up in Lawrence Ferlinghetti's *City Lights Books* on Columbus Avenue, San Francisco.

The times and tides were turning. Aside from its obvious merits, such a freeing up of poetic traditions—which originally found a good deal of its impetus in the poetics of Walt Whitman (naturally) and William Carlos Williams—the counter-culture finally species-jumped like a viral energy into '60s youth culture, powered along by the pandemic use of the electric guitar borrowed from the early blues masters. Bob Dylan replaced his acoustic guitar with this instrument and then proceeded to give greater popularity to the folk lyric. At the same time, the 'freedom train' became open house for any number of claim jumpers, pretenders, sexually narcissistic opportunists and chameleons 'in' fashion, some of whom would end up stranded high on the dry docks of post-modernism and trendy publishing houses, or find themselves gnawing at their own arses by clambering back down the *Yellow Brick Road*, resurrecting new anthologies of 'old hits' in a vain and futile attempt to claw back lost ground and prestige from the early '70s. Those far out, crazy hazy days of ego and hip clout.

I remained the confirmed outsider, something that proved an unwise career move. I guess I didn't think of writing as a 'career' in such practical terms. Somehow that seemed a particularly 'cold' term and I perhaps, stupidly, didn't plan my moves to good advantage. The literature grants and accolades went elsewhere. Writing, or particularly poetry, I regarded more as a vocation, or to use an old-fashioned phrase, as given through *divine afflatus*, a gift that I believed quite unfashionably had something to do with inspiration and an applied knowledge of technique, an art bestowed, in effect. Something you not only honoured, or felt honoured by, but cherished. I still believe it will do me more good than harm continuing to hold to this view. Writers as literary politicians and spin doctors, who paid their dues to the critics and the academics, moved along well-oiled tracks to successful appointments at universities, contemporary art museums and publishing houses, to begin the process all over again—power brokers in the clandestine game of denial and acceptance. I used to quote a few lines from the Gerard Manley Hopkins poem, 'The Habit of Perfection' which I find orphic; they suggest, at least to me, the wellspring and the fount of poetry.

> Elected Silence, sing to me
> And beat upon my whorlèd ear,
> Pipe me to pastures still and be
> The music that I care to hear.

But as yet we were still, though barely, caught within the school's progressively diminishing influence. In the last year or so, Geoff's absenteeism from school could be measured in weeks rather than days which did not endear him to the Assistant Discipline Director, Fr. Terry O'Neill. He preferred to stay home reading, or writing and re-writing snatches of novels and poems *('The lady on the sorrel rode down the boulevard' ... 'Down the boulevard the sorrel...')*. Others of our group were Philip Kennedy, John Girvan, Michael Throll, Bernard 'Barn' Kilkelly, Fred Farry and David Duffy. A few floated into focus like goldfish and drifted away again, perhaps to be intercepted at a later date in various pubs around town. Steve Murphy, usually peripheral, played a decisive role at the beginning as one of the first to help promote Geoff's literary endeavours. Murphy was an urbane individual, a womaniser (by all accounts a fine dancer), and a man of strong Irish charm with something of the 19th century decadent about him. He became a solid friend and patron to Geoff and would print and publish his first book of poems, *Images of Midnight City*, under the imprint, Hauraki Press, in 1976.

There was also a fellow named Chris, a peculiarly Wellington figure, part bureaucrat in-waiting, mostly eccentric, who developed a strong interest in pipe-smoking and folk music; he enjoyed singing roistering sea shanties and folk ballads at full throttle and without the slightest provocation. Yet four of our number would be dead in as many years. David Duffy, a solidly build and round-faced Irishman given to enthusiastic blushing and clownish humour, died of cancer at the age of sixteen. He was a talented and serious-minded cricketer. John Girvan shot himself during the Duke Hotel era, an act which came as a deep shock to all who knew him. Michael Throll leapt off the Kelburn Viaduct to his death—an awkward, ginger haired and freckled boy who tried desperately to be a part of the more robust boys' antics, but became too pressured by impossible expectations, and by a claustrophobic and deep sense of worthlessness. He had apparently read innumerable volumes of official church history. Sadly, he could not live up to whatever vocation was expected of him, either by the priests or the group he wished to belong to. He was often the barb of our jokes.

Richard Stodart (MA) invariably wore dark or charcoal stovepipes set off with (moderately pointed) winkle-picker shoes. His jackets were stylishly outsize in light colours and sporty. I am not suggesting he looked the spiv, on the contrary, more the dandified Cambridge-come-lately who could be well cast in a supporting role alongside Alan Bates. *If* only. He and Fr. Kevin O'Donoghue were the two English teachers who had anything to do with my believing that perhaps I did have something to say, and that it was worth encouragement. One was my regular teacher, and the other I sought out at various intervals, though he took us for a few classes in the upper fifth. Richard was a slight, small boned, twenty something with thick yellow, wavy hair. He, too, was a dedicated and serious-minded teacher. He seemed more 'modern' and in touch with current culture than the general run of priests who didn't seem terribly concerned with the world outside beyond their daily and dutiful obligations. Richard introduced his students to the presentation of poetry via the lyrics of the latest Leonard Cohen, Simon & Garfunkel, and Bob Dylan albums!

The year was 1965, and the rich baritone of *Fred Neil, et al.*, could be heard along with all the other big-name folk singers of the era in the clubs around Greenwich Village, on Bleecker and MacDougal streets. This announced a new decade of tolerance that would eventually see the Prime Minister Robert Muldoon meet with the Black Power gang at the Royal Tiger Tavern on Taranaki Street, Wellington, to much media coverage on the question of bikie gang warfare and social disobedience. On the corner of Willis and Manners streets, right next door to the infamous Roxy Picture Theatre, where the back rows were permanently staked out by the local bikie gangs for the late night sessions, the DUKE HOTEL was already in full generational swing as *the* gathering place for artists, poets and writers, students, renegade academics, hard-talking socialists, freaks and hippies, macho-gays and Jimi Hendrix look-alikes, rockers, the ubiquitous sexual predators and narcissists, and every other would-be dissolute and opportunist you could put a name to. The die was cast and the good times beckoned.

[1] *Either Side The Horizon*, Stephen Oliver, Titus Books, Auckland, 2005.

Gnosis, A Spark

I had started to write poetry around fourteen or fifteen years of age and latched onto it like a limpet in the light of my being otherwise a fair to average student—with the occasional flair for something that approximated to an originality of expression. Here was archaeology of the spirit. I had uncovered ancient avenues and the past came welling up to meet me in parallel time. It was like standing upon the horizon and feeling the transports of an illuminated vision sweeping 360 degrees. This world was sacred, yes—but peopled by a multitude of possibilities that might be gods, a pagan world and a belief or *gnosis* that is free flowing. We are as living-beings the sum of primal atmospherics and visions running parallel with our temporal and present lives.

Each poet, working within the tradition, must—given the allotted time-span—locate and make sense of it all for as long as the poet is functioning and prescient, and must continuously return that which is received from the world back into the world, but *charged*, reality invigorated by vision. Ego-based reportage (beware the presiding 'I') has nothing to do with poetry; if anything, it is destructive of one's ability to appreciate and recognize the genuine article. Any third-rate pretender with a few party tricks can draw a crowd. There are many examples of where this 'seeking' is evident and original. I sought intimations of what I felt, mortal or otherwise, in the more obscure works of David Lindsay, *The Devil's Tor*, for instance, and George MacDonald's *Lilith*, though these symbolist works came some time later. Earlier, I had looked at the meditations of *Thomas à Kempis*, the essays of Francis Bacon, the dialogues of Plato; and read most of the plays of George Bernard Shaw.

At this time, the most influential book, that truly affected me with its rare piquancy of thought, was the World War One letters of Teilhard de Chardin, his *The Making of A*

Mind: Letters from a soldier-priest, 1914-18. For an eighteen- or nineteen-year-old, this was the lifting of a veil, and was quickly followed by his *Phenomenon of Man*, (including his plangent poem, 'Hymn of the Universe') and *Le Milieu Divin.* This led me onto a sampling of Henri Bergson and his *Dreams*, and a text on Mariolatry and faith, from which I appreciated his definition of an agnostic as 'one who walks an intellectual tightrope'. Then H.G. Wells' *The Anatomy of Frustration, A Modern Synthesis* (1936), which in an inverted sort of way probably owes something to Robert Burton's three volume treatise, *Anatomy of Melancholy* (1893) edition—and this I had also read, plus a smattering of the metaphysical writings of Francis Herbert Bradley (1846-1924) and his work, *Appearance and Reality*, probably via T.S. Eliot who by 1916 completed a dissertation on the British philosopher titled: *Knowledge and Experience in the philosophy of F.H. Bradley.*

All through this process, I was reading the poems (more bardic than beatific) of Gerard Manly Hopkins and Thomas Hardy. Thomas Merton's *Elected Silence* (his title borrowed from the Hopkins poem) and *Seeds of Contemplation*, were a few early influences. I followed the scent where other such coincidences are famously explored as a coded system ('The Battle of The Trees') in Robert Graves' *The White Goddess*, and early Irish bardic poetry, but that came much later and has remained a continuing interest. I tracked with fascination the ancient lineage of the chromosome with J.B.S. Haldane back to wheat seeds found in 4,000-year-old Egyptian tombs; I had discovered Haldane's work (ignoring the communist tomes of Lenin, etc., party 'interpretations' of Shakespeare, etc., and *dialectical materialism*) in my father's old chest of books, stored in the weatherboard bach 'out the back' of 32 Karepa Street, Brooklyn-*west*, Wellington.

Caught up in this drag net of Russian, principally socialist literature, I discovered the folk tales of Gogol and the poems of Aleksandr Blok and Vladimir Mayakovsky. I still possess the last hardback, *Mayakovsky And His Poetry*, compiled by Herbert Marshall (1945). The frontispiece carries a picture of a glowering M. standing before a backdrop of his political cartoons. Its musty pages still remind me of the incense offered up in a Russian or Greek Orthodox church. About this time, around seventeen or eighteen years of age, I wrote a 'hermetic' poem as a result of my reading one significant, historico-scientific book from my father's library (as with the Haldane, not stashed in the chest) on alchemy, precursor to chemistry and the positive sciences. This proved a profound discovery for me with its complex medieval, quasi-pagan symbolism centred around on one hand, the transmutation of base metals into gold, and on the other the search for the philosopher's stone. Spirit and matter coupled in mystery. I wrote one poem as a result of my reading this work called 'An Alchemical Women'; the poem literally dictated itself to me in its entirety. I considered this then, the first, 'complete' poem I had written as an eighteen-year-old, sustained as it is by its inherent rhythm and melody. An incantation which came to me complete, in one rhythmic pulse. I offer it here as something of a curiosity—inspired juvenilia:

AN ALCHEMICAL WOMAN

Penelope. She prays an adept will read
The mysteries of her emerald eyes, hides
In her Hermetic womb the Philosopher's egg
Once put to love's Great Work.
Undoing the process done of love
She labours now another fire.
What Penelope in idle patience
Does, no mystic dare guess, though
She inspired men who trod away
Her ash. In time, sons of Hermes
Must illume the emblem of her hurt
    And Time's gall stone leadens
    Her Magic to near death.

It is interesting to note in this context, that the environmentalist's concerns on climate change are subconsciously tied in with a dreaded sense that, once the planet's biomass is finally decimated along with its ancient forests, we will have cut off our psychic retreat and there is no way back. Destroy the forests, you destroy memory. What will remain? Merely pockets, or *islands of wilderness*, the landscape as golf course. Welcome to the future! Museums of sensory deprivation and digital enhancement; post-modernity taken to its logical, demystifying extreme. What poet in his right mind would play curator to such an institution?

An unholy prospect when you consider that already, any number of our museums of contemporary art have all the relevance and intrinsic value of Disneyland theme parks. These are little more than tarted up 'trash & treasure' warehouses charging outlandish admission fees by the installation. Christ's crown of thorns understood as a bar code. White goods seen as nouveau tabernacles of domestic totemism. Brand names as the science of the new semiotic. Time was when the original vision, or confluence of visions, resonated with all the vibrancy and colour of the aurora borealis. One can track these origins back through the finely strung, memory-based musicality of the ancient Irish literary tradition, found within bardic and nature poetry, as in Kuno Meyer's translations of *Ancient Irish Poetry* (1994), first published in 1913:

> Bitter is the wind to-night, [1]
> It tosses the ocean's white hair:
> To-night I fear not the fierce warriors of Norway
> Coursing on the Irish Sea.

The first poem I managed to get published was quite simply about a 'tree' in full, leafy splendour which appeared in the school magazine, a stapled and cyclostyled affair called the *Patler*. Simple as the poem was, I was glad that I had started within the ancient tradition of 'nature poetry' where all poetry has sprung from; the celebration of fertility, symbol, and the cycle of growth and renewal (‘*Begin afresh, afresh, afresh.*’). At least from that point of view, I could travel the old roads and discover the towns along the way, a little like the philosopher tramp out of James Stephen’s *The Crock of Gold*, an allegorical journey of my own choosing and at my own pace. I subsequently became one of the editors of this little magazine whose presiding editor was my English teacher, Fr. O’Donoghue. These were the days of St. Patrick’s College, Wellington, an old gothic pile overlooking the Basin Reserve cricket grounds. The school, previously referred to as ‘Gormenghast’, was condemned as an earthquake hazard and demolished in 1980.

Fr. O’Donoghue was short, compact and hirsute. His hair was black, and rose in a tuft from the hairline. It was the sort of style one was born with and no amount of grooming would ever change it. He wore a pair of black horn-rimmed spectacles, and I don’t think I ever saw him without them. He had a singular way of pinching in his mouth when angry, and walked with that determined, forward bouncing, up and down movement. In public, he always stared directly ahead. He considered himself something of an intellectual I suppose, a little snobbish maybe, but there was no doubting his profound love of poetry and literature though strongly of the Romantic Tradition.

Of all the forty minute ‘periods’ that made up the school day, I looked forward to his English classes the most, for I had clambered onto the life-raft of the imagination, and I intended to cling on for dear life! Absolutely no one would take this newfound gift away from me. If I were to succeed at anything, in the event of my succeeding at all, it would be within the realms and practice of poetry, and in the exercise and journey of the imagination. Here maybe was something (I kept on telling myself) I could *genuinely* be committed to. Once I had made up my mind about that, I put some distance between myself and the 'forces of negation'. Things sped up between fourteen and fifteen years of age in quantum leaps.

Fr. Kevin O'Donoghue originally came from the South Island coastal town of Timaru, and after he had finished secondary school, went directly into the seminary. A proud South Islander, he employed, for instance, the term *crib* (South Island usage) not *bach* (North Island usage) to describe a humble sea side holiday shack. If we were discussing bucolics or the Romantic poets, he would often draw upon his own personal agrarian experiences growing up around the Canterbury Plains with some likely anecdote. It was a favourite pastime of the class to keep Fr. O'Donoghue distracted and talking about everything else except the business of teaching. He would relate to us how his grandfather, for instance, was reputedly known as the strongest man in the district, celebrated for his superhuman feats of carrying great sacks of grain across his shoulders for miles at a trot.

Or how he would secure a length of thick metal piping to the bole of an old oak tree, lodged in a cleft made suitable for that purpose, and then proceed to walk slowly around the tree gripping the pipe with arms held straight before him, as though he were pushing round a millstone at a steady pace, and unhesitatingly, bending the pipe into a perfect coil around the shape of the tree trunk. Why his grandfather did this, I really don't know, but it sounded impressive enough. These tales were invariably told in a self-absorbed and serious manner, slightly pompous even, but that didn't matter, because we enjoyed the telling hugely. He stressed that regular exercise was a wholesome thing because this got rid of the 'fatigue toxins' in the blood.

Of the books and writers we were required to study, they were the usual, though Richard Stodart (a popular lay teacher) was far too modern in his approach to bother with the 19th century preoccupations of Fr. O'Donoghue; these two teachers were as different as chalk and cheese, and given the rivalry in teaching styles, and the unbridgeable gulf that lay between them, I don't think too much love was lost either way. My relationship foundered or cooled somewhat with Richard Stodart. One of the boys in my class asked me to write a poem for him as part of an exercise set by Richard. Poetry really wasn't his thing, and so I felt happy to oblige, flattered, even.

When the boy was applauded for his efforts (which he received with a look of stupefaction) I couldn't let that pass. I had written it, after all, and decided to tell this somewhat trendy lay teacher that I was the author of the piece *and* had written it on request, to do the boy a favour. This was a cowardly act on my part. My 'owning up' was not well received, and thereafter Richard Stodart regarded me somewhat tartly, and was not so forthcoming in his praise of my writings. If I had my wits about me this writing of *vers d'occasion* might have proved a lucrative side-line if one can forgive the pun (the boy had offered to pay for the piece); unfortunately I lacked either the humour or nerve to pull it off. I guess it came down to a matter of allegiance. I began to construct for myself, in my poetics, a bridge between Tradition and the New.

From Fr. O'Donoghue we got Coleridge's *The Rime of the Ancient Mariner* and *Christabel*, the Wordsworth of *Tintern Abbey*, Keats and his *Odes*, and Shakespeare's tragedies. Even in the late '60s this sort of tuition was strangely out of fashion, and yet I was glad of it because it provided me with a deeper perspective on poetry. One had to start further back in the field as it were, and study whatever 'is well made'. At least, you didn't run the risk of confusing showy colloquialisms for poetry. We also studied the sprung rhythm and poetry of Gerard Manley Hopkins, in particular, his sonnets, though grandly culminating in his 'The Wreck of the Deutschland', and it was through him principally that I entered my apprenticeship. Of the novels, we had the usual dose of Jane Austen, the Brontë sisters, and Dickens.

We looked at *Hamlet* and *King Lear* and *Macbeth*, *Othello*.

The only modern novel that made an impression on me, and that was one of longing or nostalgia, was Hemingway's *The Old Man and the Sea*—this seemed to me more a lonely than solitary tale; humble and heroic. The writing of essays was a weekly requirement and I generally did well at this. In fact, I looked forward to the writing of them and the hoped-for accolades from Fr. O'Donoghue, where he would take the best efforts and read them out before the class. You could say that a few solid planks were thrown down for us to arrange as either walkways over a morass we wished to escape from, or scaffolding to construct something with. By this time, Fr. O'Donoghue had taken a strong interest in my early efforts at writing poetry and imaginative prose pieces, insisting I at least give him one poem a week which I failed to do, or at least on a regular basis. I would often spend time in his room after school, or during my lunch break, where we would discuss the technical aspects of composition. If anything, this is where I learned to dichotomise my life into my literary interests, and my public life which remained a reality set apart.

Fr. O'Donoghue finished up his 'wonderful apostolate of teaching' after thirty years. He left the old St. Pat's in 1978 and spent ten years at St. John's, Hastings. After that he was sent back to the New St. Pat's and subsequently gave up the teaching profession three years later in 1991. He was then sent to Futuna Retreat in Karori, Wellington. This has since been closed and demolished and Fr. O'Donoghue returned to his original home of Timaru. The last I heard was that Fr. O'Donoghue continued relieving work in parishes up and down the country, or 'supplying' as the ecclesiastical jargon has it. He was required to spend on average about two or three months in each parish 'relieving'. In this role, he had humorously referred to himself as 'a professional spare-part'. To Fr. Kevin O'Donoghue I owe a considerable debt. It was he who first encouraged me to believe in what literary abilities I imagined that I possessed.

Of the other priests who passed through the corridors and classrooms that I had anything to do with, I don't recall a great deal beyond mild recollection, except for Fr. McAteer who took me for XTD in the third and fourth forms. The class lived in fear of this man who appeared to exist in a removed, unemotional state with an intense dislike of his charges. He was, from what I gather, a fine tennis player. McAteer was olive skinned and self-consciously handsome in a Terence Stamp sort of way. You wanted to believe that he might have been a likeable womaniser in another life, but his cold, sadistic manner, coupled with supreme vanity, dissipated that fantasy quickly enough. We had to memorize endless tracts of catechism, learnt by rote and recited before the class the following morning, on command. I truly dreaded him. Any boy who got one question wrong was dispatched to either Fr. Terry O'Neill or Fr. John Silverwood for an obligatory thrashing. McAteer was a martinet pure and simple.

Yet other priests I found mild enough, and they passed by largely as shadowy figures, perhaps now many of them shades themselves, departing from and into other lives but not mine—The Rev. Burke, Hill, Egden, Taylor, Kelly, McCann, Cosgriff, Unverricht, Perry and Wysocki (who for a few terms in the sixth form took me for History, a much harried and put upon man). Then came the lay teachers: Hickey (in for the long haul, one of those peculiarly blank but dedicated individuals), Petterson, Moloney—the last a largely self-appointed Musical Director, really just some 'band master' devoid of training, a booze-red complexion and quite demented. In passing, Dennis O'Brien was nominated as school organist for the year 1966—a student one year ahead of me, and whose family also came from Brooklyn. His uncle was the self-same Labour MP for Island Bay, Gerald O'Brien, destroyed by Prime Minister Rob Muldoon, who outed and then publicly humiliated him as homosexual. Dennis would later go on to achieve some measurable recognition with his band (as keyboard player), gaining a larger following in Germany and Scandinavia than in his native country. He ended up running a Wellington record store.

We conclude our identity line up of lay teachers with Woodham, Quin, Petrus, Williams and Moriarty. Fr. O'Connor (he of the gormless aspect), could never really discipline the boys and was continuously taunted because of it. He didn't possess the jugular instinct, and took me for History in the early years, though this subject was latterly taught me by a Fr. McCann, an altogether bubbly and excitable man. One of the more interesting individuals was the Dutch Priest, Fr. Van Der Pal (Augustinians of the Assumption A.A.). He at various times during the middle period till my departure took me for most of the general subjects and XTD. I always considered him a little more worldly in his outlook than the rest, possessed of a certain European *ennui*, open perhaps to latitudes of tolerance. A man with an enjoyable, and risqué humour.

Often as not those I associated with were hardly aware of my clandestine occupation of 'poet'. You learned to be fairly careful about those you let in on the secret, especially when it came to prospects of employment further on down the track. But sooner or later the cat was let out of the bag and it didn't matter that much who knew. I had absolutely no problem in telling women of my preoccupations and, somehow, they always understood without question my involvement with poetry even if they rarely read it themselves. Women are more inclined to associate passion with an honesty of emotion than men otherwise blinkered by the competitive and destructive spirit.

If St. Patrick's (town), with its open-door policy to the Catholic community, and in many ways its rough and tumble approach, was much like any other secondary school, it was nevertheless something of a democratic institution. St. Patrick's Silverstream, the boarding school, was on the other hand an exclusive oligarchy by comparison. A friend, Paul

Glackin, who attended the latter told me, 'We were to be the leaders in politics, law and business, we were in effect groomed as the future controllers of the financial institutions and seats of power.' (Paul died sometime between the 5th and 11th of April, 2003, in Sydney. He was fifty-five years of age.)

A big ask, I thought, but that apparently was the tacit aim and it was uppermost in the priests' minds to instil this *heir apparent* attitude; after all, the church and its tentacular organization always needed money. It all added up to failure, really. No one could ever fully realize the expectations set by the Catholic schooling system, or to quote the Whanganui based minimalist painter, Peter Ireland, 'Irish Bolshie-tribalism', but what one could achieve in a concrete way was 'failure' and that qualified you for the famous, and life-long, membership of the 'Catholic guilt trip'. To sum up—one might be tempted to interpret the church's *modus operandi* as something very closely allied to what today we call globalization, or the *managerial* society. A remnant left over from the proselytising, missionary days.

Etiquette and protocol were always closely adhered to. At the school dances, for instance, the boys were required to wear white gloves at all times. 'To keep the sweat off the girls,' Paul joked. This was supposedly the elite of the Catholic, or indeed all secondary schools throughout New Zealand. The only other school that could hold a candle might be Whanganui Collegiate or St. Bede's College in Christchurch, yet who cared about Christchurch? That school was too far away to rate it as a serious contender. Fortunately for 'Paul' the grand plan was never realized. The priests did appoint him a prefect, at which point one would assume that he was well on his way to fulfilling family and the middle-class expectations of money and success, and become a strong contributing Catholic, active and high-profile in the community. His appointment had more to do with his sporting prowess—he excelled in rugby and boxing, and his elevated status might also have had something to do with his family's wealth.

His rebellion, and subsequent fall from grace, when it came, proved nothing short of spectacular and terminal. Paul smuggled whisky into the dorm, and proceeded to get riotously drunk with a few of his school mates. Sacrilege! Paul was not just summarily expelled from school, that would have been way too easy; he was banned from the school premises, *for life*. Paul was pretty much a man of his time. Four years my senior, he qualified as a '60s person who like many of his generation took full advantage of the culture of experimentation; the batteries of youth gave a seemingly endless supply of energy, and no thought was given to the possibility that one day this might be used up, and all you'd be left with would be a fragile mortality nurtured through hypochondria—and minimal job prospects.

Experience counted for everything and youth ran on forever. The 'thousand shocks that flesh is heir to' are easily absorbed but youth ends soon enough, and all you've got to show for it is the memory of a few wild interludes, a bunch of what you thought were interesting individuals who might be friends but who proved to be neither, a handful of (if you're lucky) sexually memorable relationships, a flagging idealism best left buried and of no use to man nor beast. Ah yes, the fruitful harvest of one's middle years, in which you are more likely to get caught out by heart attacks and strokes, prostate cancer or an overworked liver. That is, if you continued on with flagging steps in a grotesque parody of youth, and in a sorrowful attempt to blindly maintain the pace.

Too soon you realize that you don't have any family to speak of, or if you once had, they now belong to another country emotionally and geographically or worse, relegated to a now forgotten age. Though, all this doesn't appear too bad and is a state by far preferable to the life of any successful academic. Or corporate CEO, sitting astride his dung heap of lies and duplicity, basking in the smug aroma of riches, success and power; guarded, crusty and mean-spirited in his declining years, playing the stock market of the damned. No thanks! You continue to ask yourself, why maintain any measure of belief, if indeed this is what you are constantly pitted against? Toss a coin, what's it to be, a belief in a God or humanity, and will it do you any good either way? Whatever the odds, Paul did complete a law degree at Victoria University after his departure from Silverstream—call it a final gesture toward respectability, but the only bar he ended up successfully practising at was the local corner bar.

He travelled for about fifteen years and found himself caught up in a number of life-threatening situations, possibly involving drug-dealers and those various criminal fraternities who move across international borders with the ease of weather patterns, and which he managed to either box or talk his way out of. A generous-hearted man with a headstrong, independent Irish spirit, though given to bouts of self-pitying hypochondria, the *malade imaginaire*—and wished-for expectations of imminent death. Hardly a success by this world's motley standards. The Australian based, New Zealand writer, Martin Edmond who knew Paul Glackin well, and worked with him on various film scripts, posted this on March 1, 2016 on my FB page: 'The last work he ever did was pro bono, giving legal advice to refugees held in detention centres in this great country of ours. He did that until the dialysis meant he couldn't travel any more. He was also developing a rather good screenplay, about a crim in Queensland who became a bookbinder while inside, and befriended an old Afghan held for yonks in the same jail. True story. It was never made.'

So I celebrate that rare and endangered species who have yet guts and integrity enough to remain and insist upon being themselves. I toast the true *outlier*, sustained by an uncompromising spirit—guided by a deep honesty. Paul committed himself heartily to the pub culture. 'Beer is very important to me,' he stated to me in all seriousness. That should have been carved on his tombstone!

What then of these men in black, smelling of cigarette smoke and stale sweat, working within an educational framework closely based upon the English public school model? As boys they were subjected to much the same system we were—went directly into the seminary, became priests, and often returned as old boy priests to the same school they were taught in. Some sort of Catholic homing instinct. So they treated us much in the way they in turn were treated as schoolboys, and moved along preordained lines within the scope of a limited experience of the world.

Verily, the sins of the father are visited on the sons, *etc.*, Metaphors ('playing for his side', *Kipling*—and 'play up play up play the game', *Newbolt*), were associated with 'duty' and the measure of a (gentle) man, the ordained representative of the upper classes. Curiously, one can still detect the odour, pervasive as mustard gas, of the Post-Imperialist Englishman, a weird sort of throwback type, relocated from the 'old country' to an ex-colony, entrenched in some creative writing school complete with 'town and gown' posturing. Such a pretender occasionally lobs the odd partisan poetry anthology, 'The Best of...' over the trench works of an English department, as if it were a Mills Bomb, and into the no man's land of a non-poetry-reading public. A self-appointed 'official' arbiter of the literary canon. No pun intended. My satirical poem, 'The Lost Hurrah', from my collection, *GONE, Satirical Poems: New & Selected* (2016), attempts to capture the culprit gone AWOL:

A hard-bitten royalist's what I am,
with pipe & port, and bedroom slippers.
I play up, play on, and I play the game,
for Kipling O Kipling & fried kippers.

I'm an army brat from the Motherland,
I swim ten lengths a day in pink flippers.
My wife ran away with Bob Dylan's band,
for Kipling, O Kipling & fried kippers.

I collect old bottles from World War 1,
bayonets, boots & rusty wire snippers;
I never got to kiss Rupert Brooke's bum,
for Kipling, O Kipling & fried kippers.

This was pretty much the culture of a moribund public-school system that existed in England up until Edwardian times and ended with the World War One. Something of this atmosphere still haunted the Catholic private schooling system of my day where it was deemed *sweet and becoming to die for your faith*—that is, if you got the chance to make a noble sacrifice and offer up your life in active or passive service. However it was, the Vietnam war didn't claim my attention, and I felt no need to burrow into the Brooklyn-*west* hills of Wellington, to find sanctuary against the falling bombs or communist peril threatening from the East; no need to create my own labyrinthine set of catacombs and offer up prayer to the gods against the prevailing forces of darkness.

[1] *Ancient Irish Poetry*, Kuno Meyer, London, Constable and Company Limited, 1994.

Unposted, Autumn Leaves

I stayed on an extra year to get my UE, which I failed to do, and found the place strangely empty. The whole *Boys' Own Adventure* of school in which girls only existed at bus stops or maybe on weekends (being one of 'the boys' suggested the pack mentality), had ended for me. I left midway through 1968 while Geoff had left a year earlier without getting either his School Certificate or UE. I was finally glad to be rid of it. We had in the meantime established other meeting places in Wellington, just prior to the pub scene. There were only a handful of worthwhile coffee houses in those days that served real coffee. One was the *Casa Fontana* in lower Victoria Street and yes, there was a fountain set in a rock pool, illuminated by an eerie green light and wreathed in plastic ivy. The waitresses, who I always unsuccessfully tried to pick up, or if I did, had no success with, wore white starched shirts and tight black short skirts.

This was the first and earliest deserving of the name of coffee house. But the most popular was *Suzy's Coffee Lounge* owned by Suzy van der Kwast—anorexic in appearance and brutally blonde. She had a cut-glass manner typified by that unmistakable Dutch arrogance. I suppose one needed to adopt such a manner against the otherwise stifling provincial naivety of the day, and she served the best coffee in town. There was also a dim-lit affair in Oriental Bay called the *Beachcomber*, which became a post-pub meeting place and which had about it an air of sexual intrigue, or so you hoped. Those cosy, semi-circular booths. The décor was nautical.

It was during the mid to late '60s that Geoff and I would arrange to meet at *Suzy's*, usually on a Saturday or Sunday afternoon to discuss and exchange what we had written or were currently reading. Geoff was at this time particularly interested in the novels of D.H. Lawrence, whose poems were more to my taste. Other writers which interested him were:

Malcolm Lowry, *Under the Volcano;* the Joyce Cary trilogy, *Herself Surprised*, *To Be A Pilgrim* and *The Horse's Mouth*, the last of the three being the most popular; James Joyce, *Portrait of an Artist as a Young Man;* John Fowles; Lawrence Durrell, his novels and poems; Albert Camus, *The Outsider* and, naturally, Henry Miller. These were the very first books we discussed. From these, I veered off into Honoré de Balzac and Jean-Paul Sartre. At this time, I think the two principal poets who enthused us (after Dylan Thomas) were Thom Gunn and Philip Larkin. And for me, always W.H. Auden. The draw-card of W.B. Yeats I have largely avoided to this very day, probably warned off by Larkin who spoke of his influence being 'pervasive as garlic'.

James K. Baxter, the man and his poetry, loomed large as a messianic figure or self-styled, old testament prophet and could not easily be avoided. He had superseded most of the other poets of his generation, including, as far as I could see, all of the emerging ones; not even the academics could touch him. It was only after his death that they fed upon his ghost in order to further academic, careerist ambitions. The Baxter opus was as rich as any Graeco-Roman archaeological dig. He was all the literary and Anglo-Celtic sensibility, in the grand tradition we never had, though in fact, his poetry was quite simply the pinnacle and fulfilment of 19th century Romanticism in New Zealand. Arguably, Baxter was the last great 19th century Romantic poet writing in the 20th century. From there our literary influences radiated outward, as did our lives in an ever-increasing circle of interceptions and external activities. We compounded our metaphors through an endless parade of characters and shifting relationships, around 'the hills of home'. The following is taken from my poetry collection, *Unmanned* (1999):

WORDS TO LURE A GHOST
an exile's soliloquy

Henley Pub? I am one year from
your death, and a mad mile from your
achievement
          twenty or so years
down the track. I think you may have
killed a few of us off, brother,
who rejoiced
in your thicket of sorrows.
                                        Jim Baxter,
if a cabbage tree marks your spot by
the river,
                        I am glad of it.
After you went, we were too eager
for another Apollo, and the laurel
was tossed from
hand to poetic hand like a hot kumara.
Most dropped it. A number were swept
by the winter river with the eels
into the Underworld.
                        The God Love
and the God Vengeance sat down
in a burnt out warehouse to share out the
small morsels
          of pain.
The poets
          are playing hide-and-seek
with each other in and out of marriage.
The sharing
                  is done.
                        A southerly
whistles up over the gun emplacements on
Brooklyn Hill,
          Jim, scattering
the unposted autumn leaves.

Appropriately enough, Geoff and I cracked our first half dozen DB (Dominion Bitter) long neck beer bottles late one night behind *St. Mary of the Angels* Catholic church up on Boulcott Street. We were chased away by a vigilant priest, so I suppose you could say it was symbolic, a ritualistic departure point. Thereafter, the principal venues or watering holes we met up at were, firstly, the *Grand Hotel*, *The George* and *The Duke Hotel*, all of them in and around downtown Willis Street. Others, too, *The Forester's Arms* and *The Carlton*. These hotels and the coffee houses are long gone, including the *Royal Oak* (an infamous seafarers' bar) on Pigeon Park (now Te Aro Park) off Dixon Street, as is the city of my youth. We also spent after hours at the *Purple Onion* (or rather the coffee house appended to it) in Vivian Street, a dive for prostitutes, transvestites and a sordid array of night life, where you could smuggle in booze that we surreptitiously placed under the table. This 'night-club,' opened in 1964, was run by Wellington's most famous transvestite, 'Carmen' the boy from Taumarunui, 'made good'. Other famous 'acts' included 'The Amazing Pietro!'—an old female impersonator I subsequently met in Sydney years later, an early inhabitant of the iconic Holloway Road, that dark cleft off Aro Street—who informed me that Wellington back streets in those days hummed with clandestine, illegal gambling dens. I can still hear the pre-disco tune '*Lolla, la-la-la-lolla*' thumping from the jukebox in that dim, matt black dance zone.

After a few false starts, working as a copywriter on the first rung of a gloriously promised career (I couldn't quite work out how to marry the idea of writer and/or poet with everyday monetary existence but no longer have a problem with it), under probation in an advertising agency called *Dormer-Beck*. I was, thankfully, fired for showing the head copywriter, my boss, an Englishman, a series of Haiku I had proudly been working on during office hours. During my brief career with this agency, I had closely observed, and produced one or two 'voices' in the agency studio, and I began to get an inkling that I could do this. 'Money for jam,' I thought. A few years later, this indeed proved to be the case. I considered the job of free-lance, voice over work on a par with acting. A voice artist. After that, some sort of work editing in a publishing company lasted for a few weeks.

I decided I didn't like the office environment, associated careerist hierarchies, or the people that went with them; in fact, I didn't readily understand the mechanics of deceit, those requisite skills one needs for job security and advancement. *The Evening Post* as it turned out, offered the ideal casual employment, and I soon discovered a number of musicians, artists and artisans of one sort or another had much the same idea. You turned up about 2 pm Monday to Friday for a couple of hours work, and especially Saturdays for the biggest paper of the week, and the overtime made the job worthwhile. When the papers came off the press you manned the conveyor belt upstairs, guiding papers (and stacking them) to the wiring machine and down the chute to the loading bay. Or here you might be rostered on to heave bundles of first and second edition papers onto the waiting trucks. Of course, once you'd finished work you could have a drink at any of the pubs on Willis Street. One of the more interesting individuals I met during this time was the Dutch artist, then (and still) living in Wellington, Robert Franken. A great, gentle shambling bear of a man always dressed in black, and who executed remarkable surrealist paintings. He provided the cover illustration to my first pamphlet of poetry, titled: *Chance To Laugh*, published toward the close of 1971, though given the copyright, 1972. The following poem appears in my collection, *Night of Warehouses: Poems 1978-2000*, (2001) :

FLAGON DAYS [1]
for Robert Franken

But this one had stood three months,
brooding its yeast amongst sultanas packed
down in fathoms of vodka. Fermentation

stalked patient as a terrorist upon the
taste-buds; a Dutch custom, powerful as
an Atlantic sea squall. A late ride pillion
on Robert Franken's scooter at Pāuatahanui
out along the coast road to Paekākāriki.
The black swans of the estuary, themselves
a scattering of sultanas, glistening afloat
in the dusk. Robert, you liked things pickled
in bottles; homunculi, viscera, distorted
on the glass-plate of your surreal world-view;
a head on a stem like a cut-away tulip

titled:

TOO CLOSE TO NATURE.

That tale you told about leaving your lover's
bed before dawn to gather dewy grass,
clippings that you packed roundly into your
body-shape left warmly indented there.
You sat hard by in a chair and watched her
slowly wake, turn to embrace where you
had lain. And we took another slug from that
primal Dutch concoction filtered through
vodka-soaked sultanas, back then in '72.

[1] *Night of Warehouses, Poems 1978-2000*, HeadWorX Publishers, Wellington, 2001.

Wellington Unbound

The capital city of the new millennium is a brand spanking new CBD, streamlined in the modern international style with tinted glass and chrome, and grey stone slabs attempting to provide an illusion of angular density built around stark, open plazas for the lunch-time dwellers. Yet most of the suburbs retain much of their hill-moody, original character, striated with crumbling bitumen and pebble footpaths. Vestiges of *Pigeon Park* on Manners Street still remain though two thirds of it has been sculpted into the semblance of a Māori waka, its 'prow' pointing toward Mt. Victoria. I much preferred this overstated, cultural cliché as leitmotif carved on the lintel of 1930s Public Building entrance ways; the waka seen ploughing through cloud, or maybe my memory deceives me, and I may be thinking of the poet, Vincent O'Sullivan's poetry collection, *Revenants* (1969),[1] a sonnet sequence which in part deals with the 19th century French etcher, Charles Meryon, who went mad and saw 'war canoes' ploughing through cloud. I quote from the *Note* by Vincent O'Sullivan that introduces *Long Harbour: Twenty Sonnets on Charles Meryon*:

'Charles Meryon, the great French etcher, was the illegitimate son of a Parisian dancer and an English doctor. As a young man, he served for three years as a junior officer at the abortive attempt at a French colony in the South Island. He was stationed at Akaroa, and his mind was strongly affected by his experiences both at the colony and on cruises about the Pacific. . . . Later in his life, when his insanity was indisputable, Meryon included the Southern Alps in an etching of Paris, and had war canoes [waka] whales and chariots in the sky above the Ministry of Marine. Baudelaire, who drew attention to the artist in reviews, wished to illustrate etchings with his own poems, but the plan came to nothing. For some years before the end of his life, Meryon's insanity took the form of religious obsession. Finally, he starved himself to death in the belief that he was Christ feeding the poor of the earth.'

Thankfully, a few of the dusty old pohutukawa trees still remain to this day. St. Patrick's was finally demolished before the earthquakes did the job (I sat through several good shakes during my tenure, one of which measured about 6.2 on the Richter scale), only to be reborn in a new incarnation of glass and brick at Evans Bay. But the public library, home to the Wellington tramp and dero (sunny at the back in summer, free access provided warmth inside during the winter months), facing the sandy orange Council Chambers, '30s architecture, with its attached grassy reserve, no longer exists. The old Wellington Public Library building now serves as the Wellington Art Gallery. The steady demolition of the city I grew up in, making way for the new constructions compliant with the most up to date building codes and calibrated earthquake specifications. Resource consent and the city-state.

Gone the council vibro-block conservatorium, public seating, and whorled red brick paving on the harbour side of the library I had worked on as a brickie's labourer with the extrovert Dutch bricklayer, Kees Van Deursen. That old library was the occasion of my first court appearance. I had loaned my library card to Geoff Cochrane, my then good companion and fellow writer, who made full use of it; he had been disqualified from further use of the library's lending service, simply because he had repeatedly failed to return books on time for one reason or another. Unfortunately, his growing commitment to alcohol was now beginning to loosen the ties of responsibility at every level.

Eventually, I got a court summons to appear on charges of failing to return at least half a dozen books; I think these were D.H. Lawrence and the poems of Lawrence Durrell. *Outstanding!* for months. I claimed that my card had been stolen, and as they couldn't prove otherwise, the magistrate agreed, and the charges were dropped forthwith, much to the sour disapproval of the cardigan-wearing public servant who put the case for WCC. Gone, too, the original *Smith's Bookshop* in Mercer Street, with its internal and fluted, black metal columns and the endless bookshelves ceiling to floor, stocked with every possible edition, first, second or third editions; mostly hardback second-hand books, run by the eccentric Dick Reynolds, who was usually to be found at his centrally positioned, elevated desk, reminiscent of a lectern, much in the style of a Dickensian accountant at his books—or you'd more likely find him at *Hotel St. George* across on Willis/ Boulcott streets.

He was a rare bookseller in that he knew what went on *inside* a book. He wouldn't try to sell you *The Inferno* by Mickey Spillane, for instance. Years later I discovered another bookseller who reminded me of him somewhat, though with more sober habits: Jack Bradstreet of *Bradstreet's Books,* in Hawthorn, Melbourne. Jack was into his late seventies when I found him. There was no computer, fax or email (O blessèd and dusty silence!), not even an electronic till could be seen in his shop. I believe most of the information was stored in his head, and he knew his books, often recommending one with a fitting anecdote. I bought Norman Douglas's *South Wind* (first published in 1917), a novelist popular in the '20s and '30s but no longer read these days.

Cyril Connolly (another purchase) described Douglas, in his *Enemies of Promise*, as an 'intellectual with a strong imaginative side' and belonging to a group of (then) modern writers he called 'reformed mandarins'. *South Wind* recounted, in heightened language, Douglas's experiences of a decadent literary and artistic community on Capri (though the island is fictionalized as *Nepenthe*), and the tenor of the book suggested in a high-camp manner, the mind of a fabulist. Jack Bradstreet, when he handed me the book, said in a very straight-laced way, 'Douglas liked little boys'. Obviously, one of the English decadents of the 1890s. One of my most treasured books I bought from Jack is a first edition of *The Condemned Playground, Essays 1927-1944*, Cyril Connolly, with the Augustus John drawing of the author in the frontispiece. 'Silvery, Latin prose', a stylist and wit of the first order, and a favourite of Philip Larkin.

In the late '60s, *Smith's Bookshop* at 34 Mercer Street off Willis, was the place to plunder for poetry and playwrights (Christopher Fry's highly poetic verse dramas, and the old Penguin red or orange paperback editions of G.B. Shaw), and essayists of every era, and it was here I bought most of my early library and a hardback collection of the poetry of Roy Campbell put out by Bodley Head which I was rather proud of, though unpopular then as he is now. Yet anyone who cares to read his translations of *St. John of The Cross* might in part revise their opinion of an otherwise stilted stylist who was somewhere lampooned ('spooks in blinds') by Auden, and even C.S. Lewis in his poem, 'To The Author of *Flowering Rifle*'—'Rifles may flower and terrapins may flame / But truth and reason will be still the same'. It is right here in the detour of those branch lines, or sidings of a writer's *oeuvre*, that I discovered little flares of epiphany. This is where a rare sighting was made within a microcosm; the intake and easy rhythm of a breath caught instantaneously. Such coincidences led you off along another track as if this were all too familiar territory though it wasn't. *It is only that you think you hear the echo of footfalls, which somehow syncopate with your own heartbeat.* At best, you can say it is at these moments you experience contemplation or reverie, the true sense of the enjoyment of life. How much of it is merely youth, and the exhilaration of learning, and how much found wisdom? But this was the sort of thing that interested me, literature nobody else bothered with, or so I imagined, none of it particularly arcane, but fascinating in the digressions that ended in a *cul-de-sac* by authors who had fallen from fashion, not ever having risen to it. The art of deep reading; maybe I touched upon it once or twice.

It's the sort of thing one might find today, contrived or approximated in the hyper-texts of someone like the late Umberto Eco, or in the blurring of the boundaries between fact and fiction which appears to be superseding the novel of pure imagination in our age of the information superhighway and time-compression, where history is broken down into algorithms and lineal time has switched back upon itself and become vortex. I should add the coda that once you lose faith in life, history becomes fate, and we its inevitable victims. Somehow, one found the gaps between. The pauses in the writer's journeying where an original insight rose up into view like a lost city of the plain. *Incantation* has as much to do with listening, the patience and vigilance associated with an animal, its ears pricked—which is a sort of waiting, tuning in upon the past. You look back and attempt to sound your ancient, sensory self, and wonder whether that person still exists. Perhaps I was anticipating a similar fate and curing myself of any illusory expectations of overarching success? I discovered that reading, as much as writing, must be a learned and a practised art.

Journalism seemed the logical choice for me once out of college, feeling cosily close to the vocation of a 'real' writer. I managed to get myself accepted at the Wellington Polytechnic in Buckle Street, which ran a news and magazine journalism course (located right next door to St. Patrick's, though *that* reality was fast receding), converted over from the old Wellington Tech School-run carpentry classes we attended from Marist Brothers, Newtown, and where the carpentry teacher from the state school, who freely and vigorously used the strap, instructed us in the arts of making either a foot-stool (finished with a criss-cross plastic weave), or a kidney table. The inaugural magazine journalism course started in 1969, and as I didn't have a university entrance certificate,

I ended up in that course though my preference had been for news journalism under the late Christine Cole Catley, a respected journalist in print and television media and a regular contributor to *Time Magazine*.

This was the year that taught me, if nothing else, to socialise, meet women, smoke and drink. Philip Kennedy, another old school buddy, also found himself on the course, yet somehow most of the instructors took offence at his lackadaisical attitude to authority and blanket refusal to play the game; likeable as he was, Philip soon found himself thrown out of the course. It didn't seem to make much difference to his carefree outlook and we caught up as usual at the Duke or the Grand Hotel. One invaluable skill I learned from this one year course was the ability to touch-type under the old maidenly ministrations of our typing teacher, Miss Noble, a long-standing Quaker who, because of my off-the-cuff witticisms and attempts to amuse which she rightly considered time-wasting, accused me of 'prostituting my talents'—to which I replied, 'Yes Miss Noble, but it pays.' Laughter from the class of '69 ensued.

I also began to socialise with any number of journalists much older than myself, in the various bars around town. Of these, Ronald Malcolm became a close friend (and future best man at my wedding). He was a past *Reuters* correspondent from Aberdeen who had settled in Wellington and was also one of the tutors in the News Journalism course. He moonlighted regularly for the dailies and radio NZBC news, which was then situated in Bowen Street in the days before the Labour government under the deregistration policies of 'Rogernomics' sold off most the national broadcaster to private interests. Ron was short and bald and asthmatic, a condition which would eventually kill him at the age of fifty-two.

The was no question about his talents as a journalist and wit. I observed him on numerous occasions holding a bar in thrall with his story-telling and jokes. I never met anyone else with a comparable ability to sustain the attention of a crowd. His rather self-destructive obsessions with sex did, I think, ruin him in the end. Unfortunately, he wasted a great deal of time in pursuit of it, yet this had as much to do with his sentimental nature as anything else, and perhaps an old fashioned Scottish male attitude to the opposite sex. Ron never realised his dream of writing the novel he had already called J.A.S.O.N. I believe the letters stood for something but I can't recall what. He lived at the bottom of a damp street in a house backing onto the Karori cemetery with his wife, Muriel, a fine flautist, and their four children. He left them in the end, or they left him, and Ron ended up living in Petone with one of his girl ex-students who had loved him unconditionally for years.

A number of the journos drank either at the *Britannia*, which was situated next door to the *Evening Post* and close by to the *Dominion* in Mercer Street, or up in the house bar at *De Brett Hotel* on Lambton Quay. As to the last, you entered this via the dining room arranged in a '30s 'Raffles' style decor with cane furniture and palm potplants guarding the entrance ways. The staff was made up of superannuated individuals dressed in starched white shirts, bow tie, black trousers and red cummerbund. One of these, a Dutchman by the name of 'Bram', with a scar running down across his right eye and cheek, was always trying to sell you something from under the counter. He was one of these ex-coffee or tea plantation owners thrown out of Indonesia but still trying to recapture the lost colonial days of the Dutch East Indies, and wealth in a pathetic sort of way. Usually, the things he offered were 'rare' singer-sewing machine manuals or sales catalogues for any number of discontinued lines from say the 1920s, worthless material by any measure. I guessed that this was his way of dealing with having come down in the world.

The days of mini-skirts, pastel colours and platform shoes, from *Matinee* to *Pall Mall* cigarettes; days when you were required to go out into the city streets every Wednesday to do *vox populi* assignments on a topic of your own choosing.

One of these involved a pub crawl in which I 'interviewed' the local patrons and entrenched bar flies on the philosophic topic of why folk breasted the bar as opposed to sitting down, and how important a brass-rail footrest was to drinking etiquette. I arrived back with my fellow 'reporter' pissed and none the wiser. As it turned out, probably the most successful member of our course in magazine journalism was Louise Callan, who went onto to become a fine magazine and features writer for various leading journals like *Metro* in Auckland. Her career subsequently moved on to include script and ghost writing.

Our principal tutor was Alan Smith whose journalistic background, like every journo worth his salt (they would have you believe), was in the print media. He specialised in writing for the Tourist Commission and ran a little business on the side producing brochures and copy for the industry. He regularly used a few of the students to carry out hack work, which saved him a few bob in production costs. Whereas Ron Malcolm regularly tried to get any number of his girl students into bed, Alan Smith, a drinking buddy of Ron's but very much of the old school (dowdy grey-blue waistcoat), was also an habitué of the *Hotel St. George*, a confirmed whisky drinker and this, unfortunately, produced in him a nasty and split personality. As Dylan Thomas defined it, 'An alcoholic is a man I don't like who drinks as much as I do'. His favourite writer was *Charles Langbridge Morgan*, the writer who boasted of having spent forty years 'perfecting the comma', so beautifully parodied by Dylan Thomas in his reminiscence, 'Quite Early One Morning': '...Smoke from another chimney now. They were burning their last night's dreams. Up from a chimney came a longhaired wraith like an old politician. Someone had been dreaming of the Liberal Party. But no, the smoky figure wove, attenuated into a refined and precise grey comma. Someone had been dreaming of reading Charles Morgan.'

I guess I felt somewhat flattered hanging around with these older guys, most of them were able to converse engagingly though not at any great depth over a wide range of topics. They had their own distinctive and hard-bitten wisdom that you wouldn't find in your average university tutorial. And for that I was thankful. A breed of individual who certainly no longer exists; a mixture of the pragmatist cum sentimentalist, enforced by a strong *no bullshit* factor; professionals in their craft and raconteurs over a drink. They belonged to the world of Pat Lawler's *The Froth-Blower's Manual*. Those were days when you could leave pocket change, wallet & car keys on the bar next to your beer, and when you returned both your money and your place at the bar remained untouched and intact.

One of the legends of the era, a close friend of my mother's family from the old Dunedin days, was a highly regarded journalist nicknamed *Old tuatara* by his colleagues. Ron Jones was the archetype, the primal journalist. It was through his intercession that I managed to get enrolled into the Polytechnic Journalism course in the first place. He had originally studied to become an Anglican minister but that never eventuated. He had a profound knowledge of the Bible, and possessed a better knowledge of English grammar and how to construct a sentence than most of his contemporaries. In his days as news editor at NZBC, long before any inkling of the *de-registering* of such institutions, before the resultant centralizing of the national broadcaster meant the closing down of regional radio stations that finally marked the end of an era (and the social atmosphere of tolerance), Ron Jones was regarded across the board with fear and respect.

At one time or another he had worked on most of the important dailies and a number of the provincials in between, from Dunedin at the *Otago Daily Times* through to the Wellington-based papers. A legend in the industry. He was into his early '60s by the time he reached NZBC. These guys worked on rotation through the roster, early morning and late at night, and never missed a beat. After a late night shift they would continue on drinking into the small hours, and then get up at 4.30 am to oversee the morning news. Ron, as I discovered, visiting him early one morning at his apartment on The Terrace, always started his day with a glass of whisky and milk.

Emphysema got him in the end; years of smoking *Capstan* cigarettes finally took its toll. Even his last days under an oxygen tent in hospital weren't without incident and passed into folklore. The doctors were astonished at his ability to rally, his moments of intense lucidity coupled with profound knowledge on any number of subjects, his ability to conduct an intelligent conversation when he should have been comatose. In the end, he managed to bribe the hospital orderly to sneak out and purchase a bottle of whisky. That pretty much terminated his contract. At his request, Ron Jones, or '*Old tuatara*', was buried to the strains of Vaughan Williams's Fantasia on "*Greensleeves*". In appearance, dapper with loosely hung, soft grey suits, brick red or moss green wool ties, with a face cured and lined by cigarette smoke, he bore an uncanny resemblance to W.H. Auden. His voice sounded in a worn smoky register, and you associated that with docks and fog and late-night house bars.

Yet I never managed effectively to practise as a journalist except for a brief stint at *Suburban Newspapers* in Miramar overlooking Shelly Bay, an independent group run by a disgraced ex-*Truth* newspaper editor (if such a thing is possible), by the name of Bryant—a true grotesque who insisted upon working only with young girls devoid of journalist experience, upon whom he bestowed the ranks of either J1 or J2, dependent upon the degree to which they flirted with him. It was a question of 'beauty & the beast' and they played him like a sap. The story goes that the *Truth* board members fired him in his absence while he was overseas, on the pretext that too many protests and law suits had been lodged against *Truth* under his editorship for articles alleging any number of falsehoods, and he was costing them dearly. Usually, *Truth* was happy enough to deal in tits & bums and the general run of smut, but the recriminations were sending the firm broke. He countered with a lawsuit based upon unfair dismissal (hardly on moral or ethical grounds), and won the day *and* a big payout in damages. It was from this court settlement that he bought Suburban Newspapers Inc.

He would often fly into a black rage for no apparent reason, grip his earlobes and pull down upon them with great ferocity. I got fired from that job and the girls resumed control of the office, and him. This was an inverted experiment in equal employment opportunity that failed. I gave journalism another bash some years later, in 1973 at 4XO in Dunedin, as a newsreader, journalist and promo voice. In any case, this is still the late '60s, and it was at De Brett Hotel (and strangely, as if this were a visitant from another planet who had slipped through some weird wormhole into my present back then, or so it seems from this perspective) that I first saw in passing the leader of the Australian Trade Union Movement in all his cocky glory, the future Prime Minister of Australia, Bob Hawke; a short and noisy man, aggressively stabbing his forefinger *up at* trade union officials, emphatically making his point, rowdy as a cockatoo. The consumption of that half dozen or so bottles of beer behind *St. Mary of the Angels* with Geoff effectively draws a line between the conditioned world we were now freed from into the Wellington heading into the decade of the '70s. For the most part, our teen years were subjected to much the same influences, schooling and humours of the age. Our reading came from these revered, second-hand bookshops. As we both didn't get accredited with university entrance, we had no recourse to university libraries. I once contested this at a PEN meeting in Auckland, and the first and last, I ever attended. I had put it to Michael King (since deceased), the respected biographer and then member of PEN, that given I was an author of one or two published titles of poetry, and that these books were lodged in university libraries, logically I should be entitled to access the university library system. Michael put my case with strong conviction, and by implication, the cases of those writers in a similar position, to the convening members of the PEN committee. His petition was vigorously contested and defeated by the late Keith Sinclair, then an Auckland University academic and historian. Sinclair, in all his intellectual vanity, reckoned that if you weren't enrolled at a university you had no entitlement to university facilities, especially libraries. He hated me on sight. I found him vainglorious and elitist.

This reaction was unsettling to say the least, but to me it went to the crux of why establishment publishing houses, university presses, for instance, vetoed writers who were not trained and contributing members of the *status quo*. This 'town and gown' attitude still prevails in small communities like New Zealand where intellectual elitism is consciously fashioned within the university system and is tied up with English concepts of class and privilege, the more so because of its essential isolation and provincialism. Power plays within a limited marketplace necessarily must control limited marketing opportunities, *ergo*, university texts written by university professors for university students, in limited editions, as part of a language department series for university libraries. *Boycott*, the end justifies the means. As an *outsider*, my motion was unanimously defeated aside from Michael King's insistent support for my case.

The attitude remains firmly entrenched within establishment presses, the usual recipients of literary grants and funding, though universities have become more like corporate run enterprises these days, guided by the prevailing economic rationalistic ethos. Arts facilities are slowly being abandoned, and English professors and doctors of literature find they have to step outside the precincts of universities (careerist ambitions within the university system being at a dead end), into the publishing world of the conglomerates or mainstream literary magazines. Otherwise, they launch a new literary organ as a 'bogus' counter force to conventional publishing interests —they must choose both their enemies and supporters with equal skill—which proves to be little more than a vehicle for their own personal cultural agendas.

These literary magazines invariably fold because the buying public is not terribly interested in cultural elitism and exclusivity, and the magazine either ceases publication entirely after a run of a dozen or so issues, or re-surfaces as an annual literary, or commemorative publication, sponsored by some private institution or school, to end up in the magazine section of university libraries for the purposes of student research. If indeed the magazine is in part sponsored by an 'expensive' private school, Professor 'Ersatz' as I shall call him, suffers the indignity of having to change the magazine's name from say, *Forged* (hard) to *Favoured* (soft).

The new publication now runs the risk of appearing as a *Boy's Own Annual*, as it is now required to publish the end of year literary efforts by the school's award-winning students. The editorial board has strong student union representation to safeguard these interests. Of the original series, and the remaindered numbers, Professor 'Ersatz' will endeavour to sell as many as he can, and as quickly as he can, in a 'box-set' to private libraries and collectors. The whole thing will fizzle in time. Students will leave school and go into business and show more interest in 'annual financial reports' than literary annuals. The good professor will spend the remaining days of his retirement giving the odd seminar on 'How To Edit A Prestigious Literary Magazine For The Underprivileged' or doing the talk circuit on the engaging topic 'The Dinner Party Set & The Literary Life For Me,' through local writers' centres and the National Bookseller's Association—offering a special discount rate for group bookings. Food and wine included. Professor 'Ersatz' realizes that the critical component in all this is that he must never lose his credibility in the public arena. He will be remembered as the man who stood alone outside the university system and fought a rearguard action for poetry, for poets, and for the culture of critical debate.

Perhaps an arts minister would name a literary fellowship after him for his heroic contribution? He would continue to do the occasional review on emerging or migrant novelists with an eastern European bias, and happily spend his twilight years peering through a magnifying glass with cabalistic fervour searching for the more obscure etymological origins of the word *magazine*. At what price success! The dog-eat-dog world of the private sector fight it out amongst themselves at every level tirelessly. It is not too difficult to imagine a world in which universities become progressively dismantled into rated 'economic units' or virtual colleges owned by independent business interests, where most degrees or certificates will be accessed through the internet and traded by *e-commerce*. The only university fees paid will be in the form of monthly accounts on individual 'servers' owned and licensed by Microsoft, Amazon, or similar government backed, corporate sponsored enterprises.

Professorships will exist only as honorary titles for commemorative corporate festivals. *A Brave New Campus; Whoever Sells Wins* will be the industry standard, technology that empowers transmission; and memory will become the redundant factor, and history redefined as 'immediate occurrence'. The process of erasing memory is an essential component in the structuring of a protean society whose values are traded like shares on the futures market. Information generates information endlessly. Its very nature is beyond value-added definition, and its usefulness is utilitarian and disposable. Back then, life was complicated enough in its simplicity. We didn't project ourselves into dreary nightmares. Jugs cost around 3s/6p and a favourite combination was a 'black & tan', half draught and half stout. Depth charges were occasionally indulged in, and this involved placing a whisky tumbler full of *Drambuie* or something similar at the bottom of a full jug of beer. Let the good times roll!

[1] *Revenants*, Vincent O'Sullivan, Prometheus Books, Wellington, 1969.

The Great University Break-In

The days of the rambunctious Duke of Edinburgh Hotel, cnr of Willis and Manners streets, next door to the seedy Roxy picture theatre, Wellington, in the late '60s, early '70s, were in full swing. Many participants had walk-on parts but then you always had the regular hard-core, and Friday night brought the whole cast together. Sam Hunt from 'Bottle Creek,' around Pāuatahanui way; Rhys Pasley who eventually took off to Carterton in the Wairarapa to open up a joinery business (or so it was rumoured at the time), and then completely disappeared; the late David Mitchell who came and went pursuing the 'White Goddess' in the days when women at parties lay around like 'odalisques'—or so he claimed in perhaps an oblique reference to Henri Matisse's *Odalisque with Grey Trousers*; the ubiquitous Geoff Cochrane, Vincent O'Sullivan and Alistair Te Ariki Campbell. The latter was one of the poets of the '50s who stuck it out at *School Publications* in Wellington, unlike Baxter who, as mentioned, also worked as a sub-editor in the School Publications Branch of the Department of Education, 'Carving stones in Caesar's graveyard' as he put it in his poem *Ballad of Nine Jobs.* The Māori activist, Dun Mihaka, and the quasi-literary, *agent provocateur*, Brian Bell, were regulars and cohorts at the time. That these two appeared to be 'in league' with each other about this time proved a profound mystery to me.

Sam Hunt often drank at the *Brunswick Hotel*, in upper Willis Street, an event notable for one reason only, that the publican allowed him entrance with his dog, *Minstrel*, a privilege granted only to Sam Hunt. The keys to the city granted the troubadour. School Publications offered one of the few stable jobs—the good old Public Service sinecure—aside from casual employment as a postie favoured by any number of artists back in the day. Baxter spent a little time employed by the Education Department (and worked as a postie during his drinking days, once notably discovered dead drunk in a public urinal surrounded by a scattering of mail), dozing, mostly. Alistair once bailed me up in the pub's urinal and threatened to take me to court if I dared publish a ballad I had written (since lost) on his 'legendary' womanising. Also, Harry Orsman (laughing Harry), a mid-ranking lecturer at Victoria University in Old English and Icelandic, a close friend of the poet Alistair Te Ariki Campbell, who would achieve acclaim for editing the first *Oxford Dictionary of New Zealand English*, which he had reputedly spent forty years compiling—a massive tome of 965 pages finally published in 1999.

Another scholar associated with the same university who remains less clear in my memory is an unsung hero whose name I no longer recall, and who worked along similar lines from the early '50s compiling a never-completed New Zealand dictionary. Had he and Orsman never met? At about that time, in the late '60s or early '70s, I met this lexicographer at the Duke Hotel. He had amassed carton after carton of cross-indexed references to New Zealand regional dialects and idioms (the Southland dialect, for example, with the rolling 'r' I clearly recall with a deep fascination from my early days living in Dunedin), idioms in the process of disappearing, or being absorbed into colloquial speech. The blue shimmer of suburban television sets seemed increasingly to erode speech patterns. Yet as if in direct contradiction of these recollections, Geoff Cochrane insists that the bulk of this material dealt with the Slavonic (Cyrillic) languages. These observations are as much about the 'mortality of memory' as anything else—where memory fails as fact, myth as interpretation claims the middle ground. One could easily, for instance, define an actor as one who lies his way into sincerity. Whatever the case, this scholar had lost his chair at Victoria University as a linguist, probably through a renegade individualistic approach coupled with alcoholism, and so his story is not rated a success and remains untold.

This is a *cautionary tale*—symptomatic of the brutal boycott enacted against literary individuals who dare to stand their ground as uncompromised practitioners of their respective art, against the conventional wisdoms of graft and power play that continue to be associated with mainstream publishing houses, academic institutions, and partisan anthologists. These play upon the paranoia central to the national psyche—a deep-seated insecurity, somehow tied in with a condemnatory Calvinism, peculiar to a small and insular nation like New Zealand. Claustrophobia writ large. This defines the literary political activity within the country and is a game played out for keeps—the object is to destroy the individual if that individual is deemed as different, or not for any reason (or no reason) likely to 'fit in'. Not much over the years has changed in this respect; a changing of the guard, but the basic corrupt strategy remains the same. *What could they be afraid of?*

I have finally come to realize that such an environment will endlessly favour the talentless literary predator, more concerned with prestige as he sees it, and the need to control and exclude in order to secure his place at the top of the literary dung heap. In the end, it must come down to a personal faith—in the true motivations behind the act of writing—and one's reasons for pursuing it. Vision has always been the enemy of dictatorship in any of its guises. Be advised, citizen, the literary mafia never sleeps. One wonders just how many years this polyglot had spent compiling *his* dictionary—its breadth can only be guessed at. I continue to conjecture, what *really* did become of the forgotten lexicographer's detailed and invaluable research?

I had seen this source material on a late-night junket of subterfuge and secrecy (see below) containing rare etymologies, *an invaluable reference and foundation work*, painstakingly recorded in hundreds of meticulously hand-written index cards, overflowing from dusty old cartons stored in a disused room on the ground floor at the back of the main Victoria

University building. An unresolved outcome and an odd coincidence—yet, I cannot believe that he could ever have sold out, or given away his years of research *anonymously* to assist Harry Orsman's grand enterprise! His dissolute friend, the gay psychologist, no less a curious individual, often insisted in conversations that had anything to do with ideas (perversely, he would intersperse his intellectual ruminations with sexual fantasies of an alcoholic and quite desperate kind), that if I wished to understand the true and independent nature of authority, I should read the most profound and elegant dissertation on the question, 'a theory ushered in' by Henry VIII, and now famously known as 'The Divine Right of Kings'. Unfortunately, I never got around to reading it. The following is taken from my collection, *Night of Warehouses: Poems 1978-2000*, (2001):

BRILLIANT LOSERS
on reading Geoff Cochrane's Tin Nimbus

The gay psychologist quoting 'The Divine
Right of Kings' and the lexicographer, his life's
dream of the Great New Zealand Dictionary,

both entrenched alcoholics, both the originals
Dostoyevsky might have claimed, although
both stark losers by the world's brute standards.

Yes, I was there too, that late Saturday night
after THE DUKE, riding the Kelburn cable car up
under the shadowy, Gothic pile of Victoria

University, where furtive as hedgehogs, we found
a handhold to jemmy open an illegal window,
fossick the disused office for carton stacked upon

carton, each one packed with indexed filing
cards, meticulous references, NZ arcana, forgotten
dialects, fables rare as moose from Southland,

obscure derivations, *etc.*, incalculable musings
of an idealist (this he showed us) and dreamer. Here
lay the singular industry of a reverential scholar,

abandoned—yet thirty years on, *The Oxford
Dictionary of New Zealand English* first appeared,
penned by an academic of that self-same city.

We are the last of the witnesses Geoff, like the
derelicts who took the sun sitting behind the Public
Library, or sheltered in Pigeon Park, days long

gone (along with THE DUKE and THE GRAND
HOTEL) a city newly syllabled, yet the light remains,
much the same milky white and pale as stone.

Words and the shadows they cast, words and their weight, words round and pyramidical, words combustible and the wordscapes we constructed in our talk and across the wastes of the untracked page. We criticized each other's efforts for and against, though always with a vigilant curiosity toward each other's attempts; words in a sometime friendly, sometime not so friendly tourney and joust—jostling one another for an acceptance and respect, willing our differences to small advantage. In those first days I felt at times the presence of the painter in Geoff's poems and prose pieces, in his finely polished metaphor and balanced sentence structure which had all the gloss of a still life. As though he were proud owner of a brand-new car, putting it forward for show, stepping back from it, viewing from every conceivable angle, removing a speck of dust here, rubbing a piece of chrome there, and savouring the ownership and creation of something unique and newly constructed.

I thought then that he ran the risk of freeze-framing an image, locking up the rhythm of a sentence, or in poetry presenting these rich metaphors as quartz crystal rising from a verbal foundation too unstable to contain them. I had the sense of 'ceramic' fragments rather than completed design. But all this was worked with the skill of a practised-lapidary—a poet who doubtless had the tools and saw the intricacies of the pattern. Geoff was given to employing the quaint, rhetorical expression, somehow archaic in a *conversational* sense (as the tone of modern poetry is forced to be); this quirk would become a trademark of his stylistics in both prose and poetry. This is a lyricism of the decadent kind associated with writers of the calibre of Ronald Firbank, or put another way, a 1920s modernity redolent of the 1890s. But memory has nothing to do with fashion, more to do with an impossible and sad yearning. The abandoned Romantic spirit. W.B. Yeats made the observation that we make poetry out of our quarrel with ourselves, and rhetoric out of our quarrel with the world. Whatever the case, we both started out in lyric mode as is the case with most young poets. There are flocks of them! A veritable, posse of poets! If one can maintain and develop an informed belief in life then the lyric may give way to a sustained and original *seeing*.

The first engagement in one's writing apprenticeship is usually with the flare and brilliance of image; hopefully, and in the intervening years, the intellect and one's ability to abstract and represent ideas—construct a superstructure out of the 'small felicities' beyond metaphor. Personal vision must emerge from the image, and not end with it. Life styles as much as anything else would shape our directions and individual signatures dispensing destruction and epiphany along the way. Whether the role assumed by the writer supersedes the act is merely an individual decision. Finally, every act of creation can be no more than a *translation*—of the life lived or transformed into art. The Duke was pulled down in the mid-1970s. On the flat, bare clay building site, cordoned off from the pavement that was once The Duke Hotel, some wit soon after the demolition, had set up a wide circle of empty

DB beer bottles slap bang in the middle of the empty space. In the centre of the 'ring of empties' was placed one solitary DB bottle with a flower sticking out of it. A *Glasshenge*, no less! Salutation and homage to a sacred watering hole gone but not forgotten. As significant a gathering place for all manner of artists, outsiders and desperados as was *The Sandringham Hotel* in Newtown, Inner West Sydney, a couple of decades later. A gathering place by definition, is either celebration, or revolution. The Duke was both.

As two individuals with roughly similar backgrounds (Geoff grew up in Island Bay), and subjected to much the same influences, we were from the outset simply caught up in the dreams and the adventures of poetic expression. We were, like other young writers who took the whole business seriously, in love with the power and discipline of words. We gathered about ourselves our different literary models and discussed them, we competed in order to find out where we were, as individuals and talents, placed in the literary landscape. We pushed each other to see further, yet our rivalry and awareness of each other's wholly measurable successes was never vicious. We wanted to be writers and probably believed we were born to it.

This one common obsession had originally brought us together, and we found we had something to say to each other. How it would eventually work out we never gave much thought to back then, and so didn't plan those 'smart political moves' to secure our future in the writing profession which seems to be an essential requirement these days if you are to 'market your product successfully'. Somehow, we believed it would all take care of itself, with due diligence and belief in our own unassailable abilities. For the rest, we lived the literary life as we saw it through the immortality of youth—our early and youthful pursuits as writers in that *bridge* between the late '60s and '70s. We did not nor did we wish to follow a university career path.

I was headed for a precarious involvement with state and commercial radio following, perhaps, the Dylan Thomas edict that 'poets run away to broadcasting like sailors to the sea'. I already had a sense that I was to be defined, and likely ostracised, as literary 'fringe dweller'. Within the precincts of youth an acceptable outcome. I asked Geoff as he stepped aboard the train to return to Wellington (we had met up in Upper Hutt where I was staying at the time on a flying visit from Sydney in the late '90s), if he would send me a copy of his most recent novel at the time, *Blood*. He said he would get onto it immediately. The book turned up a few weeks later at my Sydney address. On parting, I suggested to him that perhaps we should do a hike over the Rimutakas and into the Wairarapa, in the grand old tradition of writers going on extended walking tours. The last time I had visited the Wairarapa was at the beginning of the '80s to see my dear, now deceased aunt, in cahoots with my now deceased, youngest brother, Michael, who died in tragic circumstances on the 22nd of April 2014.

Yet, maybe this proposed walking tour was to pay homage to the yearly Christmas trips the family made (invariably, a disordered pilgrimage), from our home in Karepa Street, Brooklyn-*west* to Pahiatua in the North Wairarapa. These intrepid voyages took place back in the '50s through to the early '60s of my childhood. We spent the school holidays at my aunt's residence, a genteel woman who had always accepted me without question, regardless of whatever unfashionable turn I may have taken as far as my family was concerned regarding career choices, or for that matter, any other direction in life. We all have a favourite aunt. I guess the writer's life begins before one is aware of it. I would eventually record childhood and cultural memories in my book length poem, *Intercolonial* (2013). A *transtasman* epic.

One Day In The Life Of Richard Ramos

'Wanna meet some office chicks man?'—he said.

San Francisco at the end of the '70s still had about it something of the easy-going atmosphere left over from the '60s. AIDS hadn't yet loomed on the horizon, though in retrospect, you knew it was gathering its forces, going about its work unsuspected, especially in that city. I fled Auckland at the close of 1978. You had a lot of women living alone, 'independent' women, who took what was on offer, snaffling up pleasure wherever it came within reach like at the local wine-bar or 24-hour *Safeway* supermarket, a great place for an involuntary pick up, as I discovered, way after mid-night. For straight guys, women were a matter of multiple choice.

This city was an energy grid of 'freedoms' and many tributaries fed into it. Given that most of the new social movements started out, or ended up, in San Francisco, from the gold rush days to Dashiell Hammett, from the *Grateful Dead* to the *Beats*—and that just about every social experiment of one kind or another had been played out on the west coast—you could understand without effort the plasticity and independence of the place with its attractive alternatives that made this city so vibrant. Yet, when I saw that great progenitor of the *Beats*, Allen Ginsberg, I was somehow less than impressed. Maybe the age had gone stale or I had other things on my mind. Ginsberg may have lamented and howled at San Francisco's *Six Gallery* on October 7, 1955, flanked by other poets of his generation, Gary Snyder, Michael McClure, Kenneth Rexroth (host), Philip Lamantia, Philip Whalen; and if Gregory Corso and Bob Kaufman didn't make the audience they weren't too far away for what was to come by way of 'the movement'.

'I saw the best minds of my generation destroyed by

madness,' etc, but I have always suspected *that* statement (heresy!) to be several degrees short on honesty, a truth distorted by sensationalism, a statement upon which much of the poem rests and without which it would be mere hollow rhetoric. Or is it merely the atmosphere he picked up on, the mood of the time, a mixture of the genuine and declamatory? For sure, the poem (*Howl*) bewails, mourns the failure of the *Great Democratic Experiment* caught in the maw of Moloch. For many an immigrant family promised the New Jerusalem found themselves struck down by poverty—grist to the satanic mills. To me the statement without question is overblown and mock-prophetic/heroic in tone, relying as it does on a kind of Blakean, biblical rhetoric; but in Ginsberg's case, the sentiment is little more than a sordid brand of American Puritanism, tailor-made for a bland age—of post-war American consumerism that craved for some sort of pick-me-up.

Today it is sobering to observe that we hear any number of catch phrases and musical refrains, once heavily freighted with youthful idealism, blowing through numberless television commercials and jingles. Copyright doesn't so much protect one's rights as create market value. A lyric once seen as valued social comment now endorses a brand, and in doing so transforms whatever may have remained of honourable or ethical value into mere product. So the *Beat Movement* was born, and I suppose, like God (a real cool cat), *beat* means different things to different people—beatific/synaptic/syncopated or, as defined by Kerouac in a television interview, 'sympathetic'. Aside from all the validity, huff and puffing against the 'establishment' through drugs, particularly during this time, LSD, protest marches, and the whole freedom trip—such idealism inevitably opened the door to all manner of literary and artistic charlatans and shysters, no-talent opportunists, who would stake ego-fuelled claims on the 'freedoms' offered up in the '60s, an era from which we have not yet fully recovered—any number of whom would manoeuvre themselves into positions of respectability and power in the literary, publishing and artistic stakes. Thirty years further on down the track a brand-new elitism lay in wait.

The American playwright, Richard Greenberg, has observed that, 'regardless of economic reality, everybody in America *likes* to think he's middle-class'. Greenberg was echoing President Clinton's statement made in a speech during his first term, that he 'wanted to be the president to the middle-classes'. A statement which he says, shocked him at the time, until he realized that such a wish exists alongside every God-fearing citizen's democratic right to a share in the American Dream. Such remarks are without reservation tied up with promises of the economic benefits bestowed equally on all; health care, education, housing, etc. The youth revolution and movements of the '60s, tailing out into the '70s, were at base a middle-class phenomenon, though at a deeper level, this was more a dream of absorption and predominating world culture. *Freedom become Cultural Imperialism.* Sadly, the American Dream can distort into the American Nightmare.

You can't imagine, for instance, peace, love and flowers being benignly celebrated in the ghettos of America, not unless it was in a Mel Brooks movie. The 'rights of privilege' came into play in the adult years of these youthful participants, whose concerns were more to do with immediate gratification rather than anything long-term, orchestrated specifically for the benefit of humankind. You could say it was more fashion than future planning. Inevitably, the middle-class mentality closed ranks around itself to preserve that privileged position. Amongst the middle aged, so called baby-boomers, you have the spectacle of endless power plays by any number of surviving pretenders, acting in a manner little different from the establishment they laid siege to a generation past—claiming for themselves respectability by excluding anyone who confronts the fundamental lie and hypocrisy of these self-styled guardians and arbiters of all things culturally hip; a social privilege, they believe, granted to a very few.

I got to see Ginsberg and his entourage perform in 1979 at a commemorative reading hard by *City Lights Books*, at 261 Columbus Avenue, but it didn't do much for me. He sat on stage, Buddha-like, dressed in a white flannel suit looking for all the world like an overweight deity upon whom a train of lackeys attended with awed reverence. His boyfriend and fiercely devoted lover, Peter Orlovsky, mopped his brow every two minutes. Just like in the last days of an Elvis, Las Vegas performance. Then Ginsberg, hand-pumping a concertina, chanted mantra style 'tiger, tiger, shinning bright, in the forests of the night'. I still couldn't see what all the fuss was about. Then the owner of City Lights Book Shop, Lawrence Ferlinghetti, got up and shouted a poem about a large nun flying out of L.A. airport, at which point I left for the nearest bar. Way before that, in a thousand tales like it, Gerry Mulligan in 1952 with his baritone sax departed the brownstone canyons of NYC, hitched west to the California girls with eyes blue-bright as swimming pools—into the cool, west coast sounds of 'Pacific Jazz' just waiting for Gerry to turn up and make it happen. And there he ran into Chet Baker, and they got into the Big Band Jazz ensembles, played some smooth grooves together, and the rest is recorded counterpoint and history.

Gerry made the baritone sax popular in the territory where alto and tenor sax had hitherto reigned supreme. In his time, the Jazz clubs gave birth to the excesses of chic heroin, pimps and prostitutes; the cool of the '50s, or at least, so it appeared in the Jazz world, but that 'cool' faded out with the close of the decade; and Gerry, whose heyday lay behind him, could never quite got a handle on that whole '60s thing any which way. Everyone at some time gets to vote on happiness. That great corridor through which the American Dream passes (in real time, the iconic Route 66) fell into disrepair and now exists as a tawdry tourist strip manufactured anew with each generation. By now the mythical journey 'to the land vaguely realising westward', as Robert Frost laid down, as though in the aftermath of the dream, in his poem, *The Gift Outright*, had re-routed northwest through conifer country, and retreated into the last habitable wilderness (Alaska waits) up there in software city, Seattle—giving onto grizzly territory. But back in the largest gay city in America, with the '70s cooling off, playground for most emerging and alternative lifestyles, the women of San Francisco, with its gay population, had an expression, 'Straight guys are at a premium', and I was straight.

Of course, you had the oddballs and eccentrics. You got a heap of those like some sort of hangover from the good old days of love, flowers in your hair, peace and weed. There used to be a character down near *Pier One*, though you never actually saw him, hidden inside this—what looked like an up-ended wardrobe with a little red curtain across a mini-stage about head level. You expected a sort of medieval Punch & Judy show. All you heard when you walked by, usually around mid-day, was psycho-babble or a mantra-chant coming at you real fast from behind the curtain where you guessed the head might be. Then the curtain would shake like crazy, followed by the sudden appearance of a kid's toy yellow trumpet and yells of '*tra la la*, *tra la la*, repeated several times over, which would as quickly disappear, followed by further violent shakings of the curtain. More low mumbling. The guy had been performing this routine for years, his call to come buy weed. In the end, the cops came by and took him away, and that was that.

About then I hung out occasionally with a guy called Richard Ramos, an old Haight-Ashbury freak. There he'd be shuffling toward me, longhaired in his beige gabardine coat and a pair of wire-rimmed glasses. He'd greet you with a huge smile, '*Hey man, what ya doin?*' Richard was one of my favourite people back then because he was so laid-back and had these brilliant one-liners. He was real easy to be with. We used to meet at a bar off Polk Street in the city; anywhere in the city was San Francisco, and everyone knew it. Every street corner announced an adventure. Polk Street (like Castro) was one of the main action streets and the central gay district, and still is. We'd meet at this little bar called *The Rose*, up past the *Sukkers Likkers* liquor store on Polk & Pine, and about the only straight bar in the area at the time, except for the ensemble of freaks.

And no, I wasn't a local. Though it was so easy to slip into that mode—San Francisco made you feel as though you belonged to it. I had even (forgetting for a time I was merely a traveller within grasping distance of the legendary green card) been introduced to a dude who could procure me my passport to freedom for about $500. The promise of this dissolved as soon as the 'relationship' I was in began to look shaky. I did try to find work and almost scored, first with a Jazz station, non-union work for about $5 an hour. Another radio station offered me casual late-night announcing; it wasn't so much a matter of getting there, it was more a question of breaking the picket line in order to get into the building. Finally, Jerry Nachman, 'old style newshound' from New York who managed a key news station in San Francisco CBD, seemed impressed. To have someone trained in news reading, with a 'transatlantic voice' on station, would have proved an almost affordable luxury.

When I got to the first interview he welcomed me 'into his space' and talked big money promises, and 'how's that for just stepping off the boat'. Sure enough, the American Dream seemed to be casting its dawn-breaking light upon me. I got to the third interview stage when my relationship, *and* available funds, came to a close, in that order. I didn't, in the end, have time to wait around for the final decision. Somehow, everything seemed to be taking too long to get there. It was easier really, during the wait period, to remind myself that I was a 'free agent'—though I had already stayed well beyond my three-month visa period, with responsibilities to nothing more than my immediate appetites and the next, convenient destination. That is, if I could give up the comfort of a bed and woman to move on. In the end, I opted to let things just ride until my money ran out, which would ultimately decide my immediate fortune without my having to make a cold, rational decision. Live in the moment is where I have always been at.

When Richard wasn't going down to the 'dock of the bay' or Golden Gate Park where he used to sit (long after the sun had burned off the early morning fog that rolled in up the harbour and under the bridge), with a bottle of cheap red, looking out over the bay, or wandering the streets of San Francisco, you'd usually find him up at *The Rose* late afternoons or evenings. We'd sit around genially hunched at the bar drinking beer, laughing a lot, assessing each other's reactions (scratch an American, you find a *hard-assed* cynic. Puritanism is really an old colonial thing, more for public display), and swapping one-liners. Usually stoned or mildly tripping. The atmosphere was easy.

And if you got sprung having a 'number' in the back alley up behind the pub by a cop some fifty metres off down the sidewalk coming toward you real fast, yelling for you to 'stop!' that was no problem either as you scouted round the corner into the pub to disappear amongst the freaks ranged from one end of the bar to the other. You sat at your bar stool, sandwiched between the black dude in the bowler hat and cubed vest, bright as a neon chessboard, and the Texan loud-mouthing ('how do I get to Texas if my wheels don't turn!') to anyone. The two cops came in and immediately gave up the chase as hopeless, and the barmaid never looked twice or hurried, but shifted maybe to engage you in meaningless conversation, and told you to stay put and drink your beer and look at her until—well, just so you'd settle down. Richard wasn't in the least bit paranoid, it was, after all, his city.

At night, you'd find some sort of band hard at it which we

chose to ignore. This was just background. The acid wasn't that strong either, but enough to see the men's toilet walls crawling with insects under the naked light bulb. But then we'd just sit at the bar and watch the varnish lift off the surface. One night I asked Richard what he thought of the 'American Dream' while we were sitting around doing that—just watching the varnish lift off the bar surface, while some sort of band fused itself into a ball of black fuzzing energy up the back—an amped up swarm of bees. All he said was, '*Whose American Dream you talkin' about, huh?*' But then, this was in the twilight year of 1979. The memory of Haight-Ashbury lingered on in a few Saturday morning garage sales, or dimmed in the far-away eyes of a few burnt out freaks, phase-locked into the moment of an epiphany that had never arrived via the magic bus forever seen rocking down the Yellow Brick Road. Yet, in the aftermath of youthful reflection, you soon realised that America is not just any dream, it is *the* dream of self-fulfilling prophecy.

Modern America is a freeway running between two great toppling waves, the Old Testament and the New Testament; it is the history of the contemporary moment. It has always been and so it continues to be in order to assuage its guilt—in words writ large upon the great rhetorical tablets held aloft by Walt Whitman and Hart Crane, witnessed in bloodletting by the roar and pain of Puritanism over a land without saviours. To which one might add, sorrowfully, 'Moral Integrity' as either bald epitaph or footnote. For to claim a dream for reality is to displace the self; yearning, lost innocence, some remembered Eden, and all the rest of it. Part the seas at your peril, brother!

In defiance of the pilgrim ethos of the New Jerusalem, and the continent being set apart in God's design as a continuance of the Garden of Eden, America—eternally made new beginnings, a place without history, because any historical attachment automatically brings with it anathema, the blight of original sin. The Pilgrim Fathers creeping through the

American deserts bowed before the burning shadows of the mesas. In his essay, *The Archives of Eden*, George Steiner observes: 'Time and again, American consciousness would turn its back on the blighted past; the restlessness of hope points west. The conflict is unresolved. From it springs much of the creative wealth of the American temper. From it, as well, spring essential uncertainties and frustrations in respect of "culture", of the life of the mind in society, as this life has, *mutatis mutandis*, been construed and experienced in the "old West" since Hellenistic times'.

And yet, I wonder what Richard Ramos would have made of his own place in history as he sat down by the Golden Gate drinking red wine, at home within his city, and living in the afterglow of the '60s? Few of us these days can reassuringly attach to metaphysical conceits. Does knowledge exist before birth? Most of us are caught out because we fail to read the signs that tells us youth dissipates. We may slowly become aware that what is left is the damage and experience of disappointment, *but of what, exactly?* A sort of enforced knowing without wisdom that we have been expelled from *something*. Dreams of the past are graveyards. Maybe new definitions of culture are applicable, without direct relation to historical truth as precedent, through a re-ordering of those same inherited sensibilities that customarily define cultural value in relation to that which is learned and accumulated. Time honoured habits of history and culture. Maybe there is to be found a 'richlier' harvest in the *Nostalgia of the Immediate*, beyond that sense of endangering loss; living in America, as in any new world country, is as much incident as incidental. The following is taken from my collection, *Night of Warehouses: Poems: 1978-2000*, (2001):

THE DECADEERS

Yi-yippee-yo! The picket line of
verse slingers stretches back to the '50s.
The decadeers ride on in anthological
gallop to blaze the way with found
poetry into one more famous sunset.
Kerouac is laid back on the trail, strung
out beneath the bo tree. Bukowski has
lit out for the Badlands of L.A.
Stead's skull hangs over the ripped off
limbs of embryo poets at El Academia.
Jacques Derrida signs up, notches
a trope on the butt of language:—
they ride on off the page onto the stage.
All that day smoke rose untroubled
from the desk-top mesas into a blank sky.
In the borderless regions the racist
ape yawled through the stadiums of Europe.
Then night came fast as a fax,
and as they leaned into saddles on that
wordless waste, each writer pondered: what
had been altered by the observation of it?
The *furor poeticus* sang like a
great wind down the Information Highway.

Gulls Dreaming At The Mast

I

My great-grandfather, Thomas McCormack, was born in Dublin in 1841 practically at the beginning of the Great Irish Famine. He left his native land at the age of six (at the height of the famine) and arrived in Hobart, Tasmania, in 1847. In 1851, at the age of ten he relocated to Melbourne. Twenty-seven years later, Victoria went through a period of depression, and so in 1877 he thought he might try his luck in New Zealand and set sail for Dunedin aboard the steamship *S.S. Ringarooma.* I was not aware of the coincidence at the time, but when I landed in Australia, I was the exactly the same age as Thomas McCormack, thirty-six years, when he first sailed into Port Chalmers, Dunedin, all those years before. It seems that I had unconsciously retraced his steps, made my *right-hand circuit* as was the practice of the Irish ancients, when I ended up living in Melbourne some time later for three years. I wrote a poem as my first address to him in acknowledgement and passing salute—in my poetry collection, *Unmanned* (1999):

YOU DON'T REMEMBER DYING

Least, that's what the Old Londoner
told me who didn't learn to relax till well
past fifty, seated alongside his two
mates: a Norwegian: 'You're not the same
person now as you were ten years ago.'
And the Irishman: 'I like the music, it's
the noise I can't stand.' Each one,
orphaned and aphoristic, deep into his sixties.
NZ born and much younger, I offered:
'You're not the same person tomorrow as
you were today.' And then, 'To your
arrival in Melbourne,' they singly toasted.

(Great-grandfather, Thomas McCormack,
arrived here in 1851. Twenty-six years later
in 1877, he set sail for Dunedin aboard the
Ringarooma). So our tale of the two cities
unfolded: *Sydney, is get what you can.*
Melbourne, what have you got to offer, are
we really interested. The afternoon floated by
as did the trams with dry, asthmatic rush
in this mellow town of bungalows and brass.

In this context, one can see the significance of the title a little more clearly (beyond the wry, off-hand tone), containing as it does echoes of parallel time and atavistic memory. It was by first addressing this displacement of circumstance and memory, that I had hoped to uncover an imagistic mosaic where I could identify my origins as a *transtasman* poet, moving within an historical continuum. Yet at the time I wrote this poem, I was not consciously aware that Thomas McCormack had spent such a substantial period of his life in Melbourne prior to his New Zealand existence. Could it be that I was being guided by his ghost or *taisch* for reasons not entirely clear to me? Perhaps revelation can never be made fully manifest beyond certain moods and atmospherics, and within a given 'climate of influence'. Ancient landscapes shape our imagination and synonymously our memory in the first instance; certain things must reside and atmospherically inform our moods, instincts and inspirations—and such visitations are not solely unknowable or unsettling chimeras, but *familia* by which we can retrace our comings and goings, under the guidance of these 'spirit guardians'.

That which exists is what we give name to, and poetry by this interpretation is the naming of those regions imagined, visualized and released from the past, or indeed any projected time zone. The point at which imagination becomes truth is debatable, as is the point where histories become fictions; what ceases to exist, exists—it is a matter of how we locate these 'psychic trig-stations' within time and space and our own *collective* frame of reference—recalled through a syncopated culture, in other words. Yet there is no reason to assume we cannot communicate with our ancestors, and that this exchange is more than likely outside of time, and multi-dimensional. The mind automatically functions by associative cognition to push back the barriers, break through spiritual and historical dimensions, in an effort to connect up with psychic-spatial, living systems of consciousness, both received and generated.

I am only now beginning to glimpse the existence of these processes, and sense the implications and directions for my own mortality as it radiates outward as I grow older. I can do this by placing complete trust in my own immediate past, that it is as *ancient and modern* as any other or ancestral profile connected with my lineage, and that this can be seen as such if I choose to review what I have learned, or apply myself to what those discoveries meant at the time, even if not fully realized. As I have suggested elsewhere, this applies directly to my own personal poetic and mythology. Paradoxically, mortality seems a condition designed and set up to explore beyond the inherent limitations offered up by death (and as death is a void we can have no knowledge of it), though we invariably pull back from the brink at the very thought, and deterministically accept our fate as laid out through evolution. One can understand why materialism at base means nothing more than the celebration of failure (physical) predicated on an interchangeable value system, reliable as quicksand, while we rewrite the rule book (ethical) to accommodate our designer faults (genetic) and vacillations on the stock market.

We accumulate in order to forget. If progress is the road into the future, then it doesn't exist and you wonder what the acceleration is all about. I firmly believe that the antidote for our irreconcilable fear and panic (for that is what it has come down to), the illusory pointlessness of our existence, can be found in attuning our senses to the past which never ceased to exist. Culturally we refuse to admit to ourselves that our beliefs are dead, that they now only serve as conventions. When beliefs ultimately fail, whether in a single or a multiple system of gods, then the only thing left is an active knowledge of destruction. The terrifying reality is only now beginning to come home to roost: *we do not want to belong to our own species.* At least, when we put our faith in the dramatics of seasons, and the seasonal changes, we could believe in our gods and address the vastness of the horizons. Inspiration is elemental, after all, and is made spiritual through an act of interpretation. If the gods at times erred in their judgements at least they erred divinely.

I can't say much is known about Thomas McCormack's youth in colonial Australia, though it is certain he was largely the self-educated man, a voracious reader from an early age who had that dogged pursuit and hunger for knowledge and learning one usually associates with the autodidact. He married one Elizabeth Anne Briggs in Melbourne in 1869. It was latterly in Dunedin that he established for himself a literary reputation, both in discussion and in the publishing of essays with the Catholic paper, *The NZ Tablet* and through the *St. Joseph's Literary Society*. McCormack, with the support of one or two others, founded the first (economic) *Protection League* in New Zealand. He was also a committee member of the 1889 Centenary Celebrations. His obituary in the *Tablet*, December 6, 1923 says that he died on November 30, 1923 at the age of 82 years. Interestingly, the great Victorian poet (and novelist) Thomas Hardy, his contemporary, was born a year earlier in 1840, and died five years after the death of McCormack, in 1928. I don't believe that the latter, a proud Catholic Irishman, would have referred to himself as a Victorian. McCormack is described in his obituary (reproduced in full at the close of this essay), as 'A man of fine intellect and remarkable literary attainment, he having at different times won various open essay competitions on such themes as "Protection and Free Trade", "The Colonial Youth", etc. He won the prize essay on Irish literature some years ago, a competition promoted by the "N.Z. Tablet" Company. He was a frequent contributor to the "Tablet" columns on subjects connected with Ireland.'

McCormack celebrated the egalitarian spirit and championed the underdog in his writings, and one of his earliest memories is recorded in his essay, 'The Colonial Boy', first published in *The NZ Tablet*, August 10, 1894, in which he defends colonial society against charges of 'a stratum of speculators ... overlaying a substratum of convicts', or the prosperous city of Dunedin being written about as 'a community of petty bankrupts', and like opinions offered by visiting writers, 'some of whom possess literary reputations more or less brilliant, and others, reputations more or less otherwise, and to judgements contradictory and diverse'. He put forward the case that the 'colonial boy ... is not easily impressed by externals which his keen intelligence informs him is but the covering that may or may not envelope a vast amount of respectability'. 'In short,' he says, 'his surroundings have developed in him, that freedom of thought, and directness of speech, which is his most pronounced characteristic.'

He then recalls an incident, perhaps a treasured memory, from his own childhood in Tasmania:

'By way of illustration I will relate an incident which many years ago happened to myself. It is a rather pronounced case in point, showing the deceptive nature of appearances. When quite a boy I had occasion to travel by coach from Hobart to Launceston in Tasmania. During part of the journey the passenger who sat beside me was a well-dressed, staid-looking man, of middle age and thoroughly respectable demeanour, who patronised me, and in a very entertaining way, pointed out and described whatever was interesting on the way. As the day wore on, I noticed that the passengers in our vicinity or the guard, who sat with us, never once addressed him, nor did he attempt to join in their conversation, but devoted himself exclusively to your humble servant. The arrival of dinnertime, however, brought with it an explanation of this apparent churlishness, on the part of our fellow travellers. All having alighted with the exception of my very respectable friend, who proceeded to eat his dinner where he sat on the roof of the coach, we entered the hotel and sat down to table, when mine host, in a loud voice thus addressed the driver "Well, Phil', I see you've got Solomon with you this trip." To which Phil' replied, "Yes, that cove in Launceston is to be turned off to-morrow, he's a'goin' up to scrag him." From this, and the conversation which ensued, I learned that my patronising fellow-passenger was the notorious Solomon Blay, the common hangman. I finished my dinner early, took a fresh seat, and gave the other travellers a chance, as I did not wish to further monopolise the attention of so prominent a citizen.'

For more on the infamous hangman, see my epic poem, *Intercolonial* (2013). Once identified, this hangman must have seemed to the boy, Thomas McCormack, like that other cloaked coachman, the rumoured figure of Death in Irish folklore, the one who draws his blackened coach stealthily up under the bedroom window in the depths of night, sable horses standing at the ready, who lifts his hollow stare to whisper sinuously, *'There is always room for one more,'* and moves silently on through the cobbled ways.

As mentioned, he arrived in Melbourne from Hobart at the age of ten. It was not long after that he was apprenticed to Messrs. Phillips, Chambers and McWalters, a well-known and prosperous business which conducted the Victoria Foundry at 7 Victoria Street, East Carlton. About the age of twenty-one, McCormack had gone into business 'on his own account' as an iron founder and lived in Carlton. These were the years in which he developed and perfected his metal-work techniques and originated various designs and patents for cooking ranges, veranda castings, tomb railings, gates and all manner of wrought iron work of diverse repoussé and ornamentation style. In 1883, six years after his settling in Dunedin, he established the firm of Barningham & Co, iron founders (previously, *Guthrie Larnach & Company*) on a site in King Street, opposite the public hospital. His business expanded, and five years later, the firm relocated to new premises at 325 George Street, opposite Knox Church. An advertisement to that effect appeared in the *New Zealand Tablet* on Friday, January 6, 1888.

BARNINGHAM & CO.,
Ornamental Iron Founders and
Range Makers,
HAVE REMOVED
from Great King Street to their New Premises
VICTORIA FOUNDRY, GEORGE STREET
(opposite Knox Church)

He also pursued his literary interests, continued to read widely, and was attentive to the current social and political scene. In the same essay, 'The Colonial Boy', we find him defending the 'nasal twang' attributed to colonial youth, and refuting the charge against him of 'precocious depravity':

'There is another matter which obtrudes itself in an unpleasing manner upon the notice of the critics. At most it is but a superficial blemish, which calls for no apology. They tell us that the colonial boy speaks with a pronounced and most un-English "nasal twang". Let us suppose such is the case (which I do not admit). Is there anything so very dreadful in that? If he does utilise his nose in speaking his utterance is always understandable, and in that respect often in marked contrast with his father's. No Somerset burr or Scottish idiom obscures his meaning. His speech, in short, might be considered perfect had it but the flavour of the "brouge." Having had some considerable experience of this colonial boy's English, a nasal twang, in my opinion, is not by any means its weak point. That, I consider, lies more in the direction of its painfulness, frequency, and freedom, and the slang mosaic with which it is occasionally overlaid. This most objectionable feature cannot be ignored, but I hope the rapid decay of bullock driving will produce an ameliorating effect in this much-needed direction.

Of all the charges levelled against the colonial boy the most serious is that to which I will now briefly refer. I admit his ability to compress into a given time a greater amount of misdirected energy than most other boys, but the indications of "precocious depravity" so patent to his critics I altogether fail to perceive. Of course, we are all aware, that for some considerable time, a consensus of opinion exists among elderly people that boys are not now as they used to be when they were young. That belief comes with years to most people, and is essentially but a tribute of rose-tinted recollection that memory pays to vanished youth. But no slight defect in the colonial boy can have called forth this accusation from his critics; no mere ebullition of youthful "cussedness" would justify so serious an allegation, for "precocious depravity" implies the plumbing of deeper depths and a wider knowledge of the ways of evil. The colonial boy is precocious, that few will deny, but is he depraved? His ranks contain, no doubt, a full proportion of the vile and undesirable, but what nation is free from that reproach? Is the moral and social atmosphere his critics are accustomed to breathe unpoisoned, or are the youth of their own land his superiors in this respect? I could quote statistics to prove that they are not, but knowing how inconclusive figures are in such cases, I will not inflict them upon you. The old adage concerning those who live in glass houses, applies in this case, and his critics should remember that the "precocious depravity" of the young colonial has never yet blossomed into the full blown scoundrelism of a "Deeming," a "Peace," or a "Jabez Balfour."

Even in the criminality of the young colonial, there is something not altogether unmanly, his bush-ranging exploits have shown a degree of pluck and daring, that in a good cause, would be most admirable. Take for instance, the Kellys in Victoria, Vane, Gilbert, and O'Malley, and other misguided youths in New South Wales, who in the sixties were led away by the glamour which enveloped the notorious Gardiner. These, no doubt, were precociously depraved, yet their misdeeds are a pleasing contrast to the brutalities perpetrated by imported practitioners in the same line, such as Morgan, or the Levy and Burgess gang in this Colony'.

McCormack then goes on the celebrate the physical virtues of 'Colonial Youth' favourably against those of his father's generation:

'Until recently, gentlemen, we were told by critical people whose acute vision enables them to see as far into a tar barrel as the rest of us, that the colonial boy was physically a failure. He was, they said, a weed, long and ungainly; a slab-sided lout who gave every indication of physical degeneracy. But now all that is changed. In rowing, cricketing, football and other athletic games he more than holds his own, whilst as a boxer, he had literally "knocked spots off" most opponents. If he does not carry as much flesh as his progenitors, it is not for want of a frame to hang it on. He may not possess the red and white of their complexions, but his fibre is as tough and his courage as enduring. In stature, even his most captious critic must admit, that his tendency is upwards, indicating that nature has determined to make of him a bigger, if not a better man than his father.'

II

Dunedin, the main city in the province of Otago, situated on the lower east coast of the South Island of New Zealand, was at this time a vibrant harbour city, with a robust economy built on the industry of the gold fields in Otago and, later, farming, timber and the Mosgiel Woollen Mill. Accelerated growth in Dunedin started in 1862, and Otago yielded more than half a million ounces of gold annually from her rocks and rivers and plateaux. Port Chalmers, about 10 kilometres along the northern arm of the Otago Harbour, was the principal mercantile and trading centre for the district in the mid to late 19th century. I lived in the area (Sawyers Bay) at the beginning of the 1970s. There was migration south amongst the youth for cheap accommodation, and gallery space, in those days. It was and still is to some extent unchanged in that respect (though real estate prices have more than doubled), and continues to play host to any number of young writers, musicians and artists of every persuasion. Dunedin is now celebrated as the UNESCO City of Literature.

My generation was attracted to Otago's inexpensive real estate and the attraction of a rundown colonial city with 19th century architecture still in evidence; the complete reversal of the reasons for Thomas McCormack's migration from Victoria. I was attracted to the city for romantic and economic reasons (inexpensive living); aware, too, that much of my heritage belonged to Dunedin, and that it was the place where my mother's family, the McCormack clan, had continued to live. Indeed, one of Thomas McCormack's many great-grandsons, Patrick McCormack (deceased), was a long-time proof reader for the *New Zealand Tablet* up until 1999 when it was sold, though he continued on in a part time capacity under the new ownership. *The Tablet* finally folded as a Catholic magazine in the last decade of the 20th century, and latterly continued to trade under its original name as a 'photo laboratory'. The

McCormack family (my grandparents) ran the *City Hotel* during its heyday in the '30s and '40s. This perhaps was one of the more opulently designed hotels in the Dunedin of its day, situated at Princes Street and Moray Place and built in 1877 by the architect, A.T. Brindley of Brindley & Stewart, with its fluted columns surmounted by carved consoles, and by a delicately modelled parapet, which not only hid an ordinary roof, but also screened the attic accommodation of the staff from public view. The urbane Lawrence Olivier and Vivien Leigh, and many celebrities of stage and screen stayed here during this time. My cousin, Louise Sligo (eldest daughter of Nance Sligo née McCormack, my mother's eldest sister), recalls as a small child meeting Vivien Leigh on one of the actor's sojourns at the *City Hotel* in the '30s with this wistful anecdote:

'Vivien Leigh took a shine to me on a visit: I reminded her of her little daughter left in London. She sat me on her knee and fed me bread and butter. Her breath was exquisite and I shyly asked about it. She told me it was *Listerine* and I knew then that would be the first thing I would need to get if I wanted to grow up at all like her. She took me by the hand to a rehearsal of *School for Scandal* and I remember another woman in the cast shrieking *"A Child! Oh No. Not a child!"* and feeling devastated not knowing of such theatrical superstitions.' Louise goes on to say that my grandmother, referred to as 'Mater,' 'endeared herself to many by regularly feeding those hard hit in the Depression days. She had a soft spot for painters too, and the likes of Russell Clark, Allen Bollard, and the historian, E.H. McCormick were given liberal helpings of her largesse. They often repaid in kind with their art works. Clark, for instance, did a 'wrap around' mural of a public bar that was much heralded at the time. City Hotel heydays ran from the mid '30s till Mater's death in 1950. Apart from visual artists, the novelist and short story writer, Dan Davin was another regular habitué, and a short-time suitor of Mary's (*my aunt, one of the three sisters*). Other prominent guests included one of the Churchill clan. Was it Randolph, my dear? He would pluck a red rose from a nearby arrangement and place it beneath the benign bust of Beethoven in the dining room when he entered. There was also Anthony Eden (future Prime Minister of Britain), generally credited with 'stuffing up the Suez Crisis in 1956'. *In a subsequent email sent me in December, 2011, Louise further recalls:*

'I must add to the memory of Vivien Leigh, the presence of her famed husband, Sir Laurence Olivier. He was outside their suite, beautifully groomed and dressed and madly rehearsing his lines quietly in the corridor. Later I read in a biography that their marriage was in terrible shape at the time, having come to the bottom of the earth after an Aussie tour during which Vivien L. had fallen in love with Oz actor Peter Finch. Looking back, I am amazed at the professionalism, taking such care in such a far-flung spot to be ready for performance.' The McCormacks' tenure ended in 1950, on the death of my grandmother (the year of my birth), and the hotel was demolished in 1986. That was the year I left for Australia. My aunt Mary with her gentle spirit and accepting humour became my favourite aunt and 'pal'. I wrote a poem for her which first appeared in my collection, *Guardians, Not Angels* (1993):

MARY, DEAD [1]

Now is the season when the birds
who funnel silence to song rush to
neutralize the gaps between.
Other departures fall back upon themselves.
Mary, your gentle breath is done.
Your heart stumbled before you,
stumbled again in an empty house
your children grown and gone.

The rooms of your heart flew apart,
became the dream that awoke the silence
you once sought to impart.

'I want to as you would say, fade out'
'Do that, and you'll disappoint us all'

We drove the corridor of towns to you
(a dimmed Icon at the hearth)
entered the garden, tall and still, where
you had journeyed to what one is
away from the half-finished present to
the light caught either side;
an afternoon of years drawn back three
weeks beyond the lamp glow of my
mother's womb, and grandmother driving
to another Christmas.

A heart attack at the wheel stopped that.
I became the last and nearest to your
world and departure. Mary
under the full sky of Pahiatua,
the moon wanders through trees into dust
roads borne away to the hills.

From the outset of the gold rush, and the city's rapid growth, many fine architects moved into Dunedin: William Mason, from Auckland, Robert Lawson from Melbourne, George Mallinson and Julius Toxward from Christchurch and Invercargill, and many others. Notably the eminent W.C. Vahland, responsible for much of Bendigo's architecture. Mason is of interest because by 1862 he had already been in the colonies for twenty years, was a well-known and respected Member of Parliament, and was one of Governor Hobson's long serving officials. Mason established a working relationship with the Melbourne architect, William Henry Clayton, who had already claimed fifteen years' colonial experience, mostly in Northern Tasmania, during which time he had designed about 300 buildings, including five churches, three banks, one mechanics' institute, one theatre, three steam and water mill breweries, mansions, villas, and bridges. He was a Tasmanian by birth, trained in Brussels, and most of his work was built within Launceston and its neighbourhood. He remained in Dunedin for about six years and then moved to Wellington as Colonial Architect, the first and only man to enjoy that title. This illustrates the close-knit *intercolonial* ties between Melbourne and Dunedin during this time, perhaps at a level somewhat more sophisticated than one would otherwise have imagined. Both these cities' fortunes emerged from their respective gold fields, though Melbourne had got an earlier start by about ten years.

Mason, apparently, would design what was required of him, while Clayton followed his own preferences for interpretations of the neo-Renaissance style. Mason would be remembered for several major commissions in Dunedin, particularly for the 1865 building intended as a post office, though it was mainly known as the old exchange building—successively used by the university, the Colonial Bank, and the stock exchange. Mason was responsible for the Bank of New Zealand (1863), the exhibition building (1864) subsequently converted to a hospital, the Bank of New South Wales (1866) and many others. Clayton's influence could be seen in Edinburgh House (1865), the Provincial Council Chambers (1865), the Colonial Museum in Wellington (1865) and All Saints' Church (1864).

Mason's The Exchange (post office) he described as 'Palladian with Italian and Grecian features'. Of the Greek classical styles, he employed Doric and Corinthian supplemented by carved spandrels, friezes, cornices and balustrades. The scale of this building was quite monumental, with a ground floor story height of 22 feet and a 120-foot tower very much in keeping with European ambitions. The dramatic aspect of this building could be observed at some distance—with its tower and recessed upper story creating the triangle effect. The ground floor was largely arcaded and the overall impact was Victorian. As a result of constructing this building, Mason was the first to introduce Oamaru stone on a large, civic scale. He placed a notice in the *Provincial Gazette* and as a result Oamaru stone, it was discovered, proved ideal for cutting. Up until this time stone had been imported from Hobart to Dunedin. The Clayton-Mason partnership often tended to the overtly ornate, High Victorian Style.

The Otago Witness, recording the occasion of Sir William Grey's visit to this building site, had this to say: '... the cutters for a simple architrave were in place; and steam having been got up ... His Excellency was enabled to see how easily the stone can be worked. He stood by while ashlar was cut from blocks, by means of a steam-driven circular saw, and while men with a hand saw made deep cuts into a block which was being worked into a capital; he was shown the speed with which balusters can be turned, 36 can be finished in a day of 8 hours, by one man, so that the labour for each cost less than 4d; and he watched the first chippings by which a block was roughly moulded, in its progress towards an elaborately finished capital. His Excellency examined with great interest two beautiful cabinet specimens by Mr J.L. Godfrey, samples of real art, as well as proofs of the delicate working of which the Oamaru stone is capable; and he also saw how easily the stone yielded to the chisel of Mr Godfrey and other of the workers.'

To this day Dunedin has continued to preserve much of its 19th century character. Port Chalmers, as far as shipping and economic activity goes, was practically dead through the 1990s, except for the occasional logging truck with a load of Southland beech (perhaps that should be *pinus radiata*) headed for Japan and the wood-chip market. The port is now a moderately resourced container terminal of the southern hub, with two cranes handling the bulk of the freight from Timaru down. The terminal itself was first successfully petitioned for by the local business community of Otago in 1973, with the assistance of the local private radio station, 4XO, where vans broadcasting support for a container terminal through loud speakers cruised the streets of Dunedin and outlying districts, using the techniques one associates with an American election campaign. Messages broadcast in public places were carefully produced on-station, and 'sped up' by a few revolutions to give the message a sense of urgency, not that you would *consciously* notice the change. Your basic propaganda technique in the analogue age, at one remove from subliminal advertising with little risk of legal infringement upon the somewhat illusory freedoms of the individual. Quaint, really, when compared to today's social media platforms.

I am only too well aware of this ploy, because I worked as a journalist/newsreader and production voice on 4XO radio at the time, and observed the entire process at work first hand. One hundred years to the decade after my great-grandfather arrived in Dunedin, I had lived four years in Otago, first on Blueskin Road, in one of a cluster of houses owned by a co-op high above Careys Bay under the brow of Mt Cargill, and then at Sawyers Bay, one back from Port Chalmers. During my brief marriage in the extended romance of youth, this was the first and last occasion I ever had a hand in buying property: a rambling old, twin-gabled house built completely out of Kauri, right down to its 13 inch weatherboard blade—including the original tree-stump piles riddled with two-toothed, long-horn borer resulting in an undulating floor particularly noticeable in the front and side rooms. The house sat at the top of a cul-de-sac off *Noyna Road* (really no more than a gravelly common-way giving access to houses either side), perched grandly above the ancient tannery (long since demolished), a Dickensian shambles unchanged since the days of the industrial revolution. From the elevated front rooms of this five-bedroom villa, large casement windows commanded a 160 degree view over the road skirting the bay with its small railway station, and out across the Otago harbour channel to the Portobello settlement on the other side. The following is taken from my first poetry collection, *& interviews* (1978):

30 [2]

Spring out of October into the next month
the wind chasing bits of broken growth,

even against the deadened tree / that bird / & peeling bark
spring!

Oyster/catchers dabs of tar on the factory roof
throats noisy & in on the act right now

the whole crazy arithmetic of the species.
Sawyers Bay. Port Chalmers. Careys Bay. Deborah Bay.

• •

The severe brush strokes of the sea at Aramoana.

• •

Pulling at the tubers ferns pulling at the chopped
soil, at the neatly cropped rows

pooling the pockets of the market/gardeners
(God's yards) in on the act. Spring.

Wisteria scrambles along the weatherboard
to our casement windows, framing this.

Against cloudwork the bruise spread yellow
with some dismantling to the west.

These structures of / distance / balance / perspective
tarnish their plaques owning (not us)

: words that doodle in cloudstrokes
to remake the boundaries of the seasons.

• •

Mt Cargill continues under detonation to loosen
giant cubes   a mouth widening over the years

& elevated terraces look east to the harbour
where the dredge lets the shipping run back to the sea

bluish.

This 4XO promotion, a comparatively upbeat campaign, was all about creating employment in a depressed Otago economy, and was orchestrated by the then programme manager, latterly, station manager, the Auckland voice over and marketing whiz, the late Mike Baker, one of the original Radio Hauraki 'Good Guys' from the pirate ship, the *Tiri*, in the days of illegal broadcasts offshore—somewhere in the Hauraki Gulf—under the signature tune, 'Born Free'. The container port was finally voted in as a result of overwhelming support through a public referendum organized by the radio station (ratings and advertising skyrocketed). Mike Baker was duly appointed to the board and made station manager. The container port was finally established in the mid to late '70s.

No great surprise really, in a city desperate to create jobs, disregarding the environmental cost to the maritime area under consideration; yet the 'success' of this manoeuvre probably had little to do with Mike Baker and his slick sales pitch. Once you get past the rock & roll hype, the DJ is little more than an unemployed car dealer, every one of them a salesman and record company stooge. Timing was all. This was the burgeoning age of the container terminal, and soon cranes were to rear up, giant stick insects in all their cantilevered glory, throughout every major port (hub) in the country—like some Orwellian nightmare proclaiming the evils of progress.

But then, Port Chalmers was originally developed for the sailboat and the steamer at the height of the *intercolonial* trade, but you don't see living evidence of that any more. An historical memory reduced to a few faded photographs hung on the walls of the old town clerk's offices (now the excellent Port Chalmers Public Library), still to be seen portside. The only hustle & bustle to be noted here is amongst scavenging gulls fighting over discarded Macdonald's wrappers tossed into some ruined bus shelter or empty parking lot. The train service between Dunedin and the port was stopped years ago (a bus service now runs twice a day) because it proved in the end uneconomical to maintain a regular weekly service. It may still run once in a while on special occasions.

No burly stevedores swagger along the crowded and rope strewn, barrel- and bale-cluttered docks of a bygone age, but only the solitary crane operator who sits in his high glass cabin, silent at the controls, a minuscule puppeteer, loading and unloading the few containers that land and depart this southern hub. If there is any activity to be observed about the place, it is an occasional tourist, the stray coffee shop or gallery owner, though more likely a local resident, heading out during the weekend from the city to one of the few remaining stone hotels in the vicinity. *Chicks Hotel* (since closed down), or *Careys Bay Hotel*, last of the old Oamaru stone watering holes along that stretch of the harbour, with its picturesque scene of a few fishing boats at rest in the bay—before driving further on to Otago Heads and The Spit, where a scattering of beach houses and *cribs* remain hunched amongst the sand dunes and yellow lupin at Aramoana.

Rumour and gossip are hidden well back into the precipitate, muscling hills alive with the clack of keyboards (in my time during the early '70s in Dunedin, the clatter of typewriters) where small literary intrigues are hatched amongst the emerging *literati*, some of whom are destined for the bigger towns, bigger things and the ever-hoped-for successes and slim pickings of a writing career. The hills up behind Careys Bay, and back to Mt Cargill, overlook the entire long sweep of the Otago harbour, across the marked channel to Portobello and out toward Taiaroa Head. The ancient, creaking dredge, with its conveyor belt of rusty buckets endlessly spilling, which cleared silt from the channel for shipping, has disappeared, replaced by a brand new blue barge which does the same job, quietly and without fuss, employing the latest suction methods. Yet a few of the old hands from an earlier generation stayed on from the '70s migration, and as they grew older, either retreated into themselves, or retreated still further into South Otago and The Catlins, or headed inland to the comparatively warm, drier climate of Central Otago, at least, in the summer months.

If to walk about a city is to open a dictionary at random and discover thoroughfares and avenues named after founding fathers, hidden courtyards and monumental stone churches, lonely expanses of parks, fountains, obscure hilly suburbs, steep streets and side streets and squares, stately homes with filigreed balcony railings, an overlaying of history and atmosphere, then Dunedin exists as a 19th century first edition. My great-grandfather's foundry made the grills and gates, etc., and much of the metalwork for *St. Joseph's Cathedral* (where my mother married), designed by the architect Francis Petrie. For instance, Barningham & Co supplied two cast iron grills, each section having seven panels, measuring eight feet high and seven feet nine inches in width, which served as an enclosure for a side chapel (as seen through the archways to the right of the sanctuary) used by the Dominican Sisters. Construction started on the cathedral in 1878. The unfinished building was dedicated by His Eminence, Patrick Francis Moran, first Roman Catholic Bishop of Dunedin (1869-1895) on Sunday 14th February 1886.

Yet this city has for decades sustained a depressed economy that fluctuates to the present day, though real estate prices have soared as they have everywhere in New Zealand. The Mosgiel Woollen Mill faced bankruptcy in 1979, revived under new ownership, but closed for the final time in 1999. The site is now an industrial estate. The long-established, Dunedin based

Shacklock Ltd closed its doors in 2007, moving its operation overseas for cheap labour. The farming sector barely ticks over though horticulture in Central Otago remains a reasonably healthy economy. Otago's extended economy depends on the 'knowledge economy', tourism, the university, light industry, retail, and timber.

The gold fields are a memory of the 1860s, preserved for the tourists in such old gold rush towns as Arrowtown and Queenstown in Central Otago—the last a goldmine in itself with the tourist industry dependent upon the ski-fields and lodges located around *The Remarkables*, Coronet Peak and the Southern Alps. Real estate is as expensive around Queenstown (the jet setters' and movie stars' capital of New Zealand), and Lake Wakaitipu, as any 'trophy home' you would find in an inner city, Sydney suburb, or 'McMansion' in Seattle. It is principally winter sporting activities and service industries that bolster up the local trade here. Elsewhere, much of the agricultural industry, still the mainstay of the country's economy, is funnelled into the northern latitudes, major centres of greater population growth like Christchurch, Wellington and, especially, Auckland—practically becoming a 'republic' unto itself.

The waterfront buildings at Port Chalmers, remain (thankfully) largely preserved in an extended time warp of 19th century grand architecture; Oamaru stone and public buildings suggestive of Scottish Presbyterianism and the stoic spirit, 'built of local stone after local traditions', ornate Victorian residences and weatherboard disappearing into the surrounding hills. Or as the business sector would otherwise define it, a city sinking without protest into a haze of continuing 'economic downturn' (the perfect refrain for a new national anthem). Dunedin survives principally as a university town and in a quiet, melancholic sort of way, as a haven for the writer and artist, fanciful or romantic (but no longer the lure of cheap accommodation and inexpensive property), enhanced by the natural, old world charm of a harbour city, with gently enfolding hills and the soft play of rinsed, Antarctic light.

A city anaesthetised by the camphor smell of history. A real estate agent will tell you that nowhere about the city or its hilly environs is more than fifteen minutes' walk, or five minutes' drive away from the CBD and the Octagon, presided over by the much-celebrated statue of Robert Burns, seemingly indifferent to all weathers, yet comfortable in it. The great poet of the Scottish Lowlands who loved mountains and winters ('a breezy blue-skyed noon and calm sunny day about the end of autumn, these time out of mind, have been with me a kind of holiday', he opined). Doubtless, he would have found more than adequate enjoyment here, rambling about the Otago hinterland, a country of 'loch, crag and brae' in the sharpness of the seasons, as many a poet has done since. His statue is a constant reminder of the Scottish forefathers and the Burns family who helped settle Otago. The poet has a writer's fellowship named after him; in fact, one of the first to be made available in New Zealand, established in 1958.

The *Robert Burns Fellowship* continues to offer a yearly residency, equivalent to a senior lecturer's salary, and is these days biased numerically toward the younger writer, as indeed most university residencies for literature in this country are, thereby further strengthening the university publishing houses' stranglehold on the availability of new and emerging talent. Ambition and youth as qualities are co-dependent and in endless supply, which translates to a ready-made market directed and controlled by the agencies of higher learning, those purveyors of current literary taste and theory. In any event, the city gradually declined through the 1930s depression and never fully recovered. Dunedin, boom city of the 1870s, was to become the final home of my great-grandfather, Dublin born, Catholic, *litterateur*, businessman and essayist; and if he was not entirely latitudinarian he was certainly open-minded, a modernist by all counts, and very much a man of his time. When Thomas McCormack finally sailed into Otago Harbour, he would have seen the scaffolding still up on the recently completed grand folly, *Larnach Castle*, situated high on the North-West arm of the Otago Peninsula.

In an early essay titled, 'A Word of Advice', addressed to fellow members of the Dunedin Literary Catholic Society, and subsequently published in the *New Zealand Tablet* on Friday, June 23, 1893, Thomas McCormack with a certain drollery, or as much as his 'informal', Victorian prose style would allow, put forward one or two light-hearted introductory remarks about the value of self-education (and naturally, he was himself a confirmed autodidact) and then proceeded in a tone just short of banter, so that we have in mind something of the mock, 'Cautionary Tale', to ruminate on:

On tact:
'Tact has somewhere been described as a sixth sense, and is without doubt a valuable possession. Unfortunately, it is by no means evenly distributed in individuals, some having but a very small modicum, whilst others are blest with considerably more than a fair share .... Burns' "Scots wha hae" is universally admired, but is not calculated to arouse the enthusiasm of an Englishman. And the reason is obvious, for if when firing a skyrocket, we give our neighbours a singeing we cannot with any show of reason expect them to admire the accuracy of our aim or the beauty of the projectile.'

On humour:
'This is a matter calling for candid criticism, affecting as it does our literary taste. As a general rule I think members would exercise a wise discretion, if when selecting a reading, they left the comic business severely alone. A celebrated cricketer once sagely remarked that "good bowlers were born;" so also is it with efficient exponents of humorous literature. Nature

has gifted such fortunate individuals with qualifications the average man may sigh for in vain, and lacking which (although possessing perhaps a large amount of ability in other directions), precludes him from shining in a humorous role.... I believe the average humorous reading to be as effective in forwarding our literary self-education as grinning through a horse-collar.'

On critics:
'A definition of the difference of the various styles of playing football in the home countries, which I have read, will convey to our critics exactly what I wish to say. The writer described the "rugby game as kicking the ball," the "Association" game as "kicking the man when you could not kick the ball," and the "Gaelic" or Irish game as "kicking the ball when you could not kick the man". ... We should regard the function of the critic as being in the highest degree useful, and a very important factor in our literary self-education. If occasionally severe, we should always be just, if sometimes we find it necessary to condemn, we should always be ready to encourage and stimulate. These are some of the attributes which distinguish right criticism from mere quibbling, fault-finding, or the savage onslaught of the literary Thug.'

III

Thomas McCormack set sail from Port Phillip Bay, Victoria, to Dunedin aboard the packet steamer *S.S. Ringarooma*, in 1877, under Captain Chatfield. The journey took him *via* Foveaux Strait, between Stewart Island and the Bluff, to Port Chalmers. Departures were usually on a Wednesday, though sailing times were contingent upon overseas mail arriving via the Suez. Given the often turbulent weather conditions, the voyage took about four to five days to cover the 1,200 miles to Port Chalmers, nestled in the Otago Harbour—travelling at an average speed of 10½ knots, running to a maximum of 12½ knots. These were the glory days of steamship travel, and the intercolonial ships were designed for comfort and luxury. The *S.S. Ringarooma* was built in 1875, along with its sister ship, the *Arawata*, by Wingate & Company, on the Clyde, for McMeekan, Blackwood & Company, Melbourne, whose other steamers were the *Albion*, *Omeo*, *Alhambra* and *Tararua*. These two steamers were considered the smartest and swiftest fliers on the often-treacherous Tasman Sea and the Melbourne-Dunedin run.

Of the two ships, *W. Lawson* in his *Pacific Steamers* [3] says: '... their tonnage was 1100 net and hp 800 nominal; length 245 ft., and beam, 80ft. They had compound surface condensing engines and everything was spick and span. One funnel and two masts, with yards on the foremast and a straight stem, gave them a handsome appearance.' Each of the ships had three decks and was schooner rigged. *The Union Steam Ship Company* soon purchased them in 1878 from the Melbourne firm, McMeekan, Blackwood & Company, along with two other ships of the line, the *Tararua*, and the *Albion*. The entire intercolonial shipping service was now in the hands of the *Union Steam Ship Company* whose head office was located at Port Nicholson, Wellington, though originally based in Dunedin.

One gets the impression that there existed a certain unbounded, equanimity of spirit throughout the colonies, an even-handedness that operated between Australia and New Zealand at this time, before the roistering cries of independence and nationhood arose at the beginning of the new century. Certainly, there was great rivalry between the competing companies for sea trade, no less so than the 'price wars' conducted between today's competing *transtasman* airlines. When the *Panama Mail Service* was put up for tender, the *Intercolonial Company* secured the contract for the Pacific part of that service. From about 1866 onwards, the fortunes of the *Intercolonial Royal Mail Steam Packet Company* merged with the Panama, New Zealand and Australian Mail Company, while the *New Zealand Steam Navigation Company* struggled against its powerful rival. After the collapse of the Panama Service,the Panama Company and the New Zealand Navigation Company competed for the intercolonial and coastal trade between the two countries. In the early 1870s both companies were dissolved. At this point, the greater part of the Panama fleet was purchased by *Messrs McMeckan, Blackwood & Co.*, of Melbourne, whereas the New Zealand Company was bought out by the emerging *Union Steamship Company* then of Dunedin. A brief history of these competing steamer companies paraphrased from W. Lawson's work is as follows:

Messrs McMeckan, Blackwood & Co was still the main player at this time, running a trans-Tasman (*transtasman*) service between Melbourne and the main ports of the South Island of New Zealand, with its 'Blue Emu Line' and had only recently imported two new steamers, the sister ships, the *S.S. Arawata and S.S. Ringarooma.* The trans-shipment of cargo, doubling as a passenger service, was still an accepted practice, particularly with valuable goods needed in a hurry, and in 1878 goods were dispatched from New Zealand to Australia to catch the 'mail-post' for England. Passengers travelled in Union Steamers to connect with this run for the return journey to London. Though expedient, this was not altogether the most comfortable arrangement. The Union Line sought a deal with the Orient Line of Steamers which had recently started a service between England and Australian ports.

On September 8, 1878, the Union Steamship Co announced its appointment as agents for the Orient Line throughout New Zealand. More importantly, around the same time, this company gained entry into the lucrative New Zealand-Melbourne trade and bought out McMeckan, Blackwood & Co's 'Blue Emu' line. This takeover increased the company's fleet markedly, and it now comprised: the *Beautiful Star*, *Hawea*, *Taupo*, *Taranaki*, *Wellington*, *Lady Bird*, *Taiaroa*, *Wakatipu*, *Tararua*, and *Albion*, along with the *Ringarooma*, and *Arawata*, both popular steamers in their day. The acquisition of the McMeckan, Blackwood fleet's transtasman run gave greater focus to the service between Melbourne and Dunedin, later to become known famously as the 'Horseshow Run' covering Dunedin, Bluff, Hobart, Melbourne (occasionally Sydney), Wellington, and thence back to Dunedin.

Boasting their company colours, these ships of the line must have presented an impressive sight as they arrived and departed Port Chalmers and Port Phillip Bay respectively, and 'across the ditch' of the Tasman Sea. On Port Phillip Bay, from Williamstown, it was common enough practice, and even something of a maritime tradition, for the *Ringarooma* and the *Arawata* to race one another full steam down the flat, wide-open bay in a riotous bet to be the first ship out into the open sea and Bass Strait—*with a bone in the mouth*, to borrow an expression from Joshua Slocum.

The colours, too, of the Union Steam ship Company were proudly displayed; the hull a bronze green with yellow band and red boot-topping (from 1845 to 1875, the last was changed to pink); the upper works white; the masts, samson posts and derricks, done out in buff, and the funnel painted a bright red with black top, two thin black bands on red. These ships offered accommodation for 80 saloon passengers, with eight large tables, and done out according to the latest fashion, in mauve and gold coloured, Utrecht velvet, a type of 'flocked' wallpaper design. There was also accommodation for 120 steerage passengers. Not only was there the saloon situated amidships and approached by a wide companionway, but each ship offered a smoking room, found under the forecastle head. The bar, according to custom, was self-contained and located at the foot of the companionway. The following two stanzas are taken from my epic poem, *Intercolonial* (2013):

baffle of winds at mid-harbour barbered the funnel smoke,
combed out black-backed gulls to the finer points of
sky around Port Phillip Bay and the steamer, *SS Ringarooma*.
Dublin born of the Irish Diaspora, and 26 years resident

in Melbourne, he departed the looming depression to try
his hand further south, under the dough shaped harbour hills
of Dunedin: great-grandfather, Thomas McCormack,
sailed for Aotearoa in 1877, clouds in lit pews before him.

IV

To conclude with a note on the ancient bardic system. Within this cycle, all roads lead to and from Tara, thereby further consolidating its position as the political centre of Ireland. These places of assembly were significantly located at burial mounds. The rites of fertility and agriculture were inextricably tied and one can sense a glimmering in the mind of the ancient Celt, which must have moved with ease between the parallel worlds of the living and the dead, around the rhythms of the seasonal year. To swear by the elements as in, for instance, 'may the white moon and the sun bless you' or something similar, is indicative of the earthbound nature of Irish pagan mysticism, and oaths—called *imbas for-osnai*, which involved acquiring prophetic visions through sleep, performed at ceremonies by poets, an account of which is contained in the 10th century glossary of Cormac úa Cuilennáin—could be worked for either ill or good fortune.

As already suggested, satire was no mere gift of the poet. It was part and parcel of his poetic armoury, his exercising certain theotechnic procedures by which, through given incantations and the recitation of specific poems, he might curse his subject or place a tabu (*geis* or *geasa*) upon that person—through complex ceremonies that could unquestionably create a climate of great fear. One of these practices was known as the *Glám dícenn* and this was an incantation designed to satirize and punish a prince or king who refused payment for the poet's services. First, the chief poet or *ollave* fasted on the lands of the king to be satirized. The poet nominated six other poets upon whom graded degrees had been conferred, namely, a *fochloc*, *mac fuirmid/fuirmeda*, *doss*, *cano/cana*, *clí*, *ánrad*, *ollam* (representing the poets' ranking, each of whom had a given number of attendants), and set off at dawn to a hill located on the boundary of seven lands.

Each of the poets was instructed to turn his face to a different land and the *ollave (ollamh)* turned his face to the land of the king who had refused payment *(dúas)*. They would then turn their backs to a whitethorn bush that grew on the crown of this hill. The wind should be blowing from the north while each man held up a perforated stone and a thorn of the whitethorn in his hand. Each of the poets would sing a verse of a composition especially composed by thirty other poets under instruction from the ollave; it was a crime for these poets to refuse the wishes of the ollave as regards the withholding of payment by the king. Gathered in a pishogue of malediction.

The *ollamh* as chief poet would lead with his own verse, and the other six, chanting in unison, would follow his lead; each man recites a quatrain on the king and the *ollam* recites his quatrain before them firstly, and they recite theirs together after him. Each of the poets would then place his stone and thorn under the stem of the whitethorn, and a clay image or doll (*delb do criaidh*) of the king for whom it (the satire) is made, and a thorn from the whitethorn (*delg don sgiaich*) in the hand of each man, they stabbing the image with their whitethorn thorns. If the poet was wrong in his satire the hill ground would swallow them all, but if the king was in the wrong, the ground would swallow him and his wife and son, his horse and his hound, and his kingly robes. The satires were played out thus: the *mac fuirmid/fuirmeda* on the hound, the *fochloc* on the robes, the *doss* on the arms, the *cano/cana* on the wife, the *clí*, on the son, the *ánrad* on the horse, and the satire of the *ollam* fell on the king. Such was the power of poets in pre-Christian times. Such is the impotence of poets in our time, who appear to have been swallowed up whole by an analytical void of their own making, in the hyper-ventilation of text—leading down the virtual road to nowhere. The following poem, mysterious as it is, serves as incantation:

CREATION OF THE WINDS WITH THEIR COLOURS [4]

King who ordained the eight winds
advancing without uncertainty, full of beauty,
the four prime winds He holds back,
the four fierce under-winds.

There are four other under-winds,
as learned authors say,
this should be the number, without error,
of the winds, twelve winds.

King who fashioned the colours of the winds,
who fixed them in safe courses,
after their manner, in well-ordered disposition,
with the varieties of each manifold hue.

The white, the clear purple,
the blue, the very strong green,
the yellow, the red, sure the knowledge,
in their gentle meetings wrath did not seize them.

The black, the grey, the speckled,
the dark and the deep brown,
the dun, darksome hues,
they are not light, easily controlled.

King who ordained them over every void,
the eight wild under-winds;
who laid down without defect
the bounds of the four prime winds.

From the East, the smiling purple,
from the South, the pure white, wondrous,
from the North, the black blustering moaning wind,
from the West, the babbling dun breeze.

The red, and the yellow along with it,
both white and purple;
the green, the blue, it is brave,
both dun and the pure white.

The grey, the dark brown, hateful their harshness,
both dun and deep black;
the dark, the speckled easterly wind
both black and purple.

Rightly ordered their form,
their disposition was ordained;
with wise adjustments openly,
according to their position and their fixed places.

The twelve winds,
Easterly and Westerly, Northerly and Southerly,
the King who adjusted them, He holds them back
He fettered them with seven curbs.

King who bestowed them according to their posts,
around the world with many adjustments,
each two winds of them about a separate curb,
and one curb for the whole of them.

King who arranged them in habitual harmony,
according to their ways, without over-passing their
limits;
at one time, peaceful was the space,
at another time tempestuous.

The ancient poets employed highly complex rhyme schemes which even today would gaff and baffle our more 'formal' poets. One singular, and precise example, is enough to confirm their early supremacy in technique. These systems involved the use of alliteration, internal rhyme, and a technique found in the earliest known Irish metre, and perfected in rhyming verse with lines of equal syllables, around the fourth or fifth century. This technique, known as *rinn*: *airdrinn*, used in *Deibide* (later *Deibhidhe*, *Deibhí)* which means *cut in two* metre, was used in the earliest poetry and is a peculiar invention of the Irish. Here a trisyllable instead of a dissyllable rhyme could be used as an end word for the second line if the first line ended with a monosyllable. Given this additional syllable, the rhyme in the second line, for example, fell on the penultimate syllable, not necessarily the last as is the now familiar practice these days. This *shuttling* back and forth of rhyme between syllables within any given word of say, two or three syllables from line to line, suggests to my mind a *circular or spiral pattern (for growth) and may have originally been integral to those ritualistic and mnemonic chants of sunwise stone-circling.*

Later developments favoured the stricter pairing of rhymed dissyllables at the end of the line. These seven syllable lines did not, in the older forms of poetic composition, follow the strict metrical accent of alternating stressed and unstressed syllables associated with the conventional grammar of prosody. Such intricacies of classic Irish poetics, plus a detailed analysis of Irish social, political and literary history are beyond the bounds of this inquiry which is simply designed to give a sketch, or at best an overview of a few general principles behind the nation's development over the past 2,000 years or so; processes which helped fashion the character and attitudes of a late nineteenth century Irishman, deeply respectful of his heritage, as was my great-grandfather, Thomas McCormack.

According to Douglas Hyde, claims by reputable authorities state that the Irish first developed, before any other race, the use of elaborate and sustained rhyme *rím* 'counting, number', *rímim* 'I count'. Startling claims have been made that the Celt taught Europe to rhyme, that the *Latins* acquired the practice of counting syllables and end rhyme directly from Celtic phonology, and rhyme in the later *Latin* poetry of the Anglo-Saxons is wholly attributable to Irish influence. One of the earliest examples of perfecting this rhyme is found in the seventh century poem, *Voyage of Bran Son of Febal/to the Land of the Living* [5]. At the same period in which this poem was composed, the Germanic nations could only alliterate. Alliteration was only one of the innumerable devices employed by the Irish poet and not, as commonly believed, the one distinctive feature of it. It was in the seventh century that the Irish perfected their formal systems of rhyme of a complexity and subtlety never matched again, not even in modern times.

These disciplines belonged to the classical Irish mode of verse making as taught in the great bardic disciplines and, before the 'regulation' of these bardic colleges, became somewhat hermetically sealed in a language known only to a few. With the promulgation of the Ossianic sagas right through into the seventeenth century, through continuous adaptation and change, and with the adoption of the popular vernacular, poetic composition loosened its strict observance to a set of classical metrical codes. In other words, the language in order to grow and survive had to adapt to the more easily understood rhythms of popular speech. Probably at this point, the strict division between *fili*, pl *filid* (later *file*, *filidh*) 'poet' and *bard* began to blur, until the term 'bard' became generic for 'poet'.

In the first instance, the true poet belonged to the professional class known as the *file* (*filid*)of which there were several subservient grades, the highest of which as stated belonged to the ollave. Each of these grades practised a specialist set of rhyme schemes and the poet could not impinge upon another grade's metres. The *bards* were considerably lower in stature and skill, and were divided into two classes, the *Saor* and *Daor* bards, and there were eight grades in each class. Daniel Corkery, in his *The Hidden Ireland* [6] says of these colleges:

'The building was only an ordinary house or hut, the central figure, the chief *file*, the head *ollamh*, was indeed the school: where he went, the school went, sometimes on [a right hand] circuit from king to king. *Fili* and not *bards* it was that both conducted and used those schools, the bards, as compared with the *fili*, being a lower order, *untrained* poets, singers of songs, reciters of verse, strolling jongleurs. The word *bard*, however, in modern times, has come to include all varieties of poets ....'

As a rule, study ran for a minimum of seven years during which time the poet would work his way through the grades. This developed into twelve and in some instances, twenty years. The ollave when he had completed his studies knew, in addition to a profound knowledge of genealogy, history and law, in excess of three hundred and fifty complex and different kinds of versification. He could recite from memory at least two hundred and fifty central stories and one hundred secondary ones. Yet not everyone who went through these arduous years of training emerged as a poet; a great number functioned as historians, others were the 'journalists' of the day who recorded the histories, tracts of law, and the *all-important* genealogies, the collective memory of the nation, in the metres learned at these colleges.

The ollave must have cut an impressive figure when in full flight, either pronouncing a curse, or reciting genealogies and original compositions, calling upon his muse, the Old Celtic Goddess, *Brigantia* or *Brigit* (originally, a female poet and daughter of the *Dagda*, that is, son of one of the mythical Tuatha Dé Danann kings, *Brigit* was a goddess whom the poets worshipped), dressed in his poet's cloak, or *tuigen*. This was a highly coloured affair, and *Cormac's Glossary* describes it accordingly: 'made of the skins of white and many coloured birds; up to his girdle to the necks of mallards, and from his girdle to his neck of their tufts'. He carried a *flesc filed*, or poet's (hazel) wand, an instrument, apparently, of divining power. The poet would have always carried with him his *taibli filed* (later *taibhli fileadh*) 'poets' tablets' and *támlorg* 'sheaf of tablets like a fan', later *támhlorg fileadh* or 'tablet staves,' upon which were cut in Ogham inscription the poems and stories for which he was responsible.

Toward the end of the seventh century, the bardic schools were, as mentioned, 'regulated' as a result of a national convention called by Áed mac Ainmuirech, High King of Ireland. These bards had become arrogant to such a degree that they were ranging about the countryside demanding tribute and remuneration from the working classes. The chief bard would front up to a farm, having made a complimentary poem on his intended victim, and would chant the first verse, and each of the nine other bards with whom he travelled, would pick up on the successive stanzas. If the farmer refused to offer in either gold or silver the poet would then set about to *curse him with a satire.* The farmer would invariable pay up rather than suffer such public humiliation. Today's authoritarian equivalent of the curse is enacted through boycott—a process of slow strangulation applied through denial. The hypocritical gag of silence. That very thought engenders a Mafioso of Poets and their attendant lackeys.

As a result of this convention, the poetic grades were streamlined or, to use a modern term, deregulated, which proved beneficial to the bardic schools who now enjoyed official sanction on a national scale. For the first time, those bards who were sanctioned by the state—for none could pursue a poetic calling unless officially endorsed—were allotted property and stability. In our time, the 'retirement home' for poets was once called the *Public Service*, alas! long since regulated out of existence, now replaced with a tenure at any one of the innumerable creative writing schools that populate universities in the English-speaking world; the *corporatization* of poetry on a global scale minus the financial benefits.

The high-king, the provincial kings and local chieftains within their zones, were legally obligated to set aside property, rent free; both land and tenant (the poet) were regarded as sacred. In return, the poets were required to give open instruction to all and sundry who sought out such schools, much in the way university professors once functioned, long ago before the Humanities declined in our universities in deference to economics, and the professors became, through no fault of their own, the paid patsies of the corporate world. These bardic institutions, as systems of official learning, and quite apart from the monasteries, continued to teach history, law, language and literature, to the lawyers, judges and poets of Ireland—for roughly a thousand years, right down to beginning of the 17th century when they finally closed down.

The mind had not yet fragmented *time* into abstract units of measurement. Time was firmly grounded in the elemental, and paganism, with its intermeshed systems of belief and a strongly imagistic conceit, made this possible. In the ancient Celtic mind, *history was a living system*. Histories accumulated according to events which took place during the occupation of any one people or tribe; vast tracts of time figured, not merely years. History is an echo chamber, after all. The following is taken from the chapbook: *9/ DEADLY POLLEN*, (2003):

> Circuit; right hand wise, [7]
> homage to the sun—as did ancient
> Celts, Scythians, too—host to
> the Milesians on their last leg to
> Ireland as the first Celts castaway—
> whose home precinct the Black Sea
> the *right hand to the centre*;

memoried in standing stone circles.
Yet homage to a sun as walking
pillar of fire, with hell for a coronet?
The world's breath and mystery
end here, earth's innards engorged—
sprawled redly coast-to-coast.

OBITUARY

Mr. Thomas McCormack, St. Leonards, Dunedin

The death occurred at his residence, St. Leonards, Dunedin, on November 30, 1923, at the age of 82 years, of a well-known and much respected Catholic citizen, in the person of Mr. Thomas McCormack. Born in Dublin in 1841, he left his native land at the age of seven years and landed at Hobart, Tasmania. Three years later he, at the age of ten, left for Melbourne. Shortly after arrival there he was apprenticed to Messrs. Phillips, Chambers and McWalters, at that time a well-known and prosperous firm. At the age of twenty-one he entered into business of his own account. Shortly after Victoria passed through a period of depression, which induced him to leave and try his fortune in New Zealand, arriving in Dunedin forty-six years ago by the Ringarooma. In conjunction with Messrs. E. T. O'Connell, he established the firm of Barningham and Co., ironfounders, on a site in King Street, opposite the Public Hospital.

After five years they removed to the present premises in George Street, opposite Knox Church. Deceased, Mr. (now Sir) Robert Stout, Messrs. O'Connell, Shelton and Fitchett founded the first protection league in New Zealand, and [McCormack] was a frequent contributor to the press on various topics affecting this question. A man of fine intellect and remarkable literary attainments, he, having at different times won various open essay competitions on such subjects as " Protection and Free Trade," "The Colonial Youth," etc.

… won the prize essay on Irish literature some years ago, a competition promoted by the "N.Z. Tablet" Company. He was a frequent contributor to the "Tablet" columns on subjects connected with Ireland. The late Mr. McCormack was one of the original members of the St. Joseph's Literary Society during the administratorship of Father P.M. Lynch, and was a member of the committee in the 1898 centenary celebrations.

Quiet, unassuming, and of a most loveable disposition, he endeared himself to all. He leaves a family of seven sons and two daughters. His wife predeceased him some four years ago:—

> Messrs. R., E., L., F., A. P., and Miss H. A. McCormack, of Dunedin; W.H. McCormack and Mrs. N.O. Morgan, of Auckland; and E, J. McCormack, of Lower Hutt; and G.J. McCormack, of Hastings; also twenty-nine grandchildren and five great grandchildren. R.I.P.

—Reprinted from "N.Z. Tablet," December 6, 1923

[1] *Guardians, Not Angels,* Stephen Oliver, Hazard Press, Christchurch, 1993.

[2] *&interviews,* Stephen Oliver, Horizontal Press, Auckland, 1978.

[3] *Pacific Steamers,* Will Lawson, Brown, Son & Ferguson, Glasgow, 1927.

[4] *Creation Of The Winds With Their Colours* taken from *The Saltair Na Rann,* or *Psalter Of The Verses;* a long, ancient Irish poem on the *Creation Of The Universe* by an anonymous author (probably a monk), written down in the 8th Century. *THE POEM-BOOK OF THE GAEL,* Translations from Irish Gaelic Poetry into English Prose and Verse, Selected and Edited by Eleanor Hull, London, Chatto & Windus, 1913.

[5] *Voyage of Bran Son of Febal/to the Land of the Living* trans. Kuno Meyer, London: Published by David Nutt in the Strand, 1895.

[6] *The Hidden Ireland,* Daniel Corkery. Published by M. H. Gill & Son, Dublin, 1924.

[7] *Deadly Pollen,* Stephen Oliver, Word Riot Press, Middletown / NJ, USA, 2003.

The world was a wider, windier place then, governed by clouds in an overarching sky that seemed to unfurl from the horizon, opening out in a dream-like perspective and memory of ancient Odyssean voyages. These are other worldly moments when we involuntarily seek retreat through old as well as new ways in order to feel *surprised at life*. Memory in this sense is the act of recalling completely other chemical compositions, patterns in time and space, far removed and disconnected from any immediate sphere of existence. Nostalgia becomes the unveiling of that Edenic loss, and such absence is often felt weirdly as *foreboding*, or pre-knowledge. Prophecy is, after all, best viewed from both ends of the telescope.

A spiritual diaspora, Irish or otherwise, must have awoken in McCormack that sense of things past, of the migratory spirit echoed in the transmigration of souls, recollections of earlier migrations still, and the dispersal of the Gadhelic branch of the Celts (or at least of their language and culture) from Northern Europe; from the 'La Tène' lakes district and the Baltic coast of Germany, through the alpine passes to Italy, Gaul, Spain and thence to Britain, Scotland, the Isle of Man, reaching Ireland around BC 600. If the old story is correct, in BC 350-400 came the first Belgic invasion, a proto-Celtic mixture of the Teutons and Brythons, the latter a phylum of the Celtic race, though distinct from the Goidels, who settled in South Britain and were known to the Romans as the Druids when they invaded 'Albion', an ancient name for Britain, in BC 50. Robert Graves in his *The White Goddess*, mentions still earlier tribes; perhaps the first being the Parthólan and Nemedian tribes who, according to ancient Irish history, invaded Ireland in BC 2048 and 1718, coming from Greece via Spain. Following this Attic thread through the historical labyrinth, we find the Danaans, the *Tuatha Dé Danaan* arrived in Ireland (as dated in the *Book of Invasions* compiled, as most of these ancient tales were from much older, original manuscripts no longer in existence), in the middle of the fifteenth century BC or BC 1243.

After them, came the Milesians from Iberia (Hispania) around BC 1000 who, according to Irish legend, are said, if not to have originated in Greece, then at least to have spent long periods there, as in Scythia and latterly, Iberia, early in the second millennium BC. Like most migrations this was indirect and slow, with long periods spent moving around the Mediterranean basin before eventually reaching Ireland. Robert Graves goes on to draw a closer link between the Irish and Ancient Greeks, pointing out that the 'Milesians of Greek legend claimed descent from Miletus, a son of Apollo, who emigrated from Crete to Caria in early times and built the city of Miletus; there was another city of the same name in Crete. The Irish Milesians similarly claimed to have visited Crete, thence to Syria, and thence by way of Carenia in Asia Minor to Gaetulia in North Africa, Baelduno or Baelo, a port near Cadiz, and Breagdun or Brigantium (now Compostella) in North-western Spain.'

We must remember that Irish genealogy is as much an entanglement of pseudo-history as fact. Myth celebrates migrations of memory whose effects are heightened by the acute awareness of loss, or 'intimations' of things half-remembered. Memory becomes an act of reincarnation or metempsychosis. Such heightened effects are found in the ancient bardic poetry of Ireland and Wales. St. Patrick's hymn, *The Deer's Cry* (433 AD) has druidic overtones in that it seeks through incantation, that he and his followers on their pilgrimage to Tara to promulgate the faith, anticipating the great meeting with King Loeguire (Leary) which symbolized the division of the pagan and Christian mind—that he and his retinue (St. Patrick's Family, *see below*) be seen as wild deer and fawn, a chant as magical 'cloaking device' and protection against his enemies who lay in ambush on route. George Petrie, p. 132

(footnote) *On the History and Antiquities of Tara Hill*, quotes at length a poem that refers to 'Fintan the poet', who is said to have addressed the five eldest men in Ireland; themselves symbolic of the first colony to settle that country, and thereby serving as guardians of tradition and ancient memory:

'Fintan is here represented as addressing the five oldest men in Ireland, by whom the traditions of the country are said to have been preserved. These were Tuan Mac Cairill of Ulster, Finnchadh of Leinster, Bran of Burren, in North Munster, Cualladh of *Cruachain Conallaidh*, probably in South Munster, and Dubhan of Connaught. Fintan, himself, on whom this poem is fathered, was believed, by the old Irish Shanachies, to have lived from the time of the first colony which came into Ireland, until the reign of Dermot Mac Ceirbheoil; having during this period undergone various transmigrations. For an account of Fintan, see a curious story in *Leabhar na h Uidhre*; and for the traditional account of the five seniors here mentioned, see the *Leabhar Buidhe* of the Mac Firbises, p. 244. O'Flaherty remarks on this legend, that it might be inferred from it that the Irish Druids held the doctrine of the Metempsychosis ...'

The circular world of the Irish imagination served as an ideal receptacle for systems of belief which, taken from a distant perspective, may be seen as contradictory—but within that circle of unbroken time, dream and real, a matching could be made that might appear seamless. St. Patrick's remarkable success in bringing Christianity into Ireland might be attributed to that knowledge he gained of the culture and people. Patrick, as a boy of sixteen, was taken hostage in Gaul by the great Monarch, *Niall of the Nine Hostages* on one of his many overseas raids (Laeghaire/Leary his first son was equally famed for daring exploits), and spent his early years as a shepherd-slave in Ireland. One can easily see how Patrick came to weave the belief systems, pagan and Christian, together with all the skill of an Irish smith working rhythmic patterns into red bronze and yellow gold motifs. After his escape, and subsequent return to Ireland as the church's 'officially' sanctioned apostle—where he came ashore at the mouth of the river *Inver Dea*, now called the River Vartry in Co. Wicklow, c. 432/432 CE; John O'Donovan suggests Bray, a coastal town in the same county as a possible landing place. Whatever the case, Patrick's success was altogether assured; remarkably, he survived all subsequent attempts at assassination. According to O'Donovan, in his translation of the *Annals Of The Kingdom Of Ireland, Vol 1:*

'But whoever will read the *Tripartite Life of St. Patrick*, as published by [John] Colgan, will find that the Pagan Irish made several attempts at murdering Patrick, and that he had frequently but a narrow escape. He will be also convinced that our modern popular writers have been guilty of great dishonesty in representing the labours of Patrick as not attended with much difficulty. Nothing is clearer than that Patrick engrafted Christianity on the Pagan superstitions with so much skill, that he won the people over to the Christian religion *before they understood the exact difference between the two systems of belief* [my italics]; and much of this half Pagan, half Christian religion will be found, not only in the Irish stories of the middle ages, but in the superstitions of the peasantry of the present day.'

This 'half Pagan, half Christian' dialogue (a shifting between the visible and invisible worlds), found extensively in the debates held between Ossian in the pagan camp on the one hand—representing the fathomless yearning as ancient memory recalled, found in the later melancholy of the Irish spirit—and a somewhat crusty old Patrick rigidly attempting to broker a somewhat uninviting conscription to heaven. One is tempted to speculate here that the voluminous collection known as the

Ossianic cycle of poems could never have successfully risen to the truly Homeric epic narrative form for this very reason—that Christianity broke forever the historical thread of ancient Irish memory. With the coming of the one God, the clocks started ticking. *Clocks—which continue the symbolic vigil of the right-hand circuit making of the standing stones.* Traditionally, it is the Monarch of all Ireland, Cormac, who first established the custom of making the right-hand circuit around Ireland, visiting the subordinate kings in turn and taking hostages from them. A practice not entirely dissimilar to this is attributed to certain other eastern cultures. R.A.S. Macalister in his, *Tara, A Pagan Sanctuary of Ancient Ireland* (quoted elsewhere in this essay), in his tracing of the distinctive features of Tara, based upon his reading of the *dindshenchas,* or 'History of Strongholds,' compiled about a thousand years ago, and in searching for evidence of 'Cormac's house', summarily dismisses a statue of St. Patrick on this site as follows:

'We have not quite finished with Cormac's House; before we leave the Fort of the Kings, to see what lies beyond its northern rampart, let us retrace our steps thither for a few moments. We avert our eyes from a modern statue of unearthly hideousness, alleged to represent Saint Patrick, which stands upon the mound; an offence alike to Tara and to the national Apostle.'

He goes onto give an account of the most significant stones or pillars found on Tara (one standing stone is still to be seen though at some earlier time it had been shifted to a different position), called the '*Lia Fáil,* or Coronation Stone'—integral to the inauguration ceremony of the new king on Tara. Part of that ceremony was to make a circuit around the stone. If the King was legitimate, then the stone was said to cry out, though this 'sound' may have been attributed to a 'bull roarer' a piece of wood on a twine which when swung around the head, made a warbled, or 'roaring' noise. Other stone idols or standing stones throughout Ireland were said to make similar noises. With the arrival of the apostle Patrick in Ireland, all the pagan idols are said to have fallen silent, or according to another account, silence descended upon these stones at the birth of Christ. This is another tributary at which the Pagan and Christian worlds intercept, without either entirely dominating the other; a momentary 'stilling' of time. Macalister, closing his account of the Lia Fáil, concludes that there is no evidence to say one way or the other, that this is not the actual stone used in these central ceremonies on Tara:

'To-day the stone stands as mute as the harp of Tara itself, even though once each day, with the southing of the sun, the abominable statue by which Saint Patrick is outraged throws its shadow across it, and might be expected to lose its ancient tongue in sounds of bitter mockery.'

The following poem is an attempt to place myself back in that time through the imagined words of Odhran, Patrick's charioteer, in relating the delivery of the 'Coroticus' epistle on the occasion of the capture and slaughter of a number of Patrick's acolytes—taken from my collection, *Either Side The Horizon*, (2005):

THE "COROTICUS" EPISTLE

My name is Odhran, Patrick's charioteer—
and I set down this account as witness.

'There is not enough death to accommodate
the scum of the earth.'
Where it is written:

'A prophet in his own land hath no honor'
as found in St. Patrick's ' "Coroticus" Epistle'
I first heard that wide morning when he cried out—

'The day wherein my white-robed neophytes—
The chrism still wet and glistening on their brows—
Passed at the sword's edge of these murderers.'

Small consolation, I reckoned, for those slain that
they should enter the Kingdom of Heaven,
a deathless land, via death first visited.

The rest as captives sold into slavery by those selfsame
soldiers, men and women, to the heathen Picts and Scots.

Little spoil to be had from the Brotherhood of Poverty.

The Age of Barbarity is never ended, I can vouchsafe
that, it is the measure of our days, and has always
been so unto eternity.

I who delivered this epistle from Patrick to Coroticus
who ordered this crime—heard the words of
the bishop read aloud in his municipality

amidst spears beating at shields and raw echoing laughter.

I who once served as Cordwainer and Shield-maker
am trusted servant to this humble-angry man,
he has blessed me and given me bread and lodging.

Patrick, who convened the famous *Committee of Nine*
at Tara, put his objectivity of learning over the
fairy mounds of Ireland, yet during his slavehood

here as youth, found his first vision, that some call
ancient and druidic. He escaped back to Britain,
but lost the *glimmering*—returned to Ireland as apostle

to recapture brightness as Godly grace—often he
lamented this loss in the circuit of his ministry at my side.

For faith cast his mind abstract—he could no longer
see ancient memories or ways—that first gift
Ireland gave him during his youthful shepherding.

Great was his regret and belief from that time onwards.

Servant to his bondmaster, *Milchu*, I did come with
Patrick from slavery back into *Nemthur* by South Britain.

After his coming from Gaul and thirty years study under
Germanus of Auxerre—I went with Patrick into *Hibernia*.

Brogan the Scribe took down the words of St. Patrick
in his *Confessio* and *Coroticus Epistle* and I made circuit
of Ireland from *sliab* and monastery to deliver them.

My name is Odhran, Patrick's charioteer—
and I set down this account as witness.

The members of St. Patrick's family or household [1] were: *Sechnall*, his Bishop; *Mochta*, his priest; Bishop *Erc*, his judge; Bishop *Maccaeirthinn*, his champion; *Benen*, his psalmist; *Coemhan*, his chamberlain; *Sinell* his bell-ringer; *Aithcen*, his true cook; priest *Mescan* his friend and brewer; priest *Bescna*, the chaplain of the son of Alprann; his three smiths, *Macecht*, *Laebhan*, and *Fortchern*; his three artificers, *Aesbuite*, *Tairill*, and *Tasach;* his three embroiderers, *Lupaid*, (or *Lupita*, Patrick's own sister—his other sister was *Liemania*, otherwise known as *Darerca*), *Erca*, and *Cruimthiris; Odhran*, his charioteer; *Rodan*, his shepherd; the five (spiritual) sisters in St. Patrick's retinue, *Ippis*, *Tigris*, and *Erca*, and *Liamhain*, with *Eibeachta; Carniuch*, who baptised him; *German*, his tutor; *Manach*, his wood supplier; his sister's son, *Banban*; *Martin*, his mother's brother (some accounts give a *Conchessa*, as St. Patrick's mother); *Mochonnoc*, his hospitaller; *Cribri* and *Lasra*, makers of mantles; *Macraith* the wise, and *Erc*; Brogan, the scribe priest *Logha*, his helmsman *Machiu*, his true foster son.

The transformative state of oracular focus (migrations of memory) is at once memory and Edenic transfer to and from landscapes newly claimed and anciently recalled. Such incantations can be seen in the alliterative chain-verse that preceded bardic poetry, like the 'Song of Amergin'. He was the chief bard of the Milesian invasion, possessed of magical powers, who chanted his song, with great rapidity to enhance its effect (given below), when he first stepped onto Irish soil. *The Conquest of the Sons of Mil*, taken here from *The Book of Invasions*, recounts that landing: 'The sons of Mil advanced to a landing in *Inber Stainge*. The *Tuatha Dé Danann* did not allow them to land there, for they had not held parley with them. By their druidry they caused it to appear to the *Sons of Mil* that the region was no country or island, territory or land at all, in front of them. They encircled Ireland three times, till at last they took the harbour at *Inber Scéne;* a Thursday as regards the day of the week, on the day before the first of May, the seventeenth day of the moon; the Year of the World 3500.'

The Conquest of the Sons of Mil, notes that: 'The first poem written in Ireland by a Milesian is said to be the curious rhapsody of Amergin, the Brother of Éber, Ir, and Érimón, who on landing broke out in a strain of exultation:

'I am the wind which breathes upon the sea,
I am the wave of the ocean,
I am the murmur of the billows,
I am the ox of the seven combats,
I am the vulture upon the rock,
I am the beam of the sun,
I am the fairest of plants,
I am a wild boar in valour,
I am a salmon in the water,
I am a lake in the plain,
I am a word of science,

I am a point of the lance of battle,
I am the god who creates in the head [i.e., of man] the fire [i.e., the thought]
Who is it who throws light into the meeting on the mountain?
Who announces the ages of the moon [if not I] ?
Who teaches the place where couches the sea [if not I] ?

There are two more poems attributed to *Amergin* of much the same nature, very ancient and very strange. Irish tradition has always represented these poems as the first made by our ancestors in Ireland, and they no doubt do actually represent the oldest surviving lines in the vernacular of any country in Europe except Greece alone.'

In this oft-quoted piece we have one of the great fountainheads or well-springs of Celtic inspiration (*Brigit's* fiery arrows, *breo-saigit*, piercing the poet's breast), which is also the compaction of a people's memory. Mnemosyne, goddess of memory, the mother of the nine Muses, is sacred—for this is where the gods dwell, in memory, through which the poet gains access to his vision. Perhaps it is by this act of chanting, or narrating transformations of previous existences, that Amergin invoked, breathed his gods into a new home, made an offering, a repeated chant to propitiate and appease the gods of an already resident tribe, the mythological Danaans, and doubly, to safeguard the arrival of his people thereby spiritually seeding a new beginning, redirecting the tributaries of memory, and a life in a newly discovered land made sacred.

The Milesians, ancestors of the modern Irish, according to one Irish tradition landed at *Inber Scéne*—the old Irish name for the estuary of the *Kenmore* river. Given the references in the *Book of Leinster* to the Milesians coming directly across from Spain, this river's location on the coast of Ireland can without too much difficulty be seen as positioned 'opposite' Spain. *Inber Scéne* means 'river mouth of the knife' or 'knife-shaped river', a mythopoeic description of the river mouth, which cuts inland and narrows like a dagger or blade. Similarly, the *River Bann* (or mouth of) in old Irish is called *Inber Tuaige* meaning 'axe-shaped estuary'. This same estuary is mentioned in *The Triads of Ireland/Royal Irish Academy*, Kuno Meyer, no: 59: 'The three estuaries of Ireland: Inver na mBare, Inver Feile, Inver Tuaige.' [2]

Employing a similar mythologising process (this 'naming' is common to us all, from earliest childhood, as a method of mapping 'original' memory—as shared memory unifies a tribe, or family), I have often referred to the shape of Australia as that of a medieval halberd. Though when I look at it again with a slightly satirical eye, and especially at the indentation known as the Gulf of Carpentaria, the continent resembles a 'tagged sheep's ear'. The outline of New Zealand has always, quite unambiguously, resembled that of 'a broken hand gun', symbolically violent, yet diffused through an imploded paranoia as not only a national pastime but collective, national trait. Dumb compliance is fear anaesthetized.

Memory migrations; the 'holding pattern' of Celtic spirituality, though the Irish nomadic soul is as much an inspiration of forgetting as it is of recall. During the long nights and days at sea, *Cormack the Voyager*, though no abbot journeying to Iona, was perhaps the last of his kind within the context of Irish dreaming, a state easily lost to melancholy—but that, too, is an instinctive *knowing* of cultural loss. There was a natural dignity associated with my mother, Cecily Joan McCormack, and her two sisters, a profound spiritual awareness which sustained her, but there was altogether no active or constructive participation or re-building within the culture of that tradition. No decision was made—*presence* seemed enough. That, and the conservative Catholic tradition, in close alliance with a large, boisterous family, kept her pretty much tied into the daily round. Certainly, Thomas McCormack would have had time enough to reflect on his sea voyage, and in the atmosphere of his reflections;

all his world and ancestry would have risen up before him.

The name 'Cormac' crops up regularly in ancient Irish history under the various guises of provincial king, glossator, and poet. Predominating throughout are these two principal, historical figures who bore the name, the third century High King of Ancient Ireland, Cormac mac Art, otherwise known as Cormac *ulfada (long beard)*, AD 227-266, and the tenth century king-bishop of the two Munsters, Cormac úa Cuilennáin, AD 831-908. This last king bishop records in his *sanasan saltrach cormaic*, a designation of the *Sanas Cormaic*, or the 'little glossary of Cormac's Psalter,' that his name 'Cormac' derives from 'corb' meaning 'a chariot' and *mac* 'a son', because the earliest of the name, living in the first century of the common era, was reputably born in a wagon, that is, a chariot! There is a poem ascribed to Cormac úa Cuilennáin in which he lists the kings of Munster up until his time—a number of whom are descended from a Cormac Cas. Patrick himself, according to a poem by Flann Mainistrech (of the monastery) is said to be a great, great grandson of Cormac Mór (the great), who had an earlier, and no less historical name: Cormac, son of Lactighe, King of Ulster, BC 48, grandfather of Conaire Mor and husband of Etain. There is, in this context, also a Cormac of Armagh, who succeeded St. Patrick in the archbishopric of Armagh, and who died in AD 496—not to be confused with St. Cormac, bishop of Trim, Co. Meath who died in 745 or Cormac Snithine, the son of Enda, son of Niall of the Nine Hostages. Thereafter, it appears, Cormac became a common enough name throughout Ireland. The achievements of these two remarkable men would have been made present in Thomas McCormack's imaginings, and allowed him to reach still further back to the very beginnings through spiritual dialogue and colloquy—the Happy Otherworld of his vision, just as those ancestral beginnings and heart-rivalries are an ever present reaching forward. Historical lineage and genealogy are made just as valid through an act of association—death, distance and proximity, governed by the alchemy of spirit. Faith moves mountains in time and space, and what is past may merely be a momentary eclipse.

A simultaneity of hearing the dialogue of the past, co-existent with the future, is the true nature of inspiration. The gods, and the deeds of men; the transmuting belief that floated like high-voltage cables between the various invasions of successive tribes—whose defeats and conquests were celebrated through ancient bardic song cycles in a successive process of euhemerism, first told and remembered through chant and song and repetition, in the right-hand circling of 'memory stones' as the sacred *Raths* and *Duns.* All that death and the passing of time had claimed was made ever present while simultaneously being made one with the past; there was no chronological division of time as we know it. The memory rituals must have retained in the telling at least the first shock, the tracery of that consciousness, Godly in its revelation—as revelatory as the Bronze Age giving way to the Iron. This presence, a mixture of the religious and the pagan, persists. Seamus Heaney concludes in his essay 'The God in the Tree' [3] redolent of the ancient Irish tale, *Finn and the Man in the Tree*, with these intimations of immortality:

'And I want to end with a moment which, I feel, is relevant to all that I have been considering, a moment that was a kind of small epiphany. This was eleven years ago at Gallarus Oratory, on the Dingle Peninsula, in Co. Kerry, an early Christian, dry-stone oratory, about the size of a large turf-stack. Inside, in the dark of the stone, it feels as if you are sustaining a great pressure, bowing under the generations of monks who must have bowed down in meditation and reparation on the floor. I felt the weight of Christianity in all its rebuking aspects, its calls to self-denial and self-abnegation, its humbling of the proud flesh and insolent spirit. But coming out of the cold heart of the stone, into the sunlight and the dazzle of grass and sea, I felt a lift in my heart, a surge toward happiness that must have been experienced over and over again by those monks as they crossed the same threshold centuries ago. This surge towards praise, this sudden apprehension of the world as light, as illumination, this is what remains central to our first nature poetry and makes it a unique inheritance.'

A few of the stone circles that remain are, amongst others, New Grange, Muisire Beag, The Hollywood Circle, and the stones that circle the sacred lake, Lough Gur in County Limerick—yet there were many more sites now gone (these standing stones were often broken up, especially in landscapes otherwise bare of stone, by peasant farmers in later centuries to make boundary walls and cottages), that dotted the ancient Irish landscape. See *The Triads of Ireland/Royal Irish Academy*, Kuno Meyer, p. 36, (Glosses And Notes): 'Dún Sobairchi and Dún Cermna are, according to tradition, the oldest stone forts in Ireland, having been built by Sobairche and Cermna, who divided Ireland between them, about 1500 BC—the former placing his dún in the extreme north, the latter in the extreme south on the Old Head of Kinsale'.

There is also reference to a stone circle called *Deisiol* (right hand wise) earlier, *dessel* 'clockwise' (*dess*, 'right hand'), 'a lucky direction', at the seat of High Kings at Tara, but no longer in existence; one of the more significant of these stone circles as *Cromm Crúaich*, a stone idol covered in gold with twelve subordinate stone idols ornamented with brass circled round it. This is likely to have been a sun-god ruling over the seasonal cycles. A 1,000-year-old poem on Magh Slécht found in the *dindshenchas* (the word means in modern Irish, typography—originally the origin of place names), tells its story. The god, Cromm Crúaich, in the form of a standing stone, was a significant tribal centre and gathering place at which worshipped the ancient Gaels. The poem (of 14 stanzas) gives a rare account of human sacrifice:

To him without glory
they would kill their piteous wretched offspring
with much wailing and peril,
to pour their blood around Cromm Crúaich.

The poem goes on to relate that rites were performed to this idol stone on Magh Slecht (the Plain of Adoration); that there were occasions of self-mutilation and human sacrifice, particularly of children; that at least one king, Tighearnmhas (legendary), had been sacrificed to Cromm Crúaich; that these rites were performed to the god to secure good harvests; and that, finally, St. Patrick came and destroyed these stones with a mattock, or pickaxe, something I imagine like the Roman *dolabra*—in a gesture that recalls the Christ-figure throwing the desecrators out of the temple. Lines 488-489 of St. Patrick's *Confessio* reads: '*Whence now the Irish, who in former days, / Had but their idols and their rituals unclean, / Nor aught knew the Lord, have late become / The Lord's own people*'.[4] This reference to human sacrifice is by no means proven, and may well be a Christian gloss added in at a later date. The practice of dancing round stone circles, part of extended European (and in some instances, Eastern cults), can be traced back to the Labyrinth of Crete, and the palace temple of the solar bull, the Minotaur. The poem can be read in part as an account of the struggle between paganism and emerging Christianity in Ireland. Was this then a process of slow revelation, or shudder of consciousness? Ritual sacrifice passed from the real into language as sacred symbol—where myth often gave way to 'miracle'. Kuno Meyer in the journal, *Eriu vol. 11, 1905*, in a note under the heading *Miscellanea, Human Sacrifice Amongst the Ancient Irish*, has this to say:

'Instances of the practice of human sacrifice are so rare in Irish legend that Dr P.W. Joyce, in his *Social History of Ancient Ireland*, has altogether denied its existence. (Meyer goes on to quote a tract from the *Book of Fermoy*): "As the sacrifice of children to the idol Cromm Crúaich is evidently a propitiation of the earth gods ... the practice is resorted to for the purpose of restoring fertility to earth." [On] the occasion of a general dearth and famine, the druids advise "that the son of a sinless married couple should be brought to Ireland to be killed in front of Tara, and his blood mixed with the soil of Tara" .... Such a youth is afterwards found by them. "When the druids saw the youth by the side of Conn, they gave the advice that he should be killed, and his blood mixed with blighted earth, and with withered trees, for then their due mast and fruit, fish and produce, would (again) be in them".'

Whatever the manner of epiphany, the deepest soundings of poetry are at base elemental and founded in paganism, the true matrix of its ancient memory. Thomas McCormack was quite familiar with his 'associative' genealogy and tradition, and on many occasions recorded his general respect for the profundity of ancient Irish culture. Perhaps he did belong to one sub-branch of the celebrated Cormac clan around which the great Fenian cycle of poetry was written. These sagas are based on historical events and battles centred around *Conn of the Hundred Battles*, his son Art (the lonely) Cormac mac Art, his grandson, and his son Cairbre of the Liffy. Art, son of Conn, fought the Great Battle of Moy Muchruime AD 195; his great-grandson, Cairbre, fought the battle of Gabhra against Finn's Son *Ossian/Oisin*, which conflict effectively broke the Fenian power base (there were two groups of Fenians, those of Connaught and Munster) once and for all.

These poem cycles included the earlier, more literary, though not as voluminous, Red Branch Romances of *Emania* and the Kings of Ulster—perhaps centred on Tara. Tara's associated centres around Meath that we shall look at as they apply to the agricultural calendar a little later on, was founded 300 years before Christ. The palace of Emania was destroyed by the *three Collas*, sons of Eochaidh Doimhlein, grandsons of Cairbre Lifechair, monarch of Ireland in the year AD 331. The sagas were never wrought into the sustained and unbroken narrative-form one finds in Homer's *Odyssey* and *Iliad* written long after the actual events he describes had taken place, but were overlaid with prose pieces interlarded with poems in a somewhat disjointed fashion.

Prose, apparently, was not considered an art form by the Celt until sometime well after the 11th century of the common era. It was in this century that most of the Gaelic tales and myths were transcribed from much earlier vellum texts, redacted and stocked with exaggeration and embellishment. Keating, the great Irish Historian of the 17th century who wrote in Gaelic, also drew upon ancient texts which, as with so many, no longer exist except perhaps for a few fragments. Myles Dillon in his *Preface* to *The Cycles Of The Kings* [5] says:

'Of the four cycles of Irish sagas, only the Ulster Cycle is really well known, and that as a result of Thurneysen's great study, *Die Irische Helden-Und Königsage.* The Fenian and Mythological Cycles have engaged the interest of modern writers and so are more familiar to the reader. But the Historical Cycle—more properly the Cycles of the Kings, for there are a number of separate cycles—is still comparatively unknown except to a few specialists. There is no good account of it beyond what O'Curry was able to supply in his Lectures on the *Manuscript Materials of Ancient Irish History* (Dublin, 1878). The historical sagas rise sometimes to a level of emotion and expression rarely excelled in stories of the other cycles, and they contain much that is of interest for the study of political and social history.'

The Golden Age of Irish Literature can reasonably be said to cover the period from the mythical time of the Dé Danann down to the birth of Christ, and right through until the 9th century. This was the free Ireland. It was the coming of the

Norsemen, who sacked the monasteries and ravaged the land, that broke the narrative thread of Irish literature. There were two invading forces beginning from the end of the 8th century, the white invaders (the Norwegians) and the black invaders (the Danes)—who were in fact bitter enemies and fought amongst themselves over the Irish spoils. These invasions and settlements by the Danes in Dublin and Limerick, and indeed throughout Ireland, continued unabated until the *Battle of Clontarf*—recorded precisely in the chronicle, 'Wars of the Gaedhil with the Gaill' (Northmen), an historical narrative most of which is contained in the Book of Leinster, a MS put together from earlier accounts around 1150. This compilation is structured in the usual style of richly textured prose descriptions, interspersed with poems gathered from many of the poets of that time, and with eyewitness accounts of the battle. There is also included poems by the learned king-bishop, Cormac úa Cuilennáin.

This decisive battle of Clontarf took place near Dublin Bay on Good Friday, April 23, 1014, and saw the hero, Brian Boru, and many nobles of his clan killed, but which at the end of the day routed the Danes—and finally quashed their dream of a Danish Kingdom in Ireland, for though a good number of the coastal settlements of these foreigners remained causing intermittent strife, the invasions ceased from that time onwards. It was Brian Boru, heroic warrior and statesman, who rebuilt many of the monasteries, churches and schools sacked and burnt by the Danes during this dark time when thousands of valuable illuminated manuscripts were pillaged and destroyed by the invaders (though a number were smuggled over to monasteries on the continent), wholly intent upon eradicating all learning in the Island. Sages, musicians and bards were killed for practising their profession, while others went underground.

Around this time, most of the scribes, too, had perished. Boru sent those few men of high learning worthy of the name over the oceans to buy books. He also re-established the infrastructure, making 'bridges and causeways and high roads. By him were strengthened also the *Duns* and fortresses and islands and celebrated royal forts of Munster'. Boru was perhaps the last chieftain to wield power, for a short time, from the stronghold of Tara. It had long ceased to be the residence of the pagan Irish monarchs, fulfilling the prophecy and curse of Saint Ruadhán, after the reign of Diarmaid [Dairmait] mac Cearbhaill. Yet throughout this period of invasion, the brilliance of Irish poetry still somehow continued, though in not such a broad-banded fashion. Thereafter, writers continued to look back to the glory days and time of the great champions associated with Tara. It is to be noted that the Irish vernacular language in the 11th century, particularly poetry, had reached such a high plateau of technical excellence that it was far in excess of anything central Europe had to offer about the same time—and English as a language had not yet arisen!

The Fenian cycle of poems gripped the popular Gaelic imagination and evolved over a period of 1,500 years—making it Europe's most remarkable, sustained development of literature. The Fenians had for a couple of hundred years been the standing army at Tara, guarding the waterways and harbours against pirates and constant threat of invasion from the North. Fionn [Finn] mac Cumhail (whose father 'Cool' was killed by Conn of the Hundred Battles) was their famed chieftain, whom *Gráinne*, Cormac's daughter and herself a poet (a building was named after her at Tara), ran away from but eventually married. But we are getting ahead of our story—undoubtedly, Thomas McCormack believed that the Gaels were 'children of kings, sons off Milesius', and that at some point in antiquity, his family branch joined the central stem and extended back—as did the five roads of Tara—to the original seat of monarchs, nexus of ancient Irish history. The following is taken from an essay, titled 'On Resetting A Gem' first read before the Dunedin Catholic Literary Society, and subsequently published in the *N.Z. Tablet*, July 19, 1895:

'Ours was an antique and a polished tongue ere that of England was conceived. During unnumbered centuries, and through every vicissitude of unstable fortune, it continued intact and was ever vigorous, lucid and precise, expressive of every mood, and sufficient for every lingual requirement of our learned, poetic and martial ancestors. It was alike effective in the charging cheer that fires the blood and nerves the arm as in the honeyed accents of love. In the poet's verse, sonorous and stately, bright and graceful, the tongue of the Gael was proverbial for its sweetness. Druid and Breton, saint, poet, and patriot, had loved and perfected it and made it the efficient vehicle of the thoughts and feelings of an intellectual, a cultured, and a brave race. Such was the language of our heroic past. Its decline had darkened the advent of freer times in Ireland.'

He wrote this essay at a time when there was renewed interest by the Irish in reintroducing the Irish language back into the school system in Ireland, and significantly, this interest was quickly taken up by Irishmen living in the colonies. *The New Zealand Tablet* was the first public institution to introduce classes for the study of the Irish language in New Zealand. As a 19th century Irishman living in the colonies, McCormack's cultural identity had already been filtered and, understandably, redefined to some extent through his Catholic faith, made stronger against an historical backdrop of British Imperialism. This at least introduced the English language to good advantage: 'the most valuable and useful acquisition derived from our painful and unprofitable British connection'. Yet, this 'acquisition' is largely outweighed by:

'... internecine strife and disorder, [that] dissipated the national strength and the advantages won at Clontarf, and exposed our country to the greed and ambition of a more subtle and persistent enemy than the Dane. The disunion then existing among Irishmen has entailed a long and bitter penance of blood and sorrow upon their descendants. To that disunion our race is indebted for its experiences to Henry, Elizabeth and Cromwell, whose wholesale efforts to destroy our ancestors have been consistently seconded by the bigotry and greed of many of the meaner tyrants who succeeded them. All these at different times made our country a dungeon and a shamble, the sad scene of a long-continued saturnalia of atrocity unparalleled in all the annals of massacre and crime. Overriding this, the legacy of the pagan, mythic world still retains its sense of identity, giving a cohesion to this vision of self and nationhood.

When our ancestors accepted Christianity they made practice of its precepts, and more nearly realised the scriptural millennium than any other people before or since. They attained the highest degree of intellectual culture, and made our country the school of Europe and the ark of learning and civilisation. And when impending barbarism overshadowed the Western World, from the "Island of saints" there issued an army, armed, not with sword and spear as their ancestors when led by "Dáithi", but with Christian charity, and bearing the banner of the Cross to reconvert and save, to comfort and to civilise .... It is also admitted, even by those who love us not, that we possess in a superlative degree the military virtues. These opposite qualifications at first sight seem to conflict but they do not do so, for faith, hope, and charity, the spiritual equipment of the missioner, are always strengthened and rendered more effective when supplemented by the soldierly qualities of courage, fortitude and pertinacity. These are characteristics of Irishmen, which, united to the theological virtues, account for the reputation they have won in the opposite roles of priest and soldier.'

There is no ghost in the machine. The virtual world generated by the digital age is a poor simulacrum for the ancient culture of the oral tradition and memory made visual down through countless generations of Irish ollaves and Celtic visionaries. Their cumulative knowledge and shaping of myth interwove memories of tribal migration into a Celtic pattern poetically unique in European history. The river runs backwards to the Connla's well and the hazel tree whose nuts of wisdom (see below) overhang it. Therein lies the way to a profound knowledge and contemplation for the truly gifted visionary—but now much diffused, at best registered through, and misunderstood as, contemporary psychosis, which is exactly what it has become, as if certain brain receptors had ossified yet still retained trace elements of a long-lost faculty. We suffer an 'anxiety of conscience' promulgated through the machine world, which the last great bardic poet, R.S. Thomas, railed against. It is the lamentation for a memory-continuum now irretrievably lost, one in which the noise of this world, fear promoting fear, cannot seriously entertain.

And yet, we live in an age where poets, once revered as bardic historians and recorded in metre—who oversaw tracts of law, chronicles of great families and tribes, poems recounting heroic deeds, who thrived under the patronage of kings and chieftains who generously remunerated these poets for their work, whose occupation was regarded as honourable a trade as any other, and who practised an hereditary craft, whose satires were feared and could reputably induce physical illness (a *ferb*; 'the three blisters on the face', and even death, a condition we associate with *thanatophobia*), much like the tapu placed by the Māori or the Australian aboriginal peoples— are today quite 'afraid' of history.

There is also the *Briamon smethraige* which, according to Whitley Stokes, quoting Cormac úa Cuilennáin's glossary in his *Three Irish Glossaries*, is explained as follows: '... the name of an operation which poets perform on any one who refuses them. "He grinds the lobe of the person's ear between his fingers, and the person on whom he performs this operation dies."' Maybe there is an inkling here that modern poets do not possess the imaginative scope to get beyond mere self-interest, fearing in the process that exposure on a broader, historical canvas would barely earn them a passing footnote; culling them out as irrelevant and anachronistic players. Poets content to hide their lack of originality behind a cowardly bulwark of semiotic theory in a confusion of post-structuralist babble. We live in a corporate world where observation as truth is no sooner made than it is disowned.

And if memory is circular, and the horizon full blown as any sail, and the body a craft that sets out upon currents of imagining—giving out and receiving pulse and transmission endlessly down through the ages—then there is one (of many) comparatively small segments found in the *Instructions of King Cormac Mac Airt* that might easily have echoed in my great-grandfather's mind as vision. This he may have recalled and held for good fortune, a prescience refracted through the two-way mirror of Cormac/McCormack's consciousness, as he stepped off the intercolonial steamer, *S.S. Ringarooma*, having come, *tar lear* (across the sea) and placed his right foot on the ground at Port Chalmers in 1877. This segment can be seen as transmitting from the third century, by way of his common ancestor, a perfect description of the Otago climate: No 36. *Instructions of King Cormac Mac Airt* tells us: [6]

> 'O grandson of Conn, what are the best seasons?'
> 'Not hard to tell. A fine frosty winter,
> a dry windy spring,
> a droughty showery summer,
> a fruitful autumn with heavy dews.'

In this account of the Irish currents both pagan and Christian that fashioned a man like Thomas McCormack, traced back through his common ancestry and centred upon the sacred site of Tara, the primal seat of ancient memory, I have courted the notions of these two intertwined rivers of thought and vision in space-time, and the collective Celtic unconscious always at the point of revelation. As I have said in this context: *Whatever the manner of Epiphany, the deepest soundings of poetry are at base elemental and founded in paganism, the true matrix of its ancient memory.* Abstraction is fossilized memory. Perhaps the most profound text from early Christian times in Europe that brings together these two currents, the pagan and Christian, is contained in the *Hymn of St. Patrick.* This theotechnic composition was first attributed to Patrick as early as the seventh century.

He delivered this at Tara in 433 before King Lóegaire and the assembled princes in his famous attempt to convert the king (unsuccessfully), and the nobility of Ireland, to the emerging Christian faith. Patrick chose the sacred festival of *Beltane*, a druidical festival recorded by Cormac úa Cuilennáin in his *Glossary*, or the *fire of Baal*, to do this. The sacred fire of the pagan Irish was lit for the first time every year on May Day. Upon the lighting of this fire or 'two goodly fires' the Druids brought the cattle between them, to safeguard against diseases for the following year.

All other districts of Ireland were prohibited from lighting fires until the Druids had performed this sacred duty at the commencement of this yearly festival at Tara. Patrick apparently transgressed these rules by lighting a fire at his camp close by, before the Druids had lit their fire, and thereby caused offence to the King, and he was brought before King Lóegaire as a criminal to explain his actions. This accordingly gave him the opportunity to deliver his address. The date set for this festival is Easter Eve, 433. The year of the pagan Irish was luni-solar, as with the Phoenicians and Egyptians, of 365 days and six hours. As stated in George Petrie's *On the History and Antiquities of Tara Hill*, *Transactions of the Royal Irish Academy*, Vol. XVIII (1839) p. 85: [7]

'That it was divided by them, as it is among the moderns, into four *rathas* or quarters. That these four *rathas*, or quarters, were called, as, with slight orthographical variation, the seasons of the year as they are known to the modern Irish, *Samh-ratha*, Summer; *Foghmhar-ratha*, Autumn; *Geimh-ratha*, Winter; and *Iar-ratha* (now *Earrach*,) Spring; the first of these quarters commencing at the vernal equinox, the second at the summer solstice, the third at the autumnal equinox, and the fourth at the winter solstice ... that at the beginning of each of these *rathas* a religious festival was celebrated, and that though the names of these festivals, as well as those of the *rathas*, are still retained, the periods at which they were celebrated were changed by the early Christians to agree with the Christian festivals, and so obliterate the recollection of the origin of the pagan rites, which they were not able utterly to abolish.'

The Hymn of St. Patrick is as much a claiming for the Christian God as *Amergin's* earlier hymn was for the elemental gods. The adherence to a passion and belief was in many ways more physically pagan than Christian—and there is that *colouring* of such a world in St. Patrick's words. After all, the world in which he moved and taught was illuminated by a Pagan belief system. *A living system.* Here the two great belief systems face off against each other. In itself, it is a poem of such remarkable depth and memory that these two worlds upon which this incantatory poem draws (for it is both bardic *and* incantatory) are momentarily suspended in time—vision meeting faith—and the portals of each are *simultaneously* opened up to the participant. I quote the full text here for that very reason, in the majestic translation by George Petrie, also published in the *Transactions of the Royal Irish Academy*, Vol. XVIII (1839) on pp. 57–68:

At Temur to-day I invoke the mighty power of the Trinity. I believe in the Trinity under the Unity of the God of the Elements.

At Temur to-day [I place] the virtue of the Birth of Christ with his Baptism, the virtue of his Crucifixion with his Burial, the virtue of his Resurrection with his Ascension, the virtue of the coming to the eternal Judgement.

At Temur to-day [I place] the virtue of the love of Seraphin; [the virtue which exists] in the obedience of angels, in the hope of the Resurrection to eternal reward, in the prayers of the noble fathers, in the predictions of the prophets, in the preaching of the apostles, in the faith of the confessors, in the purity of the holy virgins, in the deeds of just men.

At Temur to-day [I place] the strength of heaven, the light of the sun, the whiteness of snow, the force of fire, the rapidity of lightning, the swiftness of the wind, the depth of the sea, the stability of the earth, the hardness of rocks [between me and the powers of paganism and demons].

At Temur to-day may the strength of God pilot me, may the power of God preserve me, may the wisdom of God instruct me, may the eye of God view me, may the ear of God hear me, may the Word of God render me eloquent, may the hand of God protect me, may the way of God direct me, may the shield of God defend me, may the host of God guard me against the snares of demons, the temptations of vices, the inclinations of the mind, against every man who meditates evil to me, far or near, alone or in company.

I place all these powers between me and every evil unmerciful power directed against my soul and my body, [as a protection] against the incantations of false prophets, against the black laws of Gentilism, against the false laws of heresy, against the treachery of idolatry, against the spells of women, smiths, and Druids, against every knowledge which blinds the soul of man. May Christ today protect me against poison, against burning, against drowning, against wounding, until I deserve much reward.

Christ [be] with me, Christ before me, Christ after me, Christ in me, Christ under me, Christ over me, Christ at my right, Christ at my left, Christ at this side, Christ at that side, Christ at my back.

Christ [be] in the heart of each person whom I speak to, Christ in the mouth of each person who speaks to me, Christ in each eye which sees me, Christ in each ear which hears me.

At Temur to-day I invoke the mighty power of the Trinity. I believe in the Trinity under the Unity of the God of the elements.

Salvation is the Lord's, salvation is the Lord's, salvation is Christ's. May thy salvation, O Lord, be always with us.

[1] For an account of additional personages to the household list, mentioned in a poem by *Flann Mainistrech*, i.e. Flann of the Monastery, abbot of *Mainistir-Bhuithe*, now *Monasterboice*, in the country of Louth, who died in December, 1056—see: John O'Donovan's translation of the *Annals of the Kingdom Of Ireland*, , Royal Irish Academy, Dublin, Vol. 1, Hodges And Smith, 1854, pp: 135-141.

[2] *The Triads Of Ireland* by Kuno Meyer, Todd Lecture Series, Royal Irish Academy Dublin, Vol. XIII, Hodges, Figgis, & Co., Ltd. 1906.

[3] *Preoccupations, Selected Prose, 1968-1978*, Seamus Heaney, Faber & Faber, 1980. This essay was first delivered on Radio Telefís Eireann, 1978.

[4] *On The Patrician Documents*, Sir Samuel Ferguson; see his blank verse translation of St. Patrick's *Confessio*, Royal Irish Academy, Dublin, Vol. XXVII. Hodges, Figgis, & Co., Ltd. 1885, p. 84.

[5] *The Cycles Of The Kings* by Myles Dillon, Geoffrey Cumberlege, Oxford University Press, 1946.

[6] *The Instructions of Cormac Mac Airt* , Kuno Meyer, Todd Lecture Series, Royal Irish Academy, Dublin, Vol. XV, Hodges, Figgis, & Co., Ltd. 1909.

[7] *On the History and Antiquities of Tara Hill* by George Petrie, The Royal Irish Academy, Dublin, Vol. XVIII, Hodges and Smith, 1839.

Unfreedoms Of Expression

A latter-day sermon for the dispossessed

For at least one moment in my address you will feel that *slithering* sense of self-consciousness. Embarrassment, even. I saw a man attempting to couple with a lamp-post once, but on reflection, he was actually engaged in an 'assault' upon that pole with a ferocious groin-pounding, and gripped it in the way a possum might, for dear life, working within a familiar element with a claw-like tenacity that suggested rapid ascent, or frustrated advance. What else could he mean by this futile, and (as I passed by quickly) seemingly, Gothic posture: a thwarted rebellion of some sort? Hardly tree-hugging by any stretch of the imagination; nor does violation enter into it, for you can't, strictly speaking, violate an inanimate object, only damage it or be damaged by it. Self-expression of the powerless kind. Ah, the streets of Sydney's Inner West!

He seemed somehow completely unselfconscious of his act; the embarrassment gene did not inhabit this man's psyche. What is especially *liberating*, is one's right to effectively express freedoms of thought with the emotional and intellectual grammar readily available to us. Perhaps the overriding and neutralising frustration is simply, *how to*. What is it that we wish to playback, and by what circuitry do we choose to achieve this effectively? We feel that to observe is 'to know', that our understanding of the process, is to capture the thing observed. What describes that peculiar action or event may be defined as 'truth-seeking'. Self-satisfaction, that quietly existing tectonic state of 'I' has nothing to do with 'truth'. But such a 'self-reflective' action has everything to do with narcissism. To enlarge the playback of these images (microscopic) as opposed to shrinking them (telescopic) are so many gravitational waves originating from the Self to imagined bounds, buffers which, again, remind *us-of-us*. The great illusion is that no question ever existed in the first place. The arc of the ego is self-deception.

Memory has a great deal to do with it, this business of self-expression, memory encoded as meaning and visually deciphered. Or put another way, the active ingredient in the mnemonic process is the *act* itself. How successful this proves to be is dependent upon our interpretation or understanding of the various components; our ability to scout ahead into unknown territory, for instance. This is not to be confused with the unfortunate individual in his 'lamp-post' pantomime, a performance on a limited, closed-circuit broadcast—scheduled, no doubt, for endless repeats; repetition as its own delusional security in a shut-down environment. At the extreme end of the spectrum, logical or otherwise, it's a bit like playing blind man's bluff with an aphasic God, an epithet which should be carved onto the tombstone of every suicide or, alternately, as an inverted declaration of faith, blazoned across the dedicatory pages of our more self-aggrandising poets, sure-fire acknowledgement that the God's reputation is, indeed, boundless. *Memory* and *value*: if language is the record of memory and, conversely, memory the record of language, then it is at the junction of rhyme they meet.

There is little point these days in supposing the existence of an oral culture in the traditional sense (performance artists), if you do not have an original myth to go with it; the two go hand-in-hand, or should that be, tongue-in-cheek? The mechanism of oral performance or presentation is the shuffling about of old techno/industrial props. The oral tradition is a term employed by ego-directed & overly produced 'vocal artists' who pay little or no heed to the disciplines of rhyme and metre (knowledge of prosody allows for an educated departure point), and who insist upon claiming the qualification of poet. But then, the 21st century is already an overstocked warehouse, and anybody is at liberty to choose from the endless supply of mask & costume!—their singular apprenticeship played out essentially onto paper, against a backdrop of the folk and blues traditions that in turn fed on the rapidity of change, the sunset clause or rubric of the then fast receding 20ty century.

The oral tradition in its original capacity and historical function (an *ur-act*) gave birth to written language—*ecriture.* It is just possible that in the exhalation of breath, associated with a downward gesture as the chisel struck stone to fashion pictographs—that *breath*, in effect, gave rise to each individual letter, and that the rhythm of breath fashioned speech into visual patterns we have come to know as alphabet. Writing may be seen as the alternative means of expression to the oral tradition, rather than the logical development of it. The alphabet, then, is the record of 'breath'; and yet, as language breaks down under the multiple pressures of the digital age and the simultaneity of access, the common language by which we communicate has given way to a new set of pictographs vis-à-vis computer software programs; txt and twitter speak, *et al.*

In this instance, symbol represents fact (as coda) and not myth. Myth demands an implied patience through vast tracts of immeasurable time, the fastnesses of the spirit rather than the aridity of the clock, the multiplicity of gods rather than plethora of microchips. Can one abstract a god, and that god still exist? Probably not. Or rather, not likely. For an abstraction in the case of a deity (whose habitat is myth) barely serves as an echo of the deity's passing; it is a footprint set upon the prelapsarian shores of humankind. A god by definition (or gender) is necessarily distant, a safeguard to godly reputation and essential magnitude; to imbue a god with human characteristics is to set the scene for conflict.

The human condition by any measure is that recipe for disaster, and ideas are its most potent weapons. On the other hand, the true gift contained in verse-writing, now largely forgotten, is in the giving or the repeated *turning* back (boustrophedon) of that freedom-of-expression to a reading *and* aural public, and, in that knowledge alone is contained its intrinsic value, a quality of the highest order, both in *the thing itself* and its methods of expression and content; to give is to know, it is an act of grace that *in turn* is the truest act of creation. It is common practice, and perhaps even common law among the poets of *Flatavia*—that omelette-shaped island adrift in the Southern Ocean, to indulge in unabashed character assassination of the most clandestine kind (certainly the most cowardly and effective—namely, through the vigorous applications of boycott and general back-stabbing), and employ all manner of bile and meanness in an attempt to break the spirit of any 'opponent' who shows the slightest inclination toward honesty and originality of expression. Such a person poses a threat to the established, good order of things in the time-worn battle between authoritarian pretence, and the stripping away of that pretence; that is, the several realities and versions of truth which have been constructed to benefit the culture-industry, whose programme is orchestrated by a few hipster academics working hand-in-hand with those publishers who pay homage to the corporate, global empire.

Needless to say, this equally applies to those few individuals who are intent upon widening their own personal power base in the establishing of literary theory and practice *vis-à-vis* literary publications and forums; individuals who, in effect, are the self-appointed legislators of cultural taste and persuasion. These minions serve in the roles of 'readers' to publishing houses, committee members to funding councils and arts advisory bodies, furtive essayists, cultural supremacist critics and reviewers whose fox-holes as often as not are located in university faculties—in this case, English Departments (both provincial and central), the 'war-rooms' from which operations are directed. In *Flatavia* the university system operated under an entirely different set of precepts to those propounded by the great educationalist and prose stylist, Cardinal Newman, the founding fathers not having heard of him in this time &

spatial dimension—for the universities in this country went under the collective name: *Unicorp.* The Humanities had long since become defunct as the individual's free choice of a free education. Education for all, by right. Government funding, once unconditional, now served the Global Corporate Network.

In *Flatavia*, a deal was struck around the restructuring of these public institutions. Corporate funding to universities meant that each university faculty—from the *Environmental Sciences* through to *Languages* (a dumbing down of speech and written forms of communication that became known as 'monitor-speak'), was presided over by a corporate sponsored board made up of the principal funding bodies, whose members were controlling shareholders of giant multinationals like *Petroleum Inc* or *Mining Magnates Incorp.* Every senior and junior lecturer, each professor and doctor, was according to the terms of his or her contract, legally bound to hold a business degree in management and basic economics; but more importantly, required under the conditions of his or her contract to buy a given number of shares from the guardian or major corporate enterprise who funded that respective department. Neo-liberalism as neo-comfort zone.

Only honorary degrees in what used to be known as the Humanities (the courses had ceased to exist at the end of the Analogue Age) were bestowed, based solely upon the lecturer's economic prowess. Eventually, the amalgamation of the university system grew similar to the absorption of smaller businesses by the larger extended *Unicorp's* reach into the virtual world of on-line (or) at-distance education. University systems, in real time, also ceased to exist, and became vast administrative blocks for each new generation of share-holding acolytes. Digital degrees and at-distance education prevailed as a sort of global lottery. There existed in this young *sportocracy* (that is in essence what this country represented) a culture of deceit and self-delusion. A poet, like anyone else had two choices, either to sink or swim—and invariably, because he or she wished to succeed, chose the latter which necessitated standing on the head of the nearest competitor. A sportocracy, after all, has a more immediate interest in the application of bat-to-ball and the accelerated spin of the wheel. This is the sanctioned and collective exercise in amnesia.

Flatavia then, functioned within the relativities of the moment, and history was a scoreboard of non-existent interest, a blank screen displaying endless, muted static. Even the collective soul of a nation seeks expression, no matter how dulled out or 'dumbed down' into *Yobbocracy*, and that nadir represents the most profound ache that can be reached by any self-inflicted concussion. Interestingly, the Calvinistic spirit in New Zealand bred the 'man alone' type, who suffered in solitude and silence; while Australia, a vast continent, bred a people expansive by nature—except that Australians go in for a great deal of back-slapping, usually their own, and revel in celebrating what they lovingly call 'larrikinism' as a national virtue when it is, in fact, stupidity as a species of unintelligence elevated to arrogant display. Everything or anything considered to be of any pragmatic and practical value could only happen *in* and *of* the moment. No worries *mate*!

History did not exist and conscience or guilt were concepts that had little or no meaning in *Flatavia*. Puritanical rectitude was another matter—that central support beam of 'family' walled up within its own rigid zone of bigotry. Freedom, and the individual's right to express that freedom, existed solely within the mercantile concept of—*The Lie*. On an intellectual level or theoretical plane the attempt to inform the moment, that is, to build information into the present, and by such artifice create a history where the chronological version is considered to be wanting, was the plight of the literary theorists of *Flatavia;* constructs of the ego hardly sufficed as a substitute for a medieval or bronze age tumulus let alone a Mexican ziggurat.

Illusion represented the synonym for historical fact while image and showmanship served as handmaidens in the misrepresentation of truth. The horizontal line of personal perspective became distorted into something a little more circuitous and solipsistic; after all, *lie* rhymes with *I*—it is a circular sound, with the former breathing down the neck of the latter, so to speak. Whatever constituted doubt for the poet, that gnawing in the gut, was little more than an isolation from applause; severe withdrawal symptoms of the ego. Such was the particular climate and cultural cumuli that hung over the land of *Flatavia.* If a silver lining existed, that is, if success were to be found anywhere within this drifting island, it would be in the adopting of a casual brand of nationalism coupled with the sprawling vernacular peculiar to its people. This produced not the bard or seer in this ocean-bounded country, but the poet *manqué* whose success was recognised in the bar code or ISBN number. A brand of deception played out through multi-media, journalism, academia, the public service, the private sector, governmental advisory bodies, the diplomatic service, the Department for Propaganda, the Half-Way Psychiatric Houses Association, the Writers' Guild, the Gilded Lily of Litigation, The National Confederation for Wastewater Inc. and of course, the military (air, land & sea) were virulent breeding grounds for the poseurs and impostors who laid claim to the 'Iron Laurel of High-Bombast' not forgetting, dear reader, that the claimant was referred to in the argot of the people as, *the boofardier.*

So, the true-born or bardic poet got stomped on by the lesser talented and inherently more vicious interpolators who clamorously sought that annual prize with all the attendant glories (not forgetting the butt or hogshead of turnip mead), in the headlong rush toward recognition and public acclaim. The voice of the true-born poet, Attic or Bedouin, now rarely echoed within the courtyards and corridors of *Flatavia*, nor in the Grand Amphitheatre of its largest metropolis,

Flatus; a voice roughly diminished, or discarded, scrambled through the interstices of the social media platforms. Cry the beleaguered country! And ultimately, of course, that voice became relegated to the precincts of myth, though most probably, would re-surface generations hence as a meaningless logo on a 'Good Life' Insurance Policy, or boast a brand name to a 'gamers' programme designed to assist the hearing and speech impaired of future generations of *Flatavians.* But then, given the dawn of a new genetically modulated age, who can lay claim to prophecy these days believing as I do that *poeta nascitur, non fit*?

There is no escape; thinking then, is the shock of consciousness. Whereas, at its most mundane, and without trying to sound too priggish, thinking is a process one has to get through, in order to give validity to sleep. Love on the other hand is respect for another's vulnerability, a protective regard, having little or nothing to do with sex as pleasure, or any other transient mode of release. We pair to remind each of the other's existence. We are the collective memory of each and every cell that ever existed, and knowledge is the explanation. We as sentient beings are the ever-arriving process of that knowledge; perhaps for this reason, myth is generally more interesting as reality, than reality as myth, though the latter is closer to the truth. Truth-seeking presents itself as a bridge too far, and by far more comforting to regard the world as an exercise in entertainment value; at least that way vistas take on satirical perspectives. To lose ourselves in multiplicity is to lose ourselves in the climate of the gods, but to study the self in order to find a god is to create a still life. There is no escape, and if memory possesses any lineage at all, and is in turn marked by historical event (ultimately relegated to a postage stamp or municipal monument), then history is a sequence of re-emphasised fashion.

There are, of course, the obvious daily restrictions peculiar to any historical epoch; to be held in check by the directives of gubernatorial authorities in the name of the *polis*, good order, the commonweal, democracy, capitalism, 'one vote-one-person' and other illusory devices of individual freedom not universally applicable, and where historical memory serves as an eroding force. The English class system, founded on cruelty and sustained through indifference, as one definition of 'privilege'; poverty in third world countries which breed dictators (in crisp uniforms); where, for instance, evil holds out the illusion of power, that is, the constructs that surround mortality lend to the participants a vicarious sense of the *monumentality of things*—a bogus immortality and licence which extends to limitless acts of destruction, while a workable definition of evil presents itself as: 'destruction-equals-power'; on the sub-continent and in Asia-at-large, religious conflict has become an exercise in tactical, guerrilla warfare through hard-line militia groups who at heart trumpet the dying gasp of an historic nomadism.

The Catholic religion, by definition, becomes an elitist and conservatively traditional entity whose precepts are enforced through its intellectual 'militant' arm, namely, the Jesuits (as stated), those 'storm-troopers of Catholicism'. Consider, too, the collective distortions of heroin addiction, the sudden fury (random and robotic) of the junkie who has abandoned all pretence at an evolving humanity and who has, in effect, forfeited the right to be human and certainly his humanity—an entity that merely functions (interestingly, the junkie phenomenon has been picked up by the Hollywood myth-making factory and used in the guise of 'alien' or 'vampire', those signifiers of AIDS), a pariah reduced to negation and devoid of any measure of personal or free choice. People want to die and simultaneously know it. That's why we have an irreducible, global drug crisis. The gaping maw of negation whose appetites can never be satisfied; the consumer culture fulfilling its prophecy, fed via the sordid conduits of Mexico and

Colombia, Afghanistan, Pakistan, and the Golden Triangle.

It comes down to habit, after all, the expectations of thought (the gamma rays of consciousness) that control lives though we are scarcely aware of those mechanisms at work. There is no escape from our neighbour or the activities that surround us and are directed by and at us. We are integral to the whole and our attempts at being heard result in a conflicted dialogue with all its ugly manifestations. Individual freedom is reduced to the individual's *right to react as an interpretation of freedom*, as though the very biological necessity to breathe were nothing more than a rearguard action, and the obvious clichés of existence had all but been forgotten or subsumed to a level of dire expediency. Such observations are unfashionable these days, and are bundled up and dismissed under the label 'generalisations', where at one time such perceptions would have been regarded as soundings *toward* truth.

The Australian accent (a further example of *unfreedom*) is a parody on the English upper middle class accent, now a national and distinctive characteristic evolved in defiance of authority, yet authoritative in its 'narrow band' frequency, that is, emotive nuance as vocal utterance. Sensitivity belongs to the sensible concordance of rhythm and sound, while disjunctive neologisms express an 'undisclosed' anger or 'red-necking' of the language where mere (male) cleverness serves as a poor substitute for vision and refinement. And yet, that language (accentual) is, in addition, a pastiche of the English lower working-class speech; the friction or tension between the two positions coats the spoken language in a braying, often glutinous brutality of expression, though at a considerable remove from the benign 'nasal twang' or simpering 'ocker whine' associated respectively with both New Zealand and Australia, that first came to prominence in the mid-19th century with the emergence of the mythopoeic Colonial Youth and, ultimately, found its numerical concentration in the working-class suburbs and cottages of the inner-city suburbs in each capital city.

The bush, of course, has always maintained its 'bushranging' ethos, as a self-sufficient and separate, colloquial identity, aside from the politicians' continuing blandishments toward a uniform 'Australian'—or bogus—nationalism extolling the national identity which does not exist except, perhaps, in the 'narrow gauge' minds of the prejudicial, who interpret that phrase in the dim light of their own bigotry, fear and hatred. Liberal (Aust.) and National (NZ) politicians transmit these negatives like a virus. A national identity is nothing more than an amalgam of contained cultural divergencies, each sustained in its difference in so far as each cultural group is contiguous with its neighbour. Neither better nor worse, though a given number may be economically disadvantaged by contrast, and that alone is where any future conflict will erupt. Not race *but privilege*, and that of course is where the confusions have and will originate, and where self-interested groups prefer to keep it. Asian and Lebanese 'turf wars' over drugs in Australia, for instance. Broadly speaking, economic advantages blur cultural distinctions in that for any given cultural group co-existing within the same socio-economic system, one faction will gain mercantile precedence over another.

A few obvious and current examples from our own geographical region will adequately serve to illustrate the point: in Fiji, the Indians and the indigenous Fijians; in Malaysia and Indonesia, the indigenous peoples and the Chinese (perhaps after all, the Pacific Rim of Fire is aptly named). In Australia (a continent apart) it is a case of the white Anglo-Celtic patriarchy first, and *then* the rest who must follow in a step-by-step programme as laid down by the country's legislators and white lords toward an approved *Australianoidal* posture as defined by that economically advantaged group. Australia, triumph of the ordinary! There is no escape from our neighbour, whether he is offering alms with one hand, or whether he is wielding a machete with the other. If multilingualism is associated with the almost old testament *babble of tongues*, then monolingualism is an a.k.a. 'ocker' argot that breeds conformity of accent and, by a natural process of attrition, conformity of attitude—a holding pen for prejudice, which, to give a couple of trite examples, may be seen in the so-called TV current affairs and radio talkfest programmes, along with the usual round up of frantically nationalistic flag waving 'shock jocks' in the hysterical promotion of seasonal and major sporting events, etc.

And there you have it, the common amnesia of the New World Order: history is a moment ago and just as quickly consumed and forgotten; there is no escape, or more to the point, all is escape. Within the stuttering engines of language we can yet detect some form of dialogue. The old maxim holds true, as stated by Charles Maurice de Talleyrand: '*Speech was given to man, to conceal his thoughts.*' Meanwhile, the man engaging with the lamp-post as we now view him from the other side of the road, crucified to his obsession, will always figure as one of the disenfranchised; the victim of informational overload. A few shuddering frames of memory in passing. The following poem is taken from my collection, *Either Side The Horizon* (2005):

THE GREAT UNSAYING

And the Lord came down to see the city and
a tower, whose top may reach unto heaven
Genesis 11: 4

Farther off, came lightning silent and unanswering,
the tower that emerged from between the flashes—solid
as an after-image, and then again, with each
intermittent opening out of darkness, the figure enlarged,
advanced, *message-bearer*, refugee from a tongue-
tied past, a bronze shield hanging off the darkened wrist.
He brought with him, and in the turbulence that
surrounded him, memories of words knotted along the
rope of language, the iron roar of the rabble rising
and falling, the flayed backs of the orators retreating.

Every portal round the tower consonantal, every window
an enjambment, the noise rose, a drowning roar—
unstoppable, even under the abstract gaze of the linguists;
voices shrieked back into primal colour—every
portal seemed a stopped-up mouth that spiralled the honey-
combed tower; and this monument, curled into a ram's
horn became vortex and blasphemy. Temple or tower,
he lamented what once had stood shaped to cup hand
and mind holy as a grail. Only his closeness now fathomed
the air, tumbrels of boiling cloud carried the speech,
upon whose face contorted words, and every word a leech.

The Vocal Art Of Subterfuge

Commercial radio: whorish handmaiden to the record industry. Just as DJs are groupies to rock stars and the record industry, so too are sound engineers record industry 'drones' and occasional groupies to DJs. The frustrated record producer and failed rock star syndrome. An advertising producer may foster dreams of becoming a power broker in tinsel town whose grandiose dreams end up as narcissistic TV or internet Ads. Bit-players in a feeding frenzy endlessly looping digital freeways and overpasses of the ratings-game, filtered back through the hyped, 'in-denial' philosophies of the advertising industry. Commercial radio is, by definition, an advertising agency with the volume wound up. High rotate electronic samplings, ho-hum beats, same ol' stylings and grooves. Consumerism is as much about hip, 'in-house' patois as it is about product-placement. The expedient language of addiction. *A DJ is a salesman of the record industry. A sound engineer is a manservant of the DJ.* The following sonnet is taken from my collection, *GONE, Satirical Poems: New & Selected* (2016):

DOCTOR ROCK

(*Sounding a sonnet for B.J & Associates*)

He accumulated fans each new shift:
punk, reggae, indie, maybe some swamp rock,
pumped hip-hop and Motown and techno rift;
he timed the hits to the top of the clock—

while every other night of the week
sorted the hot-spots and the top-shelf tart:
and though he figured as the total freak
could work the women with a salesman's art.

Sexual conquests confirmed the cliché,
the white convertible, black top, the blonde
caught the marble-eyed gaze of the DJ;
without a doubt he felt that he belonged.

The cowboy: *Drifter on the fm Band?*
give him his due, the drugs and one night stand.

'Roly! Roly!—behave yourself, you say … what's that Roly? Get out of here!—there's a crocodile in your soup? Nooooo..wha, noooo, argh!' Jim Healy torqued it up in his masterly brand of hysteria. The ringmaster. I ran special effects, of anything explosive, howling, cacophonous, screeching that I could find, under the voice of *Roly Bear* in the two or three minutes, kids' morning segment on *Radio Windy.* And, God help me, I was the voice of Roly Bear. *Live.* I was also, simultaneously, the morning newsreader on this Wellington radio station. Usually, directly after the 8 am news and weather bulletin, and the 'Roly Bear intro'—I went straight into it—from the serious to the unconditionally absurd, in an instant. A series of guttural, grunting, diaphragmatic, anarchic, hooting noises and whistles ensued to which Jim Healy responded in the best traditions of ad-lib. He was a master of the form and I never threw him. Jim thrived on it. *'How's things, Master?'* though more engagingly, *'G'day Dad'*, was the enthusiastic greeting, an abbreviation of *'Daddy O'*, I guess, so reminiscent of an earlier, duffle-coated, beatnik era. The horn-rimmed specs and, on occasion—as a gesture to 'style' or station promotion and party—the shiny, black leather gear. Slotted somewhere between Roy Orbison and Buddy Holly. His vocal stylistics ranged from mild hysteria to Goon-type humour. Probably the most genuine, on-air personality I ever met; never back-stabbing or sordidly ambitious (stupidity grafted onto cunning). Jim was to be applauded for that peculiar brand of honesty associated with the true eccentric; but his time was quickly passing as the

fashionable DJ. At any rate, I had a lot of time for Jim Healy.

The sort of diversity you could freely go for in those days with private radio. In 1975 I doubled as *voice over* and *newsreader* for Radio Windy as I had done earlier around 1973 in Dunedin at 4XO where I worked principally as radio journalist/newsreader. Multi-tasking in today's parlance. The climate was more loosely eccentric, less programmed and robotic than today's syndicated and centralized, pre-programmed commercial stations. The late John Clarke, alias *Fred Dagg*, came in to Radio Windy once a week and went about his business quietly, recording his country, folkloric caricature. John belonged to the 'Good Keen Man' tradition (a reference to the 'standard' advertisement placed for a rural labourer in the '40s and '50s) of the Barry Crump novels, and yet earlier still—the *Me and Gus* books. *Pure vaudeville of the paddocks.*

John kept to himself (a serious-minded professional) and had little to do with on-station rumour-mongering and political intrigues. A wise move, especially if one is career oriented. He was looking elsewhere—his career that was about to take off and would soon see him relocate to Australia where greater opportunities awaited. I had a brief interception with John Clarke while living in Sydney (though had spent three years earlier living in Melbourne where John lived). I had read a book of his nonsense verse and found it very entertaining, so posted off to him a copy of my collection, *Ballads, Satire & Salt: A Book of Diversions* (2003).[1] John courteously wrote back informing me he very much enjoyed the poems contained therein. Brian Edwards, the Belfast Irishman and self-proclaimed atheist-rationalist (a Doctor of Philosophy), who had modelled his interview techniques on Malcolm Muggeridge and Henry Bernard Levin, similarly used radio as many others had done at the time, as a springboard to a television career. First as the talkback host on Radio Windy, then as the television interviewer putting politicians and public figures in the hot seat.

There was much of the Irish puritan about this man (think 19th century frock-coat & Calvinism). He lacked the incisive, anarchistic bite of a Malcolm Muggeridge—that is, before Muggeridge abandoned socialism and went soppy on Catholicism. Muggeridge missed his calling and would have excelled as a Master Spy in the manner of Blunt & Co; though given his method of inquiry, I suppose in many ways he was something of a charming 'spook'. Alistair Cooke, a contemporary and modernist, had escaped to America, thereby avoiding fusty English academia. His relaxed cultural polish would grant him life-long tenure as popular commentator and historian on US political machinations and current affairs. Private radio had not altogether been absorbed into the mono-maniacal corporate world, whereby innumerable independents came to be owned by a few large business interests, who imposed standard formatting throughout the networks, based solely upon how many ad breaks could be crammed into the hour, along with the latest record company and entertainment-promoter recommendations, albums, and concerts. Today, it's all about competing networks as 'brands'.

In the early days of private radio, when 'pirate' radio stations had come in from the cold and been granted a licence to operate, it wasn't long before a clutch of accountants and lawyers, in cahoots with small, local businessmen, had taken over the stations from the free-wheeling, entrepreneurial founders. David Gapes, for instance, may be the most prominent and colourful amongst them, the founding father of Radio Hauraki in Auckland, whose story is well documented from its incipient shipboard days on the *Tui* (its signature tune, Matt Monro's *Born Free*), broadcasting in the Hauraki gulf, to the granting of a land licence. Business interests soon attempted to decide on-air and station policy, by appointing inept board members (major shareholders) as station managers who knew absolutely nothing about the day-to-day running of a radio station. One such appointee to Radio Windy worked in clandestine association with Muldoon's National Party, blatantly pushing the party's right wing press releases as the station news bulletins. *And I had to read them.* He burst clumsily into the studio mid-bulletin panting and sweating with a pile of carts and intro sheets and dumped them in front of me, usually with a clatter—while I was *live to air!* I didn't get on with bumbling Keith 'the stooge' Hancock 'news editor'. He was considered a consummate buffoon by the journalists under him, and in the ultimate showdown he ended up banning me—the morning newsreader—from the News Room. Pure theatre of the absurd! Keith was only kept on for his National Party contacts. In those days they recruited local celebrities to the sales team. Keith's one claim to fame was swimming Cook Strait. The real news, and the day-to-day running of the newsroom, was carried out with cool efficiency by Paddy Bergin, who would go on to become a skilled artisan in the making of acoustic guitars. I think at one stage the mile record holder John Walker worked in a similar capacity for a commercial station but which one I can't recall. A couple of years later, in 1977, I was employed as a copywriter/production voice at Radio Hauraki where the Scotsman, Robert Bruce, acclaimed wrestler in his day, then worked as a sales rep. In 1978 he set up the *Robert Bruce Ugly Agency* for stuntpeople and actors, etc. A fine man, and we enjoyed each other's company. He could not stand bullshit or egotistical wankery. Socially, he avoided the DJs like a plague!

For the most part, the bigger radio station promotions back in the day were built around concert tours that represented the El Dorado of revenue. Sales reps worked themselves into an 'on-commission' frenzy, and DJs, little more than on-air salesmen, attended rock concerts and lavish industry junkets. The world was an endless party—let the good times roll, at least, until the quarterly ratings results came out. There's nothing sadder than an ex-DJ; used car yards are full of them. That, or some small country radio station which is the equivalent to being put out to pasture, into the domain of shady perks and contra deals. Then again, many were happy to play the country circuit: life was comfortable and cheaper, where an on-air personality could enjoy minor celebrity status with impunity. Local cowboys on the lam with names like *Bronco Bolton, Chas Drader, and Shipley Shakes*, the last, with the tremulous vocal antics of Jerry Lee Lewis; country ZB announcers before they became known as DJs with the advent of private radio. A few who had made their loot in the industry might try independent business ventures like setting up a private radio station—back in the country, where they could now enjoy the privilege of hiring and firing those very same individuals who had once hired and fired them, or maybe going into 'get rich quick' boutique enterprises, like setting up a hot house tomato farm and employing the local solo mums at below award rates (cash in hand) to manage in *absentia*. Others headed out into the entrepreneurial rock-concert and promotional Badlands.

These guys survived into the early '70s in the ZM networks of state owned radio, the non-commercial counterpart to what private radio had to offer. By the mid-70s this type of jocular DJ, pretty much belonging to the *Wolfman Jack* school of cowboy, was thin on the ground. Soon enough, the laid-back DJ claimed the not necessarily higher but more expansive rock & roll ground. Whatever you may have said about them, at least they possessed *recognizable* personalities; that is, in the beginning! Perhaps more by laxity than design, indicative of a social climate with fewer checks and balances, I suppose, rather than the carefully stage-managed personas of today's *blandified* and formulaic (failed stand-up comedians) hipster dudes. So much for the fate of your everyday DJ; mere vocal footnotes to an endless list of brand names.

For a time, I lived a dichotomized existence, and youth helped. I had been attracted to broadcasting from my late teens and enjoyed listening to the recordings of Richard Burton, Dylan Thomas, Charles Laughton, Orson Welles, et al., just as a generation of writers and actors before me similarly paid homage to these great narrators, though the vocal stylistics of Thomas, irresistibly hypnotic, by now felt overly theatrical, and could not be taken *too* seriously. The last of the *big actorly voices*, at least, as far as poets went. You could see the same style employed by actors coming into prominence in the early '60s 'kitchen sink dramas' with Oliver Reed, Nicol Williamson, Alan Bates, Peter O'Toole, and Richard Harris—all the roistering and blowzy bad boys—while on the other side of the Atlantic, Lee Marvin who in a way I've always associated with Nick Nolte, growled his way in *basso profundo* through World War Two movies and westerns; a man with a charisma that Clint Eastwood could only dream of, born as he was under a 'wandering star' that would see him buried in Arlington cemetery. Real life war hero. The marlin had landed! Orson Welles morphed into a cigar smoking caricature of his former self—pushing Atlantic Salmon and Californian wines for all it was worth ('we shall release no wine before its time'); and vocal indulgence became a kind of surety. The bad boys and the Badlands, again. Somehow, a poet with a voice seemed to me the perfect antidote to the loner—*heard, but not seen.* At distance and respected. That was the theory!

My first foray came with *Broadcasts to Schools* back in 1970 with the old NZBC (which became BCNZ in 1976, now Radio New Zealand), that once great ark of writers, artists, and all manner of creative talent, alas, before the advent of economic rationalism, and the selling off and dismantling of the state's assets to foreign investors. There had been some effort made by the Labour government under Helen Clark to buy back what Roger Douglas and David Lange through to Jim Bolger had sold off to the aforementioned foreign investors. These were the glory days of state radio quickly coming to an end, and major regional towns the length and breadth of New Zealand, from Whangarei to Invercargill, had their own iconic, bunker-like studios, built to withstand all manner of audience fallout. Extensive though underutilized facilities and recording studios, that would ultimately be sold off in favour of a centralized network broadcasting out of Wellington, with fewer broadcasters on high-rotation as a cost cutting exercise.

The old system like any *Public Service* structure, before compulsory contract employment came in, attracted all manner of eccentric, boozy journalists and producers, and at least one poet who believed he had 'the voice'. Yet another poet who ran away to broadcasting like the proverbial sailor to the sea. The institution was full of enthusiastic hobbyists, the lazily gifted who became absorbed into the system, and ended up as somewhat frustrated individuals with tidy obsessions like bonsai plant horticulture, or collecting old valve radio sets for restoration—and of course, vast amounts of administrative, bureaucratic deadwood. Middle management with middle aged spread. The *Public Service Gazette*, though required to advertise employment opportunities in the public domain, invariably, before the rise of private radio, favoured internal, over 'outside' appointments. This meant that, say, a journalist or an ex-policeman might end up as a station manager in Dunedin or Gisborne or Whangarei, or if young and ambitious enough, as a programme director for one of the ZM Stations in Wellington and Auckland.

Careerist intentions—that is, knowing how to play the system while in fact hiding such ambitions—was the preferred method of dealing with most rebellious talent, with the singular goal of removing the individual who contested authority. *The triumph of the ordinary.* And of course, given that state radio remained non-commercial, this meant that appointments to popular music stations like ZB or ZM were merely strategic shifts up the public service ladder. These were true sinecures for the manipulative. As a staff member—prior to voluntary redundancy—or the selling up of the state's assets, it uniformly meant huge payouts for long-term employees. Any hierarchical and bureaucratic system is hard-wired in favour of the status quo, invariably to the exclusion of individual talent. Loose cannons belonged to, and for a while found favour with, the bounty-hunting world of first pirate, then private commercial radio.

In that fleeting Golden Age of *state radio v private*—a twilight zone between the emergence of private radio and the inevitable recognition of independent media, with the decline of 'BBC' exclusiveness ('This is the BBC. I am terribly sorry, I will read that again'.), and old world, post-colonial snobbery—a rare set of circumstances prevailed, and allowed for one brief moment in time, in that blurring of boundaries, the creative ego to flourish in a dialogue between the old world of broadcasting and the new. Ultimately though, the public service as an institution bred, as any political system breeds, the manipulative bureaucrat as opposed to free-wheeling individual talent. Either way—yes-men, answerable to still other yes-men. Corporate executives accountable not to shareholders, but to any number of other conglomerates headed by bank managers, financiers of every hue, stock brokers and politicians. The fabled land of the CEO, in other words. Idealism only has a half-life in abstract terms, after all.

But for all that, the broadcasting industry in those days survived as a romantic and labyrinthine entity, home to a diaspora of eccentrics and oddities which, if you planned on a broadcasting career, offered high standards in drama, copywriting and technical skills, and an excellent, if somewhat hidebound, broadcasting school. Sound engineers, or technicians as they were then known, originated in state radio with very few exceptions. From there one might (if brave enough to forfeit the security of 'a public service job for life'), migrate to the new and less secure world of private radio. Right up until the end of the '70s the broadcaster, *the person behind the voice behind the microphone*, equated to the modern-day equivalent of a swagman (maybe cowboy is more apt), enjoying limitless vistas that opened out before him in moving from one station to another, up and down the country, and back again. Private to state, state to private, from small town to the metropolis, and the hype of the ratings game, and back to the provinces. The DJ on the *rodeo circuit*.

Movement is youth and youth is adventure, and the new world of private radio suggested to many a would-be star, in the absence of actually meeting or becoming a rock star, on-air stardom, after a fashion—once considered a frontier militia holding out against the seemingly indomitable forces of state radio and entrenched conservatism. The last vestiges of British colonialism could still be seen and heard in the BBC, standards upon which state radio based its charter: *hold the front line against the vulgar*, at all costs! Private radio soon became a hyped-up stampede of ratings trivia, rampant commercialism, and repetitive ego. The 'good guys' had, it rapidly become clear, hi-jacked the gravy train and proved themselves to be ultimately the opportunists and neo-cons they had always been. So right wing, in fact, they were left—legs akimbo, looking up their own arseholes! These days, commercial radio has taken personality to its erstwhile limit, and with the current fashion favouring stand-up comedy performers in a duet sit-down capacity as 'morning hosts'. What next?—on probation serial killers with tin ears as drive time jocks? Militant feminists as the traffic reporting 'eye in the sky'? Ex-State Premiers as shock jocks and talk back hosts …?

For a time, as a voice artist, I lived that dichotomized existence as far as my own psychology of coping with the unrealities of the task were concerned. A detached persona; and when it was demanded, a loose cannon approach usually served, or didn't. I regarded voice work much as any actor might, a job forgotten soon as the studio door shut behind you on your way out. Money for jam. The late Kevin Black, alias, *Blackie*, *Captain Black*—one of the 'star' DJs on Auckland's Radio Hauraki in the '70s, distinguished by his unapologetic hedonism, with a voice that possessed all the tonal shifts of a heavy-duty gearbox—once accosted me on-station in the recording suite, '*So, what are we today Stephen, a DJ! DJ! poet! poet! DJ! poet! DJ?*',' a gravelly, gatling gun delivery. These days we would call this facility multi-tasking after the fashion of the DIY attitude and think nothing more of it. Whatever the case, it is still standard practice for folk, rearing up out of their intrinsic conservatism, to insist that you come neatly packaged so they can at least accommodate you within terms of their own ego-threatening doubts or judgemental fears. *A successful DJ becomes an entertainment promotion agency. A failed DJ becomes a used car salesman, or real estate agent.* There are choices, after all. I salute the fading signal of those long-vanished radio days. I farewell the analogue dream of my youth.

[1] *Ballads, Satire & Salt, A Book Of Diversions*, Stephen Oliver, illustrations by Matt Ottley, Greywacke Press, Sydney, 2003.

An Analogue Fantasy

[seven second delay c. 1975]
'... *till we could stand it no longer*'.

The sun had reached an oblique angle and dissolved into sunken rainbows upon the oil slick of the inner harbour. The boat marina at the Courtenay Place end of Oriental Bay jostled its army of spars against the mid-morning light which deflected up through the studio windows. The aquarium-like effect of yellow and white contours seemed to suspend the three, still figures across the console from Dave. He opened both mics.

'10.15 at WGTN and the three guys in the studio with me this morning are none other than *Marine Morgue* (background sounds of ship's bells, applause from group) . . . who are causing a big stir on the music circuit in this dynamic city of ours. Conrad, the lead singer, tells me Marine Morgue represents environmental rock, right?'

'Yep.'

'Ready when you are. Let's have it.'

Dave threw a friendly salute in the direction of the lead singer who shrugged his shoulders at what he considered the magnitude of the question. The hesitation though small suggested to Dave dead air. He filled the gap.

'Spaced out musicians? I believe it. The great revelation after these commercials. More of Marine Morgue. Don't go away now.'

Spinning the carousel positioned to his left, he found the cart marked *The Great NZ Restaurant* and plugged it in.

'Just look at the situation as it is, that's confidence see?' Conrad addressed the two other members of his group, hyping them up to the occasion; phrases, sentences broken with cigarette smoke. 'Don't panic   let the rest of the dudes flip out   par for the course   right?   No-one's going fast

anywhere in this world repeating the same old mistakes and disasters over and over 'cept now there ain't no more clean air space man to fuck up it's been done over with that advertising garbage pushed into the private box of the soul where's Apology stuff blocked drains of the psyche where's the head space? where's the playground Suzie? on the moon maybe? Adidas boot prints plastered all over it there's no free breathing no more them boot prints are fixed for eternity man nobody's going to sneeze them away for sure the supreme symbol of pollution up there on the white goddess and that's why we got that picture of them boot prints as our album cover SPEECHLESS our album's called SPEECHLESS and that brothers is a silent scream.'
He drummed his fingers on the interview mic. and turned toward Dave with mock surprise.

'Are we on yet?'

'Watch for the little red light.'

'*. . . the Great New Zealand Restaurant where you can take anyone twice ....*' The commercial faded out on the sound effects of revelry as the studio lights came on.

'Welcome citizens, welcome,' cried Conrad, 'to the magic environmental music show and Nostalgia Radio which takes you back to the *now.* Our guests this morning are Marine Morgue who are going to take you on a journey through the chambers of the mind with myth and fantasy that will leave you—speechless. Roll up roll up. Call WGTN right now on 79684 but first a song.' Dave let go the title track of the album, 'Speechless'—hard grinding rock with a synthesiser undertow: *'The black swans of Porirua town / are afloat on the tide upside down / as the moon passes her darkened gown / through the bay of Porirua town.'*

Babble of tongues the words a brace of hounds seven seconds behind tick-tock reality onto air empty as a stadium the moment dead on a bit of string with these three though not so crazed musicians and himself inside some perforated universe of time as he opens the phone lines voices radial from other dimensions scrambling the panel from outer suburbia computed through the traffic pile up of thought the readout of verbal sense is a connection too far off to be treated lightly light brighter than it should be coincidental with any given or taken observation and the moment big in its looping course of revelation to roll on out of mouths ballooning aerial sacks of words broadcast grains of speech on WGTN 1460 kHz fm.

The voice as if it strained through muslin breathed through the studio speakers above the heads of the musicians and became lost in a disturbance of atmospherics like the rustle of skirts. This was followed by a metallic click like an abrupt movement of some bone joint. A barely decipherable 'Thank you' lost on the Ouija board of communication.

'*Ping*. Space Invaders. That's another one down.'

Conrad slowly passed his hands across the microphone. He cackled toward Dave.

'Hell man, you didn't tell me you'd arranged a séance, a metaphysical drip-feed,' he hooted, 'tremulations on the ether.' An ectoplasm of red lights pulsed along the telephone panel. Muted voices on-hold suspended in the warp. Ghosts, lungs full of reality banging upon the substance of time. These ones were real enough, especially in the middle zone between the *Now* and *Then*. The listener was hearing, seven seconds ago, words stretched out into wraiths of sound, hanging round somewhere in the middle-air before being pumped back through the transmitter into a thousand homes, into rooms where the hearts of forests bleed in the conversations locked within the wood grain from past generations. Delay on a vaster scale. Millennia of the now ceased audio-existence of primordial consciousness. Christ, it's got to go somewhere and here we are phased into the moment between these things, among the broken ends of signals coiled like snakes. A million revolutions of copper-wire tumbling the human message over and over as the telephone panel with its navigational beacons flashed across some monstrous schism of space.

Conrad took the next call. 'Howdy. This is radio therapy.' A breathy pause.

'What I wanted to say was why do you call yourselves—Marine Morgue?'

'Aha! The great question that almost got away.' He rose to his feet pulling the microphone from its stand after him. 'The great question that almost, almost lady,' he drawled in the compeer's near histrionic tone, 'almost got a-way.'

The two other members of the group, 'J & J' retained their abstracted silence in the quiet task of sifting through a large plastic bag of weed. Already, a healthy heap of a dozen or so joints had been stacked up on the table in front of them. Throughout the interview it had been agreed that J & J would provide positive encouragement off-mic, acting the market place rabble with vocalisations in support of the renegade from Porirua. Atmospherics. They were to play no direct part in the dialogue between Conrad and his audience.

'This is a movie I don't particularly like to be in, but there it is. I didn't write the script but sure as hell I've got something to say about the musical score. Now, your mental movie, lady, is a re-run on suburbia and you're starring in it. Get it? But the movie I'm in is none of this National Film Unit stuff about ferny ravines and glimpsed deer and bird's eye mountain peaks or untouched, religious snow cascading with the strains of Lilburn—or the pretended mysticism of the synthesiser. Not even the vast panorama of 'she'll be right, Lord'. My movie's got the livid flush of chemical effluent. My pristine mountain lakes are dead as battery water. My shorelines are studded with the bellies of bloated fish. My tranquil valleys gridded into building lots. Same old song . . . and where are you calling from?'

'Grenada Village.'

'I've hooked the big one.'

'Pardon?'

'Certainly. Grenada Village. The decramastic wonderland up there on the hills overlooking the Porirua Basin. Sure, I know it. Porirua harbour is one vast marine morgue, try doing your washing in it and see what you come up with. Now listen close, 'cause I'm going to tell ya a little story—you like stories?'

'Sometimes,' answered the paper-thin voice.

'Cool. These days the harbour is either running yellow with silt from hills around about being hacked into sub-divisions, or choked up with chemical outfall from the local factories, and the rivers run shit—it's a marine morgue, see? Once the water ran red with the blood of whales from Old Tom's whaling station at Porirua back in the 1830s, and one of the first pākehā settlements in the district. Flenched blubber hung up to dry on great triangular structures the way you hang out your washing. The shoreline was littered with the hacked carcasses and bones of whales. What a sight! What a marine morgue. Huge white structures of bones big as buildings like a Salvador Dali landscape. Wind whistling through giant rib cages like a harp. But all that came about long after the original settlement took place, by the Ngāti Toa who came down from Kawhia. Man, they were the first gang members of Porirua! They claimed the entire Golden Coast, including Kāpiti and Mana islands. The gang leader, this guy called Te Rangiaeata of the Ngāti Toa, set up his headquarters on Kāpiti. Perfect. Untouchable. He knew the rival gangs would have a go: the Muaūpoko, Rangitāne, Whanganui, Ngāti Apa, Ngāti Ruanui, Ati Hau and the Ngāti Kahungunu. They got together to raid Kapiti and blow the Ngāti Toa away. And every one of 'em full patch! The great battle of Waiorua. But the Ngāti Toa won. Outnumbered, but they won. Man, those guys could mix it. After that, the Ngāti Toa became, I guess, *Peacemakers*. The guardians. They were the best. And what's that to do with me, lady? It's my whakapapa, my family album, those are just are just a few of the snaps. We belong to Porirua, right? We are Marine Morgue and we'll take anyone on, including the corporates and property developers who mess around in our territory.' Conrad banged his fist on the table. 'That's the way it goes, baby,' he said, 'old sins cast long shadows.' He summed up. 'The danger zone is what I'm talking about. The real land wars, the Aluminium Smelter at Aramoana, the gold digging at Coromandel and the Great Barrier Island, the flooding of the Clutha Valley, the Franklin Dam project in Tasmania; these are the big spiritual headlines.'

Dave's finger hovered over the delay button in case the situation moved from the original plan. Conrad was likely to terminate his rave in abuse, given the chance of declaiming to a potential 30,000 listenership.

One of the first guests on talkback radio, an outspoken Austrian gynaecologist, caught Dave off guard in the early days. His stance as pro-abortionist (and suspected seducer of women patients) alienated him from a good proportion of the public, the suburbs and a fair representation of WGTN listeners. He used a direct in-your-face approach on issues like serial monogamous relationships, sexual hang-ups, hysteria, and self-assertiveness, etc. A career woman phoned in to say sustained job-pressure had developed in her strong symptoms of depression. She feared burn out and the inevitable psychotic breakdown. The genuine, 'Type A' personality. What should she do?

'Already,' she said, 'things are getting fuzzy round the edges.'

The good doctor drew a deep breath and tilted his head.

'For the preservation of selfhood,' he pronounced, 'and to insure calmness of spirit, I advise a good fuck. It will solve *everythink!*'

Dave didn't hit the delay button quick enough and the station was thrown into panic.

'But the advice is clinically sound,' screamed the doctor as he was bundled out of the studio by security men. He was marched before the station manager, a transit-camp victim to his summary execution. The following day he made his apology to an incredulous public.

'I have consulted with the station commandant,' he said flatly, 'who instructed me that in the interests of public decorum and acceptable taste—I am not to say 'fuck'—on air.'

The press followed his progress after this spectacular announcement and reported on his more flamboyant outbursts. Undaunted, the doctor continued his ministrations to the wealthy and menopausal dowagers of Khandallah and Karori. A month after this incident, a charge was laid by a woman who claimed that the good doctor had been overly fastidious in examination of her vaginal mysteries. The case was taken to the High Court. The seminal stains found on the woman's panties (the police surgeon's report stated) could not conclusively be traced to the glands of the accused. The doctor was acquitted.

J & J nodded approval at the mimetic performance of the lead singer who swung back again into accelerated verbal hyperbole.

'Ain't that so,' he wailed. 'Lady' (the caller had hung up), 'ever since I was a delinquent in Porirua where the two arms of the harbour embraced, paddling the storm water drains, leering up in video-arcades, yahooing in the burnt out hulks of Holdens, building island refuges from the factory refuse in the Porirua harbour basin—in that vast Marine Morgue which now extends through to the Pāuatahanui Inlet, until I discovered the first tingling of puberty with some up-front Polynesian chick in the wastes of packing sheds and the back yards of state houses—to the days when I hurled my first brick into the plastic dream dome of a McDonalds Burger Bar; long before the days of Grenada Village or Whitby, when the shags lifted wings against the evening breezes, the bulrushes and the *black swans of Pāuatahanui ....*'

The rhetoric rolled on and on, incantatory, the speaker now lost to the music and nostalgia of a boyhood shaped by spirits long since evicted (or so he lamented) from the coast and hills progressively falling under the sprawl of the Wellington building boom. An adrenaline drip-feed of mana from early memory.

'.... Our sound? Jazz played underwater. The electronics of antediluvian sea-creatures caught up in the rhythms of sightless communication. An ocean-going highway of sonic babble. Genesis. The first sound that ever broke the stillness of human consciousness—the sea.'

Chevrons of gulls angling between the container cranes ranged alongside Fryatt Wharf each bird flying a streamer that read: WGTN, EASY ROCK, FM: a loop tape of cloud spinning endlessly around Mount Victoria. Tiny electrodes of light pricking the face of the harbour. Dave felt suspended between mild panic and abandoned laughter, that rarefied dream-like quality associated with mild exhaustion, a spaced-out quality. The loosening bonds of tactile reality and Conrad, poet-musician, assaulting the airwaves with his well-rehearsed, deranged rant. The voluptuous quality of some forbidden fantasy flooding into the tidy, up-to-the commercial-moment eye-level kitchens. *The 30" second housewives.* Verbal cushions of dementia flung out of a hundred transistor radios pummelling the hills (transmissions down the back-bone of Te Rangihaeata) through Wakefield, Grenada, Paremata, Whitby. Bouncing into the living rooms and bedrooms and bathrooms of the stockaded villages strung out along the Golden Coast.

The talkback winds changeable this morning on the 10th day of the 3rd month in this year of Our Lord AD and an uplifting of tides and a lowering of hills and sea shores and majesties of black swans again to the return of the flax lands and the pas and palisades and the raising of the spouts of the whales in the bays aplenty *Ho Boy* all the way from Dusky Sound to Golden Bay and the Cook Strait to Cloudy Bay plying trade the whalers and the brigs with names like the wind the *Dragon* and *Boyd* and *Urania*, *Waterloo* and *Britannia*, *Mercury* and *Caroline* on the look-out this afternoon a boarding party of winds turning southerly on the ice caps on your homebound route take care O take care.

The slow revolutions of the master-tape in the control room ground like millstones, compressing the words, the thoughts, the conversations of the morning into a solid mass of dream. Time slowed. Rolling back the verbal histories, winding the highways and the hills tightly onto the spools—pulling the terrain from out under the *black concentrations* of building in *Te Whanganui-a-Tara*, The Great Harbour Of Tara.

Smoke curled about Conrad's face. He became part shadow, part light; a psychological ambush as the coloured banners of a personal vision flew before him. He plucked at the black strands of hair about his shoulders, and watched Dave load the next bank of commercials.

'Blows 'em away every time. A few hefty clichés and they feel, well—like original.'

He regarded Dave.

'Hope I haven't blown if for you,' he said quietly, 'but you know how it is.' They grinned at each other.

Dave considered: 'Look at it this way, you've been granted sanctuary.'

'Through the looking-glass?'

Dave gestured toward the panelled glass through to Programmes, busy with the distortions of the curious. Brandon, the night-time Jock flicked into view, gave the thumbs up and vanished. Traffic personnel fleetingly peered through to the studio. Impassive and removed. The down-to-earth realities of administration divorced them from the insecurities of on-air imagination. No threat. Dave half expected a jangle of contours and the bloated, astonished face of Garth to loom out, lips sucking on glass. For the moment the power was his.

'Surprise time yet?' Conrad asked. 'I'll sandbag the door, just give the word.'
He threw his arms and spread the fingers magician fashion, vibrating his body.

'Va Voom!' he shouted, *'blamblamblam.'* He counted the invisible sandbags as they piled up in front of the studio door. 'Lock up ya daughters,' he boomed, 'the red-coats are comin'.'

Live theatre. Complete with sound effects (Can they handle it?). The whole production had been pre-arranged. He was going to put his philosophy on the line. WGTN brings the fantasy of doom to the harbour city. A tropical forest blast of alarms. A deafening roar of fire and wind. Mass panic? Radio IS live theatre. A few upset tea-cups maybe? A practical joker. A bad joke. An outrage. Tasteless. Un-civic minded. An affront to the sensibilities of the citizens. DJ plays God and destroys city. DJ punk humour puts the boot in. DJ paranoia pummels placid populace. Torch bearing mob storms radio station. Housewives pull the plug on ratings. Women's militia set up in suburbs. The Top Forty (something) faction boycott FM. Trouble brews amongst the tea party set. Tapu placed on the Tupperware brigade by mad musician. Domestic dames denounce DJ. Apocalyptical pop. The flipped-out DJ and the Talk Back Terror Show. DJ rocks and raves in padded studio. WELCOME TO THE CAPITAL CITY. Meanwhile, the sandbags pile up in a soundproof barricade and war canoes are breaking through the foaming cloudbanks across the city skyline. 'C'mon, let's do it.' *(Can they handle it?)* Live air. Struck in the stance of noble remembrance, Conrad threw the invisible switches. 'I pass my hand over this city claiming all that lies before me. Lambton Quay dissolves into the mass of Tinakori Hill. Courtenay Place erupts into an architecture of crystal. The Terrace lined with hotels and office blocks rises up to the constellations. The condominiums of Newtown fall into rank.' A spiritual invocation to his ancestors. 'Presto! The civil defence nightmare and the great paranoiac dream of the national psyche.' A deep growl from the diaphragm. 'The invasion of self-negation and psychic guilt threatening the positive industry of the spirit. The collective awareness, citizens, is an ark to float upon the tides of oblivion.'

He breathed on the dim mirror images of other selves caught up in the deflected facets of time. The contrived schizophrenia of half-remembered dimensions. For an instant, he forgot himself enough to glimpse the ancestral masks. Then the tides of rationalism overwhelmed him, and again he was lost to the present. Dead air.

'The paranoiac dream?' prompted Dave.

'Before the earth is ripped out from under our feet like a blanket and the deadly hoof-beats of the giant quake trample this city to ruin—before the chthonic nightmare begins—panic growth, *that's* the great paranoiac dream.'

'You mean a Tower of Babel, destroyed by the people's fear and arrogance.'

'Who can say? The signals are scrambled from the sleeping half of the brain to the waking half. We struggle to decode the psychic forecast. Fear runs deep in the subconscious, and there, that's where lies the power for construction or destruction. We deny the positive strengths, the bleeps from the deeper galaxy of the self. The workings of the shadow psyche—sight, touch, smell, hearing, taste—these project the negative realities. The superstructure of fear drives piles deep into the infinite belief in matter and the suicide of the spirit.'

Somewhere along the thoroughfare of Jervois Quay a siren sounded and a chorus of pneumatic drills sighed, and fell silent. A crane sagged on the horizon.

'When the crustal plates of this earth buckle the tribal gods shall rise in a ball of flame. They won't rest until their curses writhe like a pit of snakes in our chests. Already a great wind of emptiness passes through us.' He considered the evidence. 'Gang-warfare, land marches, pollution of tribal fishing grounds, mass unemployment, the dismantling of the Welfare

State. The dogs of fear snap at our ankles . . . I tell you, the whole issue's screwed.' He paused and caught his breath, then added with the concentration of sadness. 'Shadows, who would believe shadows might one day form into flesh and sinew and muscle and fist?' He hissed.

'Who the hell believes that this will happen?'

The timing was precise. A low rumbling welled up under the last five seconds of the monologue, drowning it. Each cart automatically fired off in sequence. Earthquake. Tidal wave. Fire. Wind (labelled: Pentecostal). Explosion. The complete scenario of destruction.

'This is WGTN, 1460 Khz,' Dave announced steadily, 'we are experiencing an earthquake. Stay tuned to this station for civil defence instructions. I repeat, we are now ....'

His voice crackled out and became lost under the bombardment of atmospheric static. The odd word or phrase filtered through the gauze of sound effects.

'*... Severe earthquake ... I repeat ... stay calm ... WGTN ... 1460 kHz....*'

'Christ, that nearly threw me!' yelled Conrad over the intense rumbling shaking the studio. 'I got most of my cue notes fouled up.'

Dave pulled the recorder mounted on the trolley closer to the panel and threaded up the specially prepared tape. He patched in a couple of jack-plugs to the grid under the console and spun the tape back to the paper marker. He then switched over to channel one and cued up on the audition speaker. The cone threatened to blow out of the desk.

'Great. Hope the transmitter can cope. Should be instructive.'

'D'you reckon it'll work?' worried Conrad.

'It's only a theory mate. We'll know soon enough, you can bet on that. The technician seems to think so, given small moveable objects like vases, crockery, that sort of thing. Might rattle the odd window pane if the suckers ....'

WHACK! The mechanical eyelashes slammed across the VU meters.

'Fuck it,' snapped Dave. 'Distortion. I can't be too sure but I think that's the testing frequency.'

He tried again. *TickticktickticktickticktickWhack!*

The needles quivered and again bounced into overload. He adjusted the gain-control.

'The bastards are bending.' He ground his teeth. 'Something's happening.'

'Cool enough. Can't be all bad,' said Conrad.

'The transmitter will knock most of it back. Tough on the gear, that's the only problem. I don't want to lose it.' He thought: after all, if sanity is the art of restraint, who needs it.

'Right then,' he said. 'Let's juggle a few atoms about.'

Dave grabbed the cans from around his neck and moved them slowly back and forth in an arc across the live mic, making sure that the left and right monitor controls were wound up full. At first a burning, vertical blade of sound slashed out in one vibrant beam, generating ripples in centrifugal waves through the densities of the stratosphere. Then an aural bombardment flashed through his visual horizon. The isochasm-frequency receded in cold, multi-dimensional whiteness that spread into the hypothalamus; physical pain at the primitive jerk of memory. Exhilarated, he threw the cans back onto the desk and the lights fuzzed out on the vision of a space not previously inhabited. Rehearsed hysteria.

'What, was—*that!* Conrad slapped the sides of his head. 'A goddam trepanning exercise?'

'Celestial trumpets.'

'Fine. How 'bout we keep the divine orchestration out of this one!'

The rave started up again. 'Let's concentrate on the lesser known deities doing time as a result of the Waitangi Treaty and all that horseshit. The Divine Real Estate Agents got us into this mess in the first place. The Wakefield gang and his bunch of rip-off merchants. The treatment plant of Presbyterianism and the outfall of Puritanism and the ethic of 'fairness' and missionaries stumbling about the countryside like a survey party of God driving stakes into the mythological beast . . . O paternalism, if I must with thee dwell.' Dave waved him on. ' . . . trying to understand this superimposed culture man, *pshew*.'

Conrad shuffled amongst the heap of scribbled notes in front of him, momentarily losing the thread. Dave bridged with a cross-fade of marauding mob screams under the constant rumbling explosions.

'... Is, is like trying to read the sub-titles on some foreign movie. Can't tell what the lips are really saying. If you knew that, it would scare you shitless. We're used to making noise, see? Commissions of Enquiry passing wind—what I'm talking about is a silent thing. Keep an ear tuned, citizens, and if you listen carefully, you'll be able to hear the smashing of skulls.' He took a foam coffee container, placed it against the mic. and compressed it between his palms with a sharp crack.

'Just like that.'

He repeated the act and tossed the crumpled remains over Dave's head. The spools spun through the tape-heads as the 'obliteration' continued; the non-audible frequency below 5 hertz of high intensity, pumped through loud speakers placed at key locations around the central city. Codename: OPERATION BABYCARRIAGE.

The principal participants in this scheme were Marine Morgue familiar with the layout of the Paremata—Pāuatahanui district and an ex-Radio New Zealand technician who now serviced the WGTN equipment: a low-key subversive whose theories were considered more successful as concepts than achievements. Granger belonged to a group of highly trained RNZ technicians who during the pioneering days of FM had been instructed to build a prototype-console for the provincial stations.

The race was on for FM licences between Radio New Zealand and the emergent private stations. Whoever came up with an original design would be the first to broadcast on an FM frequency. Radio New Zealand, of course, would own the patent on the adopted design, hardly an example of a market driven economy. These were the conditions set down by the Broadcasting Commission. Radio New Zealand led the FM race. A pilot transmission on new equipment had been carried out using the (mock) trainee-station run by semi-retired RNZ announcers, old entrenched and bureaucratic queens with vague careerist hopes in the big cities, and who didn't want to work the provincial stations—with encouraging results.

At an early phase in his career with Radio New Zealand, Dave had been instructed to attend (the compromise was for one week) the announcer's training school in Wellington. He had exhibited signs of private radio 'free style'. In those days, an independent broadcasting style was regarded as somewhat uncouth, and was considered anathema to the long-established broadcasting code and practices of state radio; a tradition of mediocrity founded on the BBC model. Any contrary style suggested a dangerous, or unacceptable, renegade spirit, and that had to be curbed for who knew where it might lead? Into oddly bizarre activities as it turned out. Within the closed ranks of 'Aunty' circulated a cautionary tale, most knew of it, though 'Aunty' assumed few people in the public arena had ever heard the tale when in fact it was common knowledge. Around the mid '60s an announcer from Radio National (some said from the concert programme) was sprung as the fabled 'Bird-Man of Mount Victoria'. The guy had managed to escape detection for years, yet his antics became firmly established in local folklore.

One of Wellington's more colourful oddballs and talked about as often as the famous 'bearded lady' who roamed the streets of the city at night. Eventually, he was caught in the act though his identity was never disclosed, and remained a closely guarded secret, more for the protection of Radio NZ's reputation than anything else. (Family radio and *Aunt Daisy's* cooking 'give me your heart and joy' and cleaning hints!) His activities had been harmless enough. Usually, he rigged himself out in a giant bird outfit and took to the slopes of Mount Victoria late at night, spot-checking parked cars for lovers. A strangled screech would announce his arrival. A bang on the car roof and a flash of his torch and the dazed, terror-struck couple were called forth, to be confronted by a two legged, man-size bird.

The bird man then requested in a deep, Rolls-Royce voice that his victims blow three times on a whistle (which he courteously provided), and then just as quickly, he leapt into the hillside bushes; an activity which gave rise to the fad of 'bush-jumping' amongst some of the more adventurous youth. The curious thing was, that he invariably struck *precisely* at the top of the hour, and the whistle which his victims were required to blow into, emitted a different bird call *("here's the bird")* on each separate occasion. Obviously, the New Zealand native birdcalls played on Radio National on the hour, every hour had finally unsettled the announcer. The magic incantation of bird song soaked through his brain rhythms over a period of time until he became, as it were, ornithologically biased. He believed himself to be some sort of walking demiurge. A schizoid obsession. Radio New Zealand being the maternal institution ('Aunty') that it then was held a more sympathetic view to flipped out announcers. Usually, they were discreetly packed off to Apia, Samoa (Radio NZ owned and managed a small radio station on the island), where it was hoped the tranquil lifestyle would effect a cure. Radio fatigue, stress, paranoia were part and parcel of the job and the excesses of ego that went with it.

But maybe this disturbed announcer had disturbed something a little more primordial? Māori folklore told of a taniwha who, attempting to escape from the landlocked harbour (early geological upheavals finally opened the Wellington harbour out into the Tasman), in its frustration turned into a bird and flew to the top of Mount Victoria. And to this day the winds which whistle about its peak are said to be the screeches of that transformed bird. Perhaps he had tapped into an earlier, more ancient frequency. Such tales were not to be sneered at. Wellington, particularly in the '50s, early '60s (Dave's childhood) was, uniquely, the *City of Eccentrics.*

Granger had been experimenting at that time with frequency modulations of varied intensities. On the morning of the inaugural transmission the announcer selected to broadcast the historic words had his eardrums blown out. The privates won by default. Granger was blacklisted from the Public Service only to be quickly taken up by WGTN. Two prime locations had been selected to place clusters of loud-speakers: Kapiti lookout at the head of the Horokiwi Valley, and a small battery on the hills above Mākara Beach behind Karori: the first to cover the Pāutahanui district, and the second to cover Wellington Basin. It was estimated that within a five-mile radius of each cluster a harmless, though measurable vibration would be felt. Aside from the two prime locations there were the mobile-pulses, portable amplification systems attached to 'The Loop', the reinstated tramway link. Bright yellow trams ran from the railway station in Thorndon, up through Lambton Quay and lower Willis Street, into Cuba Street and Courtenay Place, around Pigeon Park, and then back along the same route to the railway station. One continuous, cheap service for the inner-city commuters.

The Wellington City Council had been sold the WGTN Rock-Over Festival: outside broadcasts, lunchtime rock-concerts, competitions, big money giveaways sponsored by heavy retail advertising; the festival of the year in celebration of the new city on a scale never before seen. It was a simple matter then for Dave to use this event as a cover and begin preparations weeks in advance. With the assistance of

Granger, who shared the view that radio meant audio-theatre, a workable conspiracy unfolded. Granger believed himself the foil to some relentless electronic deity and was always ready to supersede the unfathomable magnetic forces he believed taunted him. The task was to design a receiver sophisticated enough to handle an 'earthquake' frequency and Granger, a purist in the most obsessive sense, whose energies were mono-directional, didn't digress in his efforts until happy with the finished product. Though his track record was questionable his genius remained undisputed.

Thought became sensation. The Brooklyn Hills folded back westward to the predominant peak of Hawkins Hill and the radar station, which harvested from the Tasman the babble of communication. The jagged line of pine trees against the sky behind Brooklyn-*west* juddered like a cardiograph. The peaks and troughs followed one upon the other from north to south. A blurred frown on the horizon. The imperturbable revolutions of the dish on Hawkins Hill picked up the clouds in its scooped hollow, and flung them out over the sky to be caught, and hurled back with blinding velocity. Again, from north to south. The clouds switched on and off in burning balls of light.

A latticework of sound spilled from Conrad into a grid of speech. '*The Runaway Babycarriage!*' He darted about the studio. 'We've done it Davie boy! I've waited weeks for this. Who the hell could have stopped us, eh?' The checkers on his shirt pulsed cubes of colour. Bands of energy, phosphorescent, flowed through the shoulders and down the arms. The medieval knight with flashing cuirass.

'The game's up. The buildings tumbling like chess pieces,' he whistled, 'man, what a movie.'

'*Actuality*—is what the journalists call it.'

All or nothing. He felt that strange, tingling warmth begin at the back of the head like the vibration of a speaker cone. An anticipatory awareness. A prophetic, sugary sensation. The splitting of matter at distance. A beam the psyche could direct, generating a frequency at phenomena, through the partitions of visible reality, to call up the mythic gods and shadow dance of the elements.

The studio door violently banged against the padded wall and a raw concentration of matter blocked the space. For an instant the bulk was absorbed into the gallery of special effects. But then the atoms visibly coalesced and found their outline in recognisable contours. Garth shuddered out toward Dave. The head detached, expanded into a boulder, and filled the door-way.

'Holy shit!' screamed Conrad. 'It's the evil Luther!'

'What the fuck's going on?' The voice, warbled, reverberated.

'I'm getting on with my show, undisturbed.'

'You've overstepped the mark this time' (a tracery of rage); 'the receptionist is being bombarded with hysterical calls. People are in a panic. What the hell are you playing at?'

'I told you before,' said Dave, 'I've total autonomy on my show. I interview the people I want. I select the topic I want. I create the effect I want, and that is in my contract.'

'We'll see about that. I'm calling a board meeting. You're up for suspension.' Dave cut him short.

'If you have anything to say to me, say it afterwards, *not* while I'm on-air—*them's* the rules, mate! *no Jock to be disturbed*—so fuck off!' Garth stepped back toward the door.

'You've lost all rights if I have anything to do with it. Sabotage, mate. You'll hang on this one. This time you've gone overboard. You,' he yelled above the fusillade, 'are up for suspension if it's the last thing I do on this station.'

'Close the door behind you mate.' A video feedback of after-images followed him out as the door pulled shut with a *whoosh*.

'A bit rich,' said Conrad.

Dave dismissed it, 'flash paranoia, *really* something to worry about,' he chuckled, 'an illusion, a nasty one, but an illusion nonetheless. "Operation Babycarriage" appears to be a success.'

'The mental barriers are tumbling.'

And that for Conrad was the definitive statement. He had come to the close of his repertoire. J & J having noticed the approach of Garth, had adeptly hidden the weed in the sleeve of an album. Now they were on their feet and ready to go, backs pressed to the glass-panel, to block the view in.

'Hold it you guys.' Conrad indicated that they should sit down again. 'Another five minutes should wrap it up.'

From the greater framework of the station an evil as mobile as mercury flowed about the studio. Temporally, Dave had pushed it back, had punched holes in that leaden reality at a seven second remove. Meanwhile, the taped and carted broadsides fired out across the city. Plate-echo thunder through a thousand living rooms and kitchens. But the after-shock of Garth lingered on like an accusation. The seismic rumours. The deep-seated bass notes gathered about Dave. It was something tactile now. The immediate, practical forces confronted the stance he had taken; the gathering of the board members and the move to have him suspended.

'... You have been brought before the Tribunal of Independent FM Broadcasters on a charge of sedition, acting in conspiracy with known members of the Porirua bikie gang, *The Peacemakers*, to defraud and mislead the public. That on the 3rd day of the 10 month you wilfully simulated an earthquake of destructive magnitude from the studios of WGTN kHz fm, thereby causing collective paranoia and mass-guilt in undermining the democratic belief in the virtues of Christian family values, a Christian God, etc., how do you plead?'

Successful. The master-tape labelled THE DISLOCATED REALITY SYNDROME is brought forward as evidence.

'You admit the charge?'

'Yes.'

The evidence is a fast-forward historical replay on the consciousness of Dave Jordan. The earthquake lights go up pockets of oxygen in the bloodstream of a diver thrown into convulsions to the surface vaporise to sheets of pain with a high charge of electricity and the easy rocks opening and the earth gives a backhanded belt to the sky stinging it with lightning over the Rimutakas bouncing back from peak to peak the gods playing volleyball with the elements within the harbour basin the Te Aro and Pipitea and Te Āti Awa tribes sold out to the new settlement long ago says the thunder says the exploding greywacke say the sheets of lightning in this open air stadium of the gods in the *Great Harbour of Tara* under the drowning applause of the Petone Hills dropped down deeper bottoming out and belly rolling across the reclaimed mud up Thorndon and Wakefield streets sluiced out is every high risk building stranded high and dry on sunken piles or drop-kicked back and forward passed amongst the gods booming for joy the tumbling masonry and the city a *runaway babycarriage* to the tide and railway lines buckling in the bottleneck toward Heretaunga and the bass notes of the fault lines sending jumbled rhythms across Mākara and Karori and Brooklyn Hills in one continuous loop-tape running round inside his head from the *gold drifts* of sand and suburbia into the Horokiwi Valley the Pāuatahanui Inlet heaved up freshly from the estuary a vast pelt of grey mud left to dry to return forever the shags and tussock and black swans who heard it coming as did he one morning when light plumped the bulrushes of Duck Creek and Wellington gasped from the south a city bent over double.

Conrad pulled on his leather jacket. 'See ya,' he said.

Dave watched the broad back seesaw out of the studio. THE PEACEMAKERS scrawled in an arc across the leather-clad shoulders.

The following is taken from my collection, *Night of Warehouses, Poems: 1978-2000* (2001):

BRADY'S GRAVE

'Listen to the moaning of the pine
at whose root thy hut is fastened.'
Old Danish proverb

In front of the old Manse,
Duck Creek weaves through
bulrushes along the hillside
striving with pine trees,
slippery with copper needles

home to magpie's carolling.
'There were three homes we had.'
Farther back into the hill,
a tilted slab of concrete, rusty
iron posts and chains mark it out

amongst the tussock clumps—
Brady's Grave makes a slipway
for the flying, full moon;
and the local cats gather into
a circle, under the yellow glare.

A questioning silhouette
of *Black Swans at Pāuatahanui*
ride easy, buoyant, on the inlet's
long tides away from view,
behind the whistling pine grove.

Afterword

The reader may be wondering why this sudden transportation into this projected world of fantasy? I had lived in Pāuatahanui 30 km North East of Wellington on the Porirua Harbour in 1972, then little more than a clutch of houses and a car mechanic business. At the time the nearby suburb of Whitby was under construction. These were the early days of my ill-fated marriage which soon terminated. I lived in what was known as the 'Old Manse', along with the Morrison family. Tony Morrison worked for the Consortium building Whitby back then. They owned the manse and surrounding land. His job was to landscape and beautify the new suburb. Tony was responsible for designing the golf course up behind the manse and part of the overall Consortium project. The golf course was studded with little islands of native bush which I have called elsewhere, *Islands of Wilderness*, a phrase I adopted many years later as title to a long poem subsequently published by Penguin Books Australia in 1996 called 'Wild Life' a four-in-one book. The series editor was the now deceased Australian poet, Judith Rodriguez.

Tony Morrison, originally a thatch maker by trade, a 'ten pound pom', was something of a Lawrencian figure with a big ginger beard; a dedicated man of the outdoors who enjoyed regular weekend tramping excursions up into the Tararua Ranges in the Wairarapa district. He would trudge above the snowline, squat there, smoke a cigarette, all the while looking quint-eyed off into the distance through a flurry of snow—man of the 'thousand mile stare'. He subsequently died on one of his tramps by falling down into a steep gully. Tony enjoyed woodcarving, but once he had finished a piece summarily burnt it. A self-sabotaging romantic. His favourite poem was William Blake's 'The Mental Traveller'. That part of my life, now so far removed, seems dreamlike. While living at Pāuatahanui I wrote *Henwise*, the sequence of poems published by Alan Loney's Hawk Press, Christchurch, in 1975. I had worked at Radio Windy in Wellington that same year as morning newsreader/production voice and had read a news bulletin through a 6.2 earthquake without dropping a stitch! Given the radio station was built upon reclaimed land the effect of the shake was amplified. I based this fantasy tale, or prose poem of sorts, upon these experiences, and in doing so recalled much of the landscape around Pāuatahanui where I had lived three years earlier, embellished with some aspects of its colonial history. I believe the black swans still inhabit the inlet.

One Day In The Life Of Vicki Viidikas

Jesus said, *'If one blind person leads another blind person, both of them will fall into a hole.'*

—The Gospel of Thomas: *saying 34*

'I'll go for a drink with one of my demons tonight.'—Ted Berrigan

A sharp deflection of the gin-glass slashed across my knuckles. Four little red crescents. Four neat, upturned cuts bright as smiles. The day had started out as these things do, pleasantly enough, in a couple of the Newtown pubs: *The Courthouse*, corner Lennox and Australia streets, then steadied at the *Sandringham Hotel*, past the Newtown railway station, at the Erskineville end of King Street. The incident took place in the early evening at a 'boutiqued' working man's cottage in the gentrified, middle-class suburb of Rozelle. This was home to one of the middling 'beat' mandarins of the '60s generation who had never left the area. The year was 1988, three years into my seven-year tenure in Newtown. Somewhere, it was the end of an era for somebody.

Still young enough to risk my balance, I had not yet reached forty. I felt like a man upright and cruciform, arms outstretched, on the roof carriage of an express train hell-bent. Like Jon Voight in the 1985 movie, *Runaway Train*—hurtling headlong into the blizzard and oblivion. An image projected by ultra-sound (as if onto a besmirched windscreen) eerily resembles that image transmitted by a weather satellite; it is dependent on withdrawal and perspective. As I look back upon those days living in the Inner West suburb of Newtown, I observe another person caught up in the blur and distortion of a street-wise community operating frenetically in a closed and 'islanded' space; vertiginous, but confined of movement.

This choice on my part was more by accident than design (effectively, my first flat in Sydney), a life led close to the edge, yet somehow remaining apart from it; ebb and flow, a balancing act. I chose engagement with minimal compromise, not an easy line to hold against a working-class youth culture who played uncompromisingly by their own rules. Loyalty belonged to immediate and often temporary involvement—mateship, that great democratic lie lodged comfortably in the Australian male psyche was, I soon discovered, both illusory and skin deep. Or as I wrote elsewhere, which is probably more applicable to the prevarications of a Police Tribunal than the average citizen, 'Corruption is Glorified Mateship'.

So it went. If you were out of sight you were out of mind. Allegiances were made and broken on the toss of a coin or throw of a fist. Bravado, not friendship, was the name of the game around the pumping undulations of King Street, Newtown. This was the typical urban environment in which the average male acquired the pack-instinct, the easy lie of camaraderie. Either which way, the few old inner suburban working-class hotels that had escaped 'boutiquing' back then (aside from the viral spread of pokies), could be found in the Camperdown backstreets. Like the *Royal Edward Hotel* (the pub's now gone but the building remains), corner Wilson and Forbes streets, Newtown—though you wouldn't normally frequent the joint, haunted as it was, supposedly, by a double murder that took place on the premises in the mid '70s. One of the principal locations in the early days (though by late 1987, I was 'banned for life' having called the ill-educated proprietor, a schoolyard bully type given to beating up on his customers—*a fascist*), was the *Carlisle Castle Hotel*, in Albermarle Street, Newtown.

I lived in a small block of red-brick units on Chelmsford Street situated a few minutes' walk away. The pub catered to the standard contingent, the front bar with its handful of old timers and long-haul drinkers, yellow-cab couriers and short-tempered security men (for fifty bucks you could hire a standover merchant), and a clutch of blue collar workers—while the back bar, which gave access to a bare room set aside for pool tables, attracted the local 'grunge' element, a few Sydney University students, welfare recipients, minor public servants from government departments (looking for an identity), and generally, the requisite agitating core of speed freaks, loners, downright shifty dudes and blow-ins. A Rabelaisian democracy, the 'usual suspects' and standard cliques. To me the establishment always generated an edgy 'vibe' and that probably had as much to do with my paranoia as anything else. I actually *felt* like a foreigner smuggled into the camp. If you maybe got landed with a nickname, this pretty much represented a measure of provisional acceptance. Somehow, 'the poet' didn't quite cut it with that crowd for long. If this cognomen suggested exclusivity, I couldn't have agreed more. It didn't have quite the same ring to it as 'Two-Bob Pete' or 'Have-A-Chat, *whatever*'. As a regular socializing venue, this was a clumsy miscalculation on my part. It proved entirely the wrong choice in selective anonymity. There was no shortage of drinking buddies, and you could always find a bar-stool to sit at, a conversation and banter in varying degrees of intensity. Expectation lay no more than an easy walk and public bar away.

The *Marlborough Hotel*, on the corner of King Street and Missenden Road (taking care to avoid the seriously busy *Oxford Tavern* with wall-to-wall 'ferals and goths'), offered a greater crush and diversity. Newtown, gateway to the west, from the mid '80s was undergoing a sociological shift. Various musicians, artists and poets had taken up residence—John Forbes in Lennox Street, Martin Harrison in Denison Street (poets since deceased), myself in Chelmsford Street—practically living on the same block. Interceptions, as if by sleight-of-hand, were rare. Newtown was a suburb of cheap rentals and easy accessibility to the CBD. By now the gay contingent had invaded the real estate market, and inexpensive Thai restaurants had started to open up one after the other (with adventurous names like *Thai Tanic*) along the King Street shopping strip.

At one stage I counted at least fifteen Thai restaurants within a two-hundred-yard stretch. Newtown had always accommodated Greek, Lebanese and Turkish communities, along with the Yugoslavs and their tucked away gambling rooms. Earlier still in the '60s, the neighbourhood became home to a considerable Polynesian population; a shifting demographic underscored by the founding Anglo-Celtic working-class population which originally established and defined the Inner West with its cheek by jowl barrel terraces. Around Enmore you might yet discover a narrow, open doorway and worn, creaky wooden stairs leading up to an unadorned though comfortable room full of serious gamblers. As long as you kept your mouth shut, you could stay and enjoy the spicy, pitch-black coffee. A number of the ethnic restaurants on Enmore Road offered Turkish belly-dancing. Greek and Albanian women sang in spiralling Moorish or Arabian accents and circulated amongst the diners collecting tips after their performance.

This then was largely the purlieu I circulated amongst during those days. Newtown became an island unto itself. Yet I can't recall precisely when I first met Vicki; it might have been at a poetry reading sponsored by the *Goethe-Institut* in Woollahra, and organized through the (now deceased) Austrian poet/playwright, Rudi Krausmann, or through an introduction made at the *Rose and Crown Hotel* in Paddington, a local once frequented by the poet Bob Adamson. Both he and Rudi lived in 'Paddo' up until the close of the decade. They were long-time associates in varying degrees of friendship, with Vicki Viidikas,[1] going right back to the early days of the *Wild & Woolley Press*, a small independent, relatively successful publisher of poetry. But this was long before I arrived on the scene. I landed in Sydney in 1986 (on the eve of a recession), though I had previously visited for a couple of weeks back in late December of 1978, on my way through to the Mediterranean, and the island of Crete.

My intention the second time round (a hurried escape from Auckland), was to make money quickly over a two-year period selling my 'voice' to the advertising industry, and return to New Zealand with the loot to buy a house. A place of one's own, a sanctuary to write, and be left alone to do it. Naturally, things didn't quite work out that way. I eventually got my 'break', though it took five years to reach that point. I landed a two-year period of 'voice over work' with a commercial television station which involved little more than an hour a day (or less), voicing promos for a 'current affairs' program. I got what I wanted, or thought I wanted.

However, the emotional climate of my lifestyle was such that the money simply gave me much needed breathing room; respite from poverty, which had dogged me relentlessly up until then. I knew that this good fortune wouldn't last (such is the nature of free-lance work), but at least it gave me the chance to get out and move to Melbourne for three years and centre myself. But that came five years further on down the track when I had grown roundly sick of Newtown's gritty lifestyle, and five years after the incident that I am relating here had passed into history. I lived seven years in that one-bedroom unit. Newtown baked as if on an oven plate in the hot summer months; dust and grime filtered in from across the dreary factory lands extending out west, to leave the place parched and airless.

I clearly recall my second meeting with Vicki (the same clarity that precedes an accident, frozen forever in time), after perhaps an absence of a year or so, and the events of that day which are the subject of this essay. O Newtown, dark womb of Sydney! Early 1988: Vicki was sitting outside an Asian takeaway in King Street, near the Newtown railway station, eating rice from a plastic container, so delicately, with her fingers. She had pretended that she hadn't seen me in order to act fittingly surprised when I greeted her. For a moment, I hesitated, and almost walked by. Yet, I think her pretence at not noticing gave me that momentary choice. But there was something about the delicacy of her fingers which stopped me. She looked like a frail, abandoned bird. I think she may have stayed at my one bedroom apartment that night, and a couple of days later, we caught up at the *Sandringham Hotel* for one of the confused poetry readings they ran in those days (which we were responsible for), prior to the band starting up on a Saturday afternoon.

Of the afternoon itself, there is not much to relate. We continued on into the early evening and returned to my 'studio' apartment in Chelmsford Street. We commandeered a ride with an upstairs neighbour who now joined the party, 'the boy from Gippsland,' over to Rozelle and the house of the 'beat' mandarin, about ten minutes' drive away. Thankfully, he was not in residence at the time. Conveniently, I knew one or two of his New Zealand house guests. We continued to grog on steadily, getting into the groove and entertainment on the strength of this rather tenuous association. A couple of hours drifted by in that fashion. It was then (though I can't recall in what context) that I asked Vicki—was it true that she had at some time married an Aborigine (I heard she had, and I was simply interested), which precipitated a sudden and unabated blind fury on her part (I didn't realise at the time it was junkie fury), where she hurled, with deadly force and velocity, a full glass of gin straight at my face. The frail bird had transformed itself into a raptor. Pure reflex saved me, for the glass surely would have found its intended mark and more than likely blinded me. While I was dealing with this, she suddenly had the 'beat' mandarin's *Olivetti* portable typewriter clasped in both talons, held high above her in a somewhat Old Testament, avenging stance—momentarily poised, ready to dash the thing on my head! No way could I have deflected *that*. Maybe the sight of blood streaming from my slashed knuckles, or that her wrath on this occasion, suddenly ceasing as quickly as it came before she had a chance to cause greater damage, saved the situation. The stunned guests managed to somehow placate her, at least long enough for her pathological fury to cool. We managed to drive to the *Royal Prince Alfred Hospital*, my hand wrapped in a blood-soaked tea towel, situated back in Missenden Road. I got an injection stabbed into my wounds, viciously pulled open by a sadistic Irish nurse, and finally, a pretty row of stitches for my trouble. The evening tailed out over a few apologetic drinks once more, in a 360-degree sweep, back at the Sandringham Hotel. The dazed, and slowed comfort of exhaustion. For a moment, the planet had stalled. *What the hell was I doing in this neighbourhood—leading this life?*

A few weeks later there was a compounding incident involving her new junkie boyfriend or co-conspirator, a thug bikie; a hair-raising ride on the back of his motorcycle to Eastlakes, off Gardeners Road past Rosebery, where she had found free accommodation with Rudi Krausmann's ex-wife in a Housing Commission block (where I had previously stayed on first arriving in Sydney), and a threatening incident involving a monkey wrench. At that point, I decided the woman was disaster incarnate and I refused outright to have anything further to do with her. And finally, there was a residue meeting of sorts at my place, but that too deteriorated into a drunken shambles, and I kicked her out into the wet and wintry night around 3 a.m.

This was the summary of events which precipitated her poem addressed to me, freighted as it is with cross-currents of pleading for acceptance, guilt, and anger at rejection. The graveyard she refers to in her poem is Camperdown Cemetery, attached to *St. Stephen's Church*, distinguished by its age and a few notable occupants; the *Wreck of the Dunbar* memorial site with its giant, rusted anchor; Sydney's first mayor, the raffish 19th century lyre player, Nicolas Charles Bochsa. A poem of the same name originally appeared in my collection, *Guardians, Not Angels* (1993). Bochsa was rumoured to have been poisoned by agents of Napoleon III's regime. The woman upon whom Charles Dickens purportedly modelled his character 'Miss Havisham' in the novel, *Great Expectations* was also interred here. One monstrous Moreton Bay Fig tree (shelter for many a late-night, post-pub gathering), overhangs the wrought-iron gateway to that old cemetery.

The poem, which concludes this account, was placed in my letter box (as a personal letter addressed to me) not long after this last, frayed interaction. In essence, I originally saw Vicki as a special, gifted individual possessed of a large heart. Her reputation had gone before her. I had heard about Vicki through a New Zealand poet and collage artist who had lived in Sydney during the late '60s and '70s. The late John Goodall a.k.a. John MacNamara, himself a hell-raiser known to the Balmain literary fraternity of the day, and something of a legend in his own right—a close associate of Dorothy Hewitt, Bob Adamson, John Forbes, and that whole incestuous scene. Dorothy, in fact, had taken a title from one of John's collage works, 'Alice in Wormland', as her own for a volume of poetry published in the late '80s, without acknowledgement. The one book produced by 'John Goodall' (John MacNamara) called *The Savages, Poems 1964-1978*, Señor Press, published in Sydney, 1979, is now considered a collector's item. Interestingly, the typesetting was done by Lyn Tranter, wife of the poet. Typically, one day John, without warning or giving notice, surreptitiously scarpered back into Henderson and the backblocks of Auckland around 1980—and there I first met him, at the (deceased) poet Dave Mitchell's famous *Globe Tavern Poetry Readings.*

I subsequently experienced and witnessed first-hand, as many others had, the blind and unabated fury of the hopeless junkie, the complete destruction of the individual. These creatures ultimately became little more than the walking dead, completely stripped of the last vestiges of humanity. As I have suggested elsewhere, one is tempted to conclude that they have unequivocally 'forfeited their right to humanity' because they have ceased to be human. Sadly, I can see no saving grace for heroin addiction this side of the grave. The victims all follow the same boring, predictable and totally nihilistic path. To be quite frank, they are anathema and beyond the reach of compromise. Politically correct notions of 'shooting galleries' for instance, are futile. Such 'comforting' gestures are merely designed to assuage middle class ruminations of collective guilt. 'Junkies,' as an 'occasional' user once told me, 'like their rooms *close*.' They will shoot up anywhere—a garage, a park, an alleyway, it just doesn't matter—*and* they don't need an officially sanctioned club in which to do it. I had once inadvertently stumbled slap bang into the middle of the infamous Eveleigh Street, Redfern, via a back lane which led onto it, and intercepted in that fateful lane a bunch of junkies sitting in a garage and shooting up. There must have been at least twenty of them! I crept past like a ghost. I refer to this incident in Sonnet 52. *Bad Mistake*. A full explanation of this incident can be found in the 'Notes' section at the back of my collection *The Song Of Globule/80 Sonnets* (2020).

These laboured compromises represent society's complete inability to come to terms with its own self-plundering consumerism. Addiction is no more nor less than the sinister side of the same appetite that goads us onto greater acquisition in our relentless pursuit for more of what we already have. A negative drive increasingly popularized in labels like *Macsumerism*. Even a sense of irretrievable loss can be reduced to a playful brand name. If the devil walked this earth in human form today he would do so as an economist. Junkies are the black bile of that self-same greed, a sign that we are being eaten from the inside out. As a state of mind-numbness, this self-serving paranoia leads us down a blind to where, we suppose, analytical declensions can finally assume the functions of hard-wired realities. The introspective world of the self can only blur into lurid vistas of half-realized desires, directionless in the addict's appetites yet perpetuated by them.

Some call this circular panic 'living' in the modern world. But *that* person is never the person you imagine you are dealing with; communication ossifies, and becomes synonymous with entrapment.

Vicki sought shadows without restraint in a relentlessly harsh, bright land. She made that inward journey to taste the spirit's dark liquor. Fundamentally, her Estonian soul dreamt of birch-forested hills endlessly stretching toward horizons, thick as the backs of wolves. The innocent failures and miscalculations of ordinary people made her laugh and easily engage. Her warmth displayed itself in an ingenuous enjoyment of the charade that is, at base, everyday life. In the end heroin overpowered her—travelling back and forth to India for cheap junk, reduced (the subcontinent and Asia deeply attracted and inspired her) and ultimately destroyed, so that, quarantined within that hopeless addiction, she dragged the chains of destruction behind her, and became pariah to everyone she met. In the end no one wanted to know her, and that included me. You got the impression that she had outstayed her welcome in other people's lives and haunted, rather than lived on this planet. So it is with the terminal junkie. She had retreated, or something had passed her by.

Vicki was by birth a genuine talent; and without doubt would have become one of the finest poets to emerge from the '60s youth culture in Australia. Her prodigious output was largely undisciplined but undeniably original. She had a true, deep honesty that few of her peer-group possessed, for she carried something broad and antique in a vision uniquely hers. She came closer in style and emphasis to the Russian poets of the '20s and '30s, than to the conversational mimicries of the '50s and '60s American poets, and legions of post-colonial spin-offs. Though much of her later writing (particularly the last collection, *India Ink*, Hale & Iremonger, 1984), centres on her travels throughout South East Asia and the sub-continent, the *spiritual tenor* and emotional slant of her work strongly registers that of certain Russian poets of the early 20th century. Her genetic 'Slavic' disposition (though her father was Estonian) leaned more toward, for instance, the linguistic dynamism of Velimir Khlebnikov, Vladimir Mayakovsky and Marina Tsvetaeva, than, correspondingly, Sylvia Plath, Ginsberg (though his influence was unavoidable for those caught in the endless summer of the illusory '60s), Ashbery and Frank O'Hara, or alternately, the San Francisco group.

In Australia, she had as much right to membership of the so-called group, *Generation of 1968* (a boy's own adventure story), as John Tranter, John Forbes, Ken Bolton, Martin Johnston, *et al.*, never truly defined as a coherent school of poetic endeavour. For that, you need to go back to a group of Spanish intellectuals and poets who revitalized Spanish culture and rediscovered its great heritage known as the *Generation of 1898*, whose members included Unamuno, Azorín, Machado, Baroja and Valle-Inclán—bound by an artistic manifesto like, for instance, the early 20th century Symbolists, Acmeists, or Imagists. This, on the other hand, was merely a loose confederation of local competitors, around about the same age, provincial and imitative in their Americanisms, who happened to vaguely share similar drinking habits, sexual opportunism, and literary preoccupations. As amorphous as the earlier 'Sydney Push'.

Deprived of any living history in the deeper, European sense, most of our better artistic endeavours succeeded as competent second-hand models short on originality and honesty—if by *honesty* you mean the unequivocal admission of cultural and individual shortcomings. Self-conscious, imitative models at best. George Steiner in his essay, 'The Archives of Eden', gives a masterly dissection on American cultural mores, and speaks of '... the development of culture as craft, as specialization ... this organization will take on the prevailing cast of economic valuation'.

At any rate, a shared and universal immediacy was to be found in the urban American environment, especially in the architectonics of John Ashbery, an elegance romanced to the point of stylistic anonymity, and in the musical, conversational tonality of Frank O'Hara. How could anything truly outstanding emerge from a system of disposable values which is, in effect, what the '60s was—*a nostalgia for the new.* The bland shall inherit the earth and become the new status quo. How could it be otherwise? As individuals, the so-called 'Generation of '68' and other groups like it (the same label applies to the corresponding number in New Zealand), were more likely to be unified by petty dislikes, prestige and 'sexual pedigrees', by the city in which you lived with its inherent rivalries, than by anything as vital as a collective vision.

Originality became confused with novelty; spontaneity with lack of discipline; and casual, conversational technique passed itself off as innovative poetic form. These 'unfreedoms of expression' we can now see as little more than an off-shoot of easy consumerism. An Age of Comparative Innocence, under the guiding star of youthful exuberance, passing on into the land of *rock 'n' roll* to announce nothing more heroic than the Age of Social Media. Now, advancing unsteadily into the new millennium, what has become our inheritance? We shelter under the free-trade umbrella of globalization where the weak shall be made weaker, and the strong, stronger. Yet what worthwhile alternative can we offer in a desperately depleted environment beyond the rearguard action of damage control which President Bush 'the Younger' attempted to protect with a 'defence shield'.

The American way pushes on into the last great unconquered, economic wilderness that is China (and by implication, further closes down Russia to third world status), with an eye to the subcontinent and India, and into Indonesia, but not without, one suspects, a possible redeployment in the form of further disruption to the populace, and involuntary migrations of refugees to the wealthier, western-style economies. The greater Pacific by its very nature is diffuse, and small, dependant island-states present little challenge and even less threat. American aid in exchange for long range missile bases remained an option as part of the projected 'defence shield' strategy. Meanwhile, it is a matter of setting up a free-trade stranglehold in a pincer-like movement around the middle-east. Globalization means compulsory membership of trade blocks. We can see it now: all that hoopla and experimentation of the '60s 'counter-culture' was a small tremor within this entire, and evolving process. The workings of a contributing consumerism, in other words. We did not possess the perspective on a greater historical process, or the vision to see what had arrived. Duped by a sneak attack.

There never was any revolution, only a hedonism made public which fed the fashion industry, created a few bad dance fads and mock-pioneering communities, and an even cheaper, popular music culture. Hits twenty years hence destined to become the stuff of commercial jingles, *'like a rolling stone / Austral paving bricks'. 'Snap! Crackle! Pop!' / quoth the poet.* The open road may have beckoned, but offered little more than a retreating, rubescent sunset, the death throes of a moribund pioneering spirit hankering after a lost agrarian existence. No matter how fast the youth culture moved, or how far out, the suburbs had got there long before they had. After all, a road leads somewhere. Rightly, we are not alone: what it comes down to in the end, is you and me, the mortgage, and inevitable retrenchment. What we do have in common, though, is our collective sense of boredom, vertigo, and increasingly—displacement.

Vicki Viidikas was just one more victim, a casualty of her generation. She may have knocked repeatedly on that door (Generation of '68) seeking acceptance, but by the time it was grudgingly opened an inch or two (even then in the poetic grand stakes, women were mostly relegated to the role of party objects), she had disappeared back onto the streets. She was not one of those imitators of the American schools who became the very establishment they sought to change. Unlike many of her literary peers, she was not governed by cold-hearted, careerist ambitions, nor by a cowardice of spirit. Unlike many of her generation, she was not one of those who risked nothing in the frantic quest to gain everything; and she was not crippled by petty rivalries and fear. Unlike a number of her colleagues, she was not dispossessed of that generosity of spirit which reveals itself in a small, mean talent.

Vicki Viidikas was alert to the inherited histories that rose and fell in her Estonian soul (her father was an Estonian and a violin maker, her mother—an Australian), with all the pull of primal, migratory tides. What is it any one of us truly recalls? If conflict is the glue of history, it comes by way of a slow burning revelation: we are, as a sentient species, caught in the glare of consciousness, afraid, suspecting that this 'awareness' is not our own, but the infiltration of an *other;* that it is we who are under surveillance, made all the more vigilant because of it. The *will to destruction* unfolds before the emerging shock, that throughout most of our lives we have played host to an inner, corrosive spy—suspicion.

It is reasonable to assume the darker currents of historical memory flashed across her psyche, and that she gave automatic and uninhibited expression to them. In many ways, her life had become anachronistic, indeed, she did not have any 'defence shield'. She did not compromise herself as either 'product' (she wouldn't have really understood the term as applied to poetry), or become an 'attention whore' to publicity and the image machine like one or two professional 'survivors' of that era in the poetry trade. It is not too harsh a thing to say that she was the abandoned child, destined never to be accepted, and she knew it. Vicki Viidikas died on November 27, 1998.

As to valedictions from her friends, I noted that the Melbourne poet, Shelton Lea, published a commemorative and generous piece in *Overland*, 'Vicki Viidikas—Spare Angel' [154.83]. There were also two significant obituary notices strongly supportive of her work: Michael Wilding's eloquent tribute in *The Australian* [11.12.98] and Gig Ryan's tough and comprehensive piece in *The Age* [12.2.99], both pleading convincingly for a reappraisal of her work—though the latter, I felt, in part appropriated Vicki's *shade* in the interests of feminism. She was aggressively non-partisan, an individual who freely functioned beyond any political agenda. Her life was one of direct action and reaction *and* was as ungovernable as that. In all fairness, the Australian literary establishment of the late '60s and '70s did open their arms to her—success was there for the taking. Increasingly though, she chose the path of self-destruction, and as heroin addiction tightened its grip on her life, she became marginalized and opportunities soon evaporated. Both of these obituaries note the early praise bestowed on her books of poetry, and quote the distinguished writer, Christina Stead, who said earlier, 'As for V.V., her portraits of men, instant and sharp, could only have been done by a girl who took these chances [and had talent.] She has tremendous talent.'

One can only ask of her enlightened and influential literary associates that they take time out from more pressing, careerist engagements to see into publication the remainder of her unpublished works. [See *Afterword* below.] As it stands, Vicki's literary reputation is relegated to that of an interesting footnote on a talented generation that had its flowering in the '70s. Friendship like loyalty demands the preservation of memory. Regrettably, the rational processes of globalisation and the strict profit margins set by *transnational* publishing giants, do not make it any easier for the few remaining independent publishers to rescue her reputation. That includes any other genuine poet shut out for one reason or another, condemned to subside into the lime-pit of indifference, there to become indistinguishable from the fraudulent. New fashions guarantee oblivion for some, and youth-like ambition is an inexhaustible resource (the average age for the *Microsoft* employee, for instance, is twenty-two), for which there is endless demand. As far as any redress goes since her death, we have been treated to an enduring silence and leaden echo (with the rare exception) from her earliest, and closest, literary associates of the '60s. Success stories, now happily retired back into the now wealthy precincts of Balmain, the Hawkesbury, or the Blue Mountains.

Doubtless, Vicki shared a sustained commitment and dedication to the craft of writing with any number of her fellow practitioners. Philip Larkin gave us his view of that generation in his poem and book of the same name, *High Windows*, 'And everyone young going down the long slide / To happiness, endlessly.' Not everyone, as it turns out. The prose poem, rather baldly titled: 'For Stephen Oliver, New Zealand Poet', written by Vicki and which closes this essay, is signed in her own hand and dated, *9.4.88*. She dropped the poem, typed on two sheets of A4 paper, into my letter box late at night I suspect, around the date given, like some sort of poetic indictment or summons. A gesture meant as peace offering—or so she subsequently told me. I believe I am the sole recipient of this weirdly elegiac poem, and possess the original text. Indeed, I would be very surprised if Vicky ever bothered, during the chaos of those troubling days, to make a copy of the work, though many of her papers have been lodged with the *Australian Defence Force Academy*.

I offered a copy of Vicki's poem 'For Stephen Oliver, New Zealand Poet' to the poetry editor of *Overland* but this was flatly rejected. Poetry editors, as gatekeepers, are usually appointed by a representative of some exclusive poetry clique. No matter what 'uncomfortable' sentiments are expressed in this poem concerning my person, they are addressed to an earlier, more confrontational self. The paranoia that is part of the New Zealand psyche has dissipated somewhat. I own my transgressions and am, as they say, prepared to 'cop it sweet'. Vicky had one thing that not even her 'peers' could diminish or appropriate. A soul, and it burned as 'intense as a flame at midnight'.

FOR STEPHEN OLIVER, NEW ZEALAND POET

All that wonderful verbiage
of blue and glinting waters, the South Pacific, Vanuatu, skies like
old overcoats cutting the dribble of a typical Australian pub—loud,
aggressive, ego of rock 'n' roll band, musicians playing on the bar,
your mad laugh rising above the racket, rising more, more—
you will not
be silent, do penance of dumbness, shut the battery of poetry off its
artillery fire.

All your talking, New Zealand poet,
forcing poems on drinkers, shouting at barmaids, cursing till
no woman
wants to talk with you, not purring soft lyrics at her swan neck, not
beating time with the ramparts of your heart—instead, you ask me to
'talk cold turkey,' straight from the heart, honest, why do I trust you?
You'd be as cunning as any dingo pack, in this country of literary
minors,
wimps, dressed up as roast dinners, animals, offal, their dictionaries
stuffed with trivia . . .

So we drink and shove poetry books
along the bar, back and forth like wild cats, grabbing for details, a
glint in a stranger's eye, a blonde's false smile to charm your beastly
heart, an ethnic drunk who tells us poetry is obsolete—
that makes you
even madder, sane as you are with conceit, 10 years to write a
manuscript
but you carry no pen or paper, won't recite at any time, not prepared
for instant vision—that would foil all your writer's tools.

Loud as Hell I lunge for your throat
and want to stop the gunfire words, verbiage thick as a hedge, your
BBC vanity—
who is the better poet? I won't play in your competition, damn
you for shouting about my drug habits, adding fuel to more squalid
mythology—then criticising me for being a legend in Australia.
Gossip betrays.
Should I tell the authorities which poets I've been in bed with?

All that alcohol and curry and comparisons,
so sure of your talent, don't give me twelve words for your every
twelve,
but boom me down, small, into argumentative bait, reaching
for headache pills—
how can real poetry give you a headache? Christ, it was cold
leaving your place at 3 a.m., thrown out, savage, to shelter in a
graveyard till the rain had stopped, and public transport started
at dawn.

Did you leave a lamp burning
for one honest friend who took you on pure instinct? Was it
the pickled liquor
which made you turn like a snake to viciously misread me? Was it
the sound of your own voice which never finds its equal? Seriously,
you know
Narcissus is stone cold, alone, talking to himself—that doesn't
fit your image, troubadour without a road . . .

To think women are snares,
cunning as anacondas, waiting to crush your soul? I remember
dusting your
typewriter, lending you a book, sharing cigarettes, wine, cheering
when you read, friend, of the two faced mask—Janus/Adonis,
fantasy was never
my thing, but blunt reality with romantic outposts—the surreal
or gently bizarre, the subtle drop of a tongue lapping a page—Eat my
book and try to recall my touch.

Don't get me wrong, I never
threatened you with exile, encouraged you to stay, individual, pyramid
minded, devoid of greasy slaves or women with goanna mouths.
I only ever meant
you the best, a little humbled perhaps, unbuttoned from memories
of cruel riptides, Kiwi banishments, nostalgia for a country too small
for your large voice.

When you disappear
into that long cloudy island, I will not follow (I prefer the tropics)
but address my letters to The Phantom of the South Pacific—I'll be
dead before you are, not sorry but silent, alone, intense as a flame
at midnight, utterly still, dreaming of the loved ones who left me,
listening for the song of a poet, carried through the ether . . .

Afterword

Stephen Conlon was the indefatigable hotel manager of the Sandringham ('Sando') Hotel at 'the grungy lower end of King Street, Newtown, in the late 1980s'. See reference to reviews below. It was he who booked the bands, some famously remembered like Roaring Jack, and, latterly, sanctioned the Saturday afternoon poetry readings, chaotic and vaudevillian as they often were, and gave Vicki shelter from the storm for a time by offering her upstairs accommodation when she had nowhere else to go.

This was no three star hotel, but a rough & tumble working class watering hole. Stephen was at that time completing his doctoral dissertation at the University of Sydney. He went on to become the Dean of the English Department, Assumption University, Bangkok, Thailand; a position he recently retired from, and was in addition the editor of the department's peer reviewed journal, *Asian Journal of Literature, Culture and Society*.

He reviewed Vicki's posthumous collection, 'New and Rediscovered' (poems and prose), Transit Lounge Publishing,

Melbourne (2010), Vol. 6.2 (2012); and my own book length narrative poem (a *transtasman* epic) *Intercolonial*, Puriri Press, Auckland (2013), Vol. 8.1 (2014); and later, *GONE: Satirical Poems: New & Selected*, Greywacke Press, Canberra (2016), Vol. 33.1 (2019) edition of *Antipodes: A Global Journal of Australian/New Zealand Literature*. Nicholas Birns of New York University edited the journal for twenty years up until December 2018, when he gave up his editorship of Antipodes to pursue his own critical studies and writings.

In any event, Stephen Conlon recounts in these various reviews, his recollections of Vicki and myself performing in the late '80s at the Sandringham Hotel Saturday afternoon poetry readings. It is worthwhile noting that I had offered Vicki's poem, 'For Stephen Oliver, New Zealand Poet' to her immediate family who acted as literary executors, via the publishing company of 'New and Rediscovered' (see above) who were open to publishing this poem. Nevertheless, the literary executors flatly rejected my offer, favouring as they did the softer options, and so it was not included in the posthumous publication of Vicki's work through the publisher, Transit Lounge.

[1] Books by Vicki Viidikas: *Condition Red*, UQP Paperback Poets Series, (1973); *Wrappings*, [short stories] Wild and Woolley, (1974); *Knabel*, Wild and Woolley, (1978); *India Ink*, [prose poems], Hale & Iremonger, Pty. Ltd. (1984).

Dirty Bomb Poetic

'Contempts in courts and cities dwell,
No critic haunts the poor man's cell,'
—Robert Herrick

You must first recognise your man. I say 'man' because the poet is emotionally an androgyne, and I nominate the male gender because, traditionally, this is where the greater number of poetasters, poseurs and confidence tricksters prevail. A circumstance that has something to do with the amorphous nature of poetry, especially when one departs from traditional forms. Any attempt to employ these structures by the uninitiated too quickly exposes those self-same practitioners as either provincial typing instructor, school mistress, or bookish academic intent upon building verbal monuments erected to him or herself—contradicting Ben Jonson's homage to Shakespeare, 'Thou art a monument without a tomb', by paying dues to a moribund Augustan Age, and writing endless screeds in the manner of Alexander Pope along the lines of, 'As I gazed out on the Palatine Hill / My thoughts toward Horace, Virgil, and Bill /' or scanning and attempting to emulate the classical stylistics of someone like A. E. Housman and his *A Shropshire Lad.* For such a person, The Great War happened in someone else's backyard and time stopped with Rupert Brooke, though not because Brooke was, arguably, a fine comedic poet. This he fails to see.

Our man is the quintessential modern man and is quick as a jackrabbit, already up and running. The best thing that might come his way is the middle-class expectation of a measurable success, prestige and political opportunity offered him by a Bachelor of Arts degree and appointment to an English Department in a leading metropolitan university, election to the editorial ranks of the University Press and assorted Arts Funding bodies. He doesn't consider himself a seer, but instead, something of a missionary, his dutiful obligation to impart knowledge and learning to the undergraduate, and in some politically *incorrect* instances, the female undergraduate. There are to be observed innumerable variations on a theme.

The composite poet in his academic incarnation plans well in advance; he establishes his own *Creative Writing School* affiliated with the English Department of a leading university in one of the capital cities. This allows him to clone a beehive of disciples created in his stylistic image. These chosen disciples he can then relocate strategically around the country in positions of political influence; readers of poetry manuscripts in university publishing houses, book reviewers for influential metropolitan dailies (if such a thing exists in this digital age), literary magazines, and purveyors of recommendations to influential editors of innumerable online platforms associated with the arts. Who knows, he might eventually be elevated to join the esteemed and prestigious ranks of The Academy of Literary Hogwash, in both the NZ and Australian chapters, undoubtedly—a *transtasman* accolade!

This ensures the survival his poetic 'blood line' (his clones are rewarded with publication, residencies and grants), and kills off at root any counter-force or creative individualism which may, if allowed free rein, contest his position in the public arena, his stranglehold on the country's poetic future. Again, he might have found that the freedoms of the '60s gave him his head, as it were, and his early twenties afforded him innumerable roles and guises in which to ply his trade as narcissist and arch sexual opportunist. The British novelist, Jeanette Winterson, is quoted in *The Times* as saying: 'As far as books are concerned, creative writing courses have done to new writing what slugs do to lettuce—eaten it alive. Young writers now produce the same kind of books in the same kind of way. They have found a formula and it works. Of course it works, it has been done a million times before.' *Poetry and the song lyric; poetry as infotainment.* Take your pick, slam dunk poetry dumbed down for the masses. A sustained narrative of fashionable, sexual cliché and gender politics at worst.

Our composite poet probably went to training college and got a diploma to teach in secondary schools, but only in the capacity of an Arts teacher—an indeterminate role set up in the mid-sixties because the climate allowed for such things; for instance, open-plan and experimental modes of teaching. So many individuals with questionable credentials secured these positions by strategically befriending certain poet-teachers located within the administration centres of capital cities. At the right time, and in Australia (this was during the Whitlam era) you could slip through the mesh without offering, one way or another, any defined syllabus or tried and true knowledge on the subject. *The Visual and Creative Arts* as a subject was as vague as you could possibly hope for. Once safely ensconced within the bureaucratic system, and registered as a permanent teacher 'on art subjects' his career and superannuation entitlements were secured for life. He could now cruise on a sinecure and risk nothing.

Had he come from an earlier generation, say the '50s, then a career bureaucrat would have been one of the few options open to him in New Zealand; the Education Department in an administrative capacity, or some other government appointment, maybe even a role in the *Ministry of Energy* formulating educational programmes for trainees. Years of writing inter-departmental memos would equip him with a prose style ready-made for book reviews, and little critiques on current literary theory. This is a man (or woman) who runs with the hounds and always backs what he considers a winner in the literary stakes. He will take few risks and will guard against jeopardising his standing which on most things is ambivalent. He promotes the young, up and coming writer, the prescribed leaders of a new and emerging generation.

In this way, he invests in his own literary career by shoring up support amongst the young, and against those in establishment institutions who regard him with happy indifference. If the emerging writer doesn't show, in due time, signs of fulfilling his or her promise as a person with literary and political clout, and who doesn't appear to have been accepted by the leading clique of the day—then that person is just as quickly abandoned for one who does. Our man cannot afford to be seen compromising his public persona by supporting anyone other than those who are seen as gaining positions of political leverage—*at speed.* This is done in the sure knowledge that his literary endeavours are far from laudatory, having remained on a plateau of mild but ineffectual achievement for decades. His prose style is at once 'positive' but still non-committal, underplaying the salient points of the author's strengths by patronizing his 'agreeability' within the existing pantheon of writers; a style in which he appears to say *something*, but in effect, is giving away *nothing*. This man has all the nonce of a well-seasoned old campaigner and knows how to hedge his bets with the best of them. His weekend hobby is restoring old valve radios and/or collecting 1950s film posters.

At this stage in his journey he has discovered that an 'act' or 'image' is pretty much the order of the day. But which one—who or what is the best role model? He tries a couple of combos; beat and/or beatnik, pipe and horn-rimmed specks, frantic artist—huge canvases sprayed with paint pots—and for a while it's fun riding a bicycle over them, and selling them off a la Pollock as *bona fide* works of neo-abstraction: *Cyclical Series No. I, Reclining*, and *Cyclical Series No. 2, Awakening.* Henry Miller (he has read the *Tropic of Cancer*) is invoked as his sexual guru and liberator. He buries himself in the grid system as 'a cage for the *tortured* soul', but this form demands true vision that obviously he does not possess, despises, in fact.

Finally, as he does not suffer from either a bi-polar or schizoid disorder, and isn't on the requisite 'medication' which he believes is integral to this role, he feels that there is little advantage *to himself* in continuing with that particular charade, and so abandons it. Besides, the huge quantities of alcohol that must accompany this stance are by far too ruinous and would soon blunt his opportunistic edge. The one thing that demands consistency is great cunning and an unflagging vigilance. After all, emptiness is a very big thing to hide. And never let a chance go by *babe*—especially where women are concerned.

By degrees, he falls into meanness. He achieves optimum ordinariness. If you are an Australian, you will be aware that Sydney is the best place to set up such a rort. Sydney is a town where people can freely believe in their own bullshit, and everyone is prepared to believe it along with you; this mutual acknowledgement demands a fine balancing act, a peculiar generosity. To not play this game, that is, to be honest in a supplicating way, is to be made anathema—become social outcast as opposed to acceptable social pariah. Once you've got that procedure under control, from thereon in, social acceptance is a summertime breeze, a mere formality.

The object lesson here is: *seen to be seen*. Especially with women, *again*, women as sexual object. Women as acquisition. Any woman is fair game; no mercy need be shown to other people's wives— 'When we first met on the bus, man, it was *good morning*, wasn't long before it was *good morning darling*'—and, unhesitatingly, anybody else's girlfriend. Women are paramount in all these social manoeuvres; they belonged to that social code of prestige by which our 'composite poet' measured others, and in this light, regards women as trophies, as living endorsements of his own self-gratifying ego, while the business man by contrast, not quite as 'enlightened', would regard them in similar circumstances as mere dinner party ornaments, or personal servants.

As to the teaching profession, students saw through his act in an instant, and realized that he was simply out to impress with image-sans-substance. But then, secrecy and duplicity were important weapons in maintaining the illusion of the hip and the cool designed at least to give the impression that he was actually *someone.* This had the effect of compounding his authoritarian personality in the workplace, and especially at groovy soirees around his 'rustic' table, and these 'literary' gatherings he invariably orchestrated on his own turf. He became the control freak; put-downs and power plays were the one sole currency. On those few occasions when he had to attend various other social gatherings—writers' centres, or the obligatory literary function, he would act the flaneur (let the 'chicks' come to him), be noticed by all means, but never appear to be the slightest bit ruffled, or at least, not in public. His androgynous disposition displayed itself in a bitchy undermining of other people's achievements (which he obviously felt threatened by), and in unaccountable eruptions of anger, like sunspots from the core hatred of his being—especially as he got older, but only in a one-on-one basis; that is, if he thought he could get away with it without witness. The schoolyard bully in his element.

The truly gifted, who refused to present a mask to the world, he loathed like no other. By way of a counterweight, he was regarded in the school staff room with intense distaste, especially by the up-and-coming (very PC), young gay and progressive, hipster teachers, well informed and out to make a name for themselves. Usually distinguished by either red or blue-rimmed designer spectacles. No question, careerist to their bootstraps. He was as relevant to them as an outdated combine harvester—something left over from another age; an irrelevancy—a free loader from the Whitlam era, when funding was thrown at anybody who cared to call him or herself an 'artist' which launched the careers of many a 'successful' and mediocre talent.

In short—our man seen as a dinosaur. Such a charge he would readily admit to, if for no other reason than to give himself the air of the misunderstood working-class hero. A sort of, retro-exclusivity. Still boasting the charismatic outsider he never was. Although his presence in the teaching profession was detested by student and teacher alike, much as one would an abandoned corpse in a hospital corridor, the sentimentalist in him (such is the emotional fascist at heart) wished it were otherwise.

Next, he must choose the correct location to live in and to give credence to his image. Gentrified working-class inner city suburbs meant that you sided with the lumpenproletariat. Your brand of coffee and choice of wine might suggest to the reader of *Village Voice*, or even the *New York Review of Books*, the consummate host and connoisseur. This could be forgiven (understandably, not everyone could successfully aspire to the lofty heights of a Robert Hughes) under the guise of bohemian generosity, and in establishing a reputation within your small neighbourhood as an hospitable, though not recognizably sartorial, host.

Our poet had to remember that 'contrivance' must appear haphazard, casual. He dressed down. As to the suburbs and environs, the choice came down to (in Sydney) Rozelle, Balmain and the Blue Mountains—or he may even consider a riparian existence on an 'unpolluted' waterway; the arch sentimentalist disguised as the arch lyricist. In Melbourne, Clifton Hill, Brunswick and Apollo Bay—yet the migratory paths along the east coast of Australia are a two-way flight path; and he might decide (use-by date: mid-30s) to head toward Byron Bay, or up to Mullumbimby, to nurture sweaty dreams of breeding and/or leaping upon the grooviest politically correct eco-bandwagon. In Wellington, Mt. Victoria, Newtown, Island Bay and Paekākāriki. In Auckland, Ponsonby, Grey Lynn and Piha, and extending as far as the Coromandel (home of the legendary, albino possum) Peninsula.

He did not consider himself a prolific writer, producing just enough 'cut & paste' and 'collage' verse to maintain a social profile, or pulse. His first book titled, *Getting It Up For You*, was published in the late '60s through the Woof & Weft

Press who then put out regular small print runs of poetry to an even smaller readership. This book celebrated the sexual game-playing antics associated with the 'woolly' idealism of that era, and served as a record of his real and imagined conquests within a radius of maybe five kilometres. Sort of a *dirty bomb poetic*. Strategies, parties and ruses planned before the narcissistic backward-looking reflection of his bathroom mirror. One poem from this collection will serve as a fairly typical example of the style:

HEY BABE!

Anyway, no way
          so I said to Nicole
'Stay!' don't go (for the day)
          oh, what a night
let me   take you down to the river
between your thighs
          babe, let my love flow
& do you see stars in your eyes (ha)
                                                  still?
          (Yeah) so don't go
help me up by your love handles
          'cause love is in the air
 & couscous on the menu
          so I said to Nicole
'Stay!' don't go (for the day)
          oh, what a night
but by then she had split.

This is perhaps his most anthologized piece and contains about all anyone needs to know about his philosophy on life, such as can be deduced. Rarely would he submit a poem to the small literary magazines because such an attitude he considered too demeaning, unless of course approached by the editors. His work appeared in very few literary magazines during the intervening periods between publishing two or three books with titles like (aside from the one already mentioned) *Bird*

Dog Man, *Bad Bitch Poems* and maybe *I Dreamed I Was A Jazz Giant*, published over a period of about 30 years.

Anthologies were the prestige publications he sought, believing that this provided irrefutable evidence of his prominent contribution to generations of hip poets, and the legacy of literature generally. The fact that anthologies paid a bare minimum to poets for their inclusions—and served as a ready-made money spinner for large publishing houses who might be fortunate enough to market through the education and library systems, with an outside chance of international distribution—didn't particularly phase him in the least. Given his narrow-band view of life, anthologies represented acceptance by an upbeat clique, and something he elevated in his own mind to the status of privilege. As the author of this essay has written in his collection, *Ballads, Satire & Salt: A Book of Diversions* (2003):

YOU SEE THE ANTHOLOGY MAN

I am you see the anthology man,
very much the fashion, and so today,
I will let you into my little plan.

I adopt a style to seduce the fan;
(one feels *freed* in a familiar way)
I am you see the anthology man.

I shift with fashion, a chameleon,
the man for all seasons, and so today,
I will let you into my little plan.

I am a poseur but of marked élan;
(as the ego-gathering tides hold sway)
I am you see the anthology man.

A solipsist does whatever he can,
the devil take the rest, and so today
I will let you into my little plan.

Any talent challenging me I ban;
(mine is an exclusive brand of poesy)
am I you see the anthology man?
I will let you into my little plan.

The American critic and poet, Dana Gioia's provocative essay, 'Can Poetry Matter', first appeared in *The Atlantic Monthly*, in May 1991. In it he contends that poetry has become a subculture that has lost its link with a wider, reading public, and is now relegated to academic institutions and the endemic factories of 'poetry-as-product' otherwise known as creative writing schools. His essay immediately precipitated reaction and counter-reaction from teacher-poets and literary critics alike. His remarks on poetry anthologists I find unerringly relevant and satisfyingly instructive:

'A clubby feeling also typifies most recent anthologies of contemporary poetry .... More than one editor has discovered that the best way to get an anthology assigned is to include work by poets who teach these [creative writing] courses ... many of these anthologies give the impression that literary quality is a concept that neither an editor nor a reader should take too seriously.

The editorial principle governing selection seems to have been the fear of leaving out some influential colleague. Poetry subculture no longer assumes that all published poems will be read. Like their colleagues in other academic departments, poetry professionals must publish, for purposes of both job security and career advancement. The more they publish, the faster they progress. If they do not publish, or wait too long, their economic futures are in grave jeopardy. The slow maturation of genuine creativity looks like laziness to a committee. Like subsidized farming that grows food no one wants, a poetry industry has been created to serve the interests of the producers and not the consumers. And in the process the integrity of the art has been betrayed. Of course, no poet is allowed to admit this in public.'

Such beneficence is yet to be bestowed upon our man. So, to return to the profile. At intermittent periods throughout his career, and according to the fashion of the moment, he will produce the occasional cyclostyled or Gestetner-produced literary magazine (collated and stapled at his rustic dinner table), with a careful blend of women and post-beat writers, though mostly emerging, and young women writers—a tokenism offered up by the 'boys' club' to offset criticism of nepotism—the gamble being that one or two will become famous down the track, thereby ensuring literary and historical relevance in the great scheme of things, with short, informal poems reminiscent of a text-speak, and hip self-help snippets from real estate and travel advertisements, smirky off-the-wall and zany personal contact notices like 'Fun loving Sagittarian seeks leather-clad chanteuse for meaningless relationship', revamped Robert Crumb and Archie type cartoons, mixed in with found and concrete poems, list poems, urban cowboy and anti-intellectual poems, dope and Dada poems, poems about oral sex and poems about the oral tradition in a bleary-eyed production of retro '60s nostalgia and bric-a-brac couched in a North American patois with a flavour of 'throw-away' disposability about it. A Poets' Digest of small-town flapdoodle.

It should be noted here that although Dana Gioia states in his new 'Introduction To The Tenth Anniversary Edition' of *Can Poetry Matter?* (August 2002, Graywolf) that a good deal has changed for the better in the promotion of (American) poetry—and that it now reaches a broader demographic base than ever before through radio programmes, festivals, newspaper columns, the internet, etc (the same largess, however, does not apply to the Australian poetry scene where the opposite appears to be happening) beyond the academic institutions, he notes, too, 'that the state of poetry criticism and reviewing remains deplorable'.

Doubtless understandable, when you consider that the conservative mind will invariably react with fear, even hatred when challenged; this applies to a particular underclass of book reviewer, happy enough to pass off ill-considered opinion and ignorance as informed, critical judgement. The democratic process may be the 'guardian of free speech', but it simultaneously lets into the backyard the rabid dogs of bias, bigotry and personal agenda. Without question, the biggest backyard operating at present is the internet. An open range playground for the dispossessed.

Internet zines then might run to maybe five or six issues over a two-year period and then cease. A banner title would sound an attitude in the manner of STOKED [or] GET OVER IT, BUKOWSKI'S BABY—even, dare I say it, published under the imprimatur, WAY COOL UNLIMITED. This proves to be an effective DIY exercise using outdated technologies that illicit a peer-group nose sniffing and an indulgent, passing interest amongst the younger literati. As a ploy in drumming up pre-publicity for our man's next book of poems, advertising and selling through public readings and putting in for literature grants, this works well enough.

As a strategy, this is no answer to such institutionalized national magazines as The *NZ Listener*, for instance, and, increasingly, celebrity coffee table magazines like *The Australian Book Review*, or any number of assorted dailies with their 'token' book review supplements (little more than outlets for commercial, 'establishment' book publishers, those servants of the multi-nationals), tired old matriarchs of the mainstream, limping dowagers of conventional taste still aping the mannerisms of post-World War Two literary mores like the *New Statesman* or *The Spectator*. Stylistically groaning under the weight of 'precious' advertising copy, outdated cryptic crossword puzzles, and celebrity interviews, stricken by interchangeable book review editors who align themselves in the most partisan fashion to popular taste, whose editorial judgements often as not are informed by 'suspect' third party recommendations, and the dirty politics of the literary rumour-mill. Journalist hacks who wouldn't know a bard from a Buick, an ode from an omelette. Journeymen, without a creative bone in their bodies, whose cultural refinement exists in an uncanny ability to kowtow before the established presses of the day, and to take advantage of every A-list dinner party thrown their way by the self-proclaimed, 'official' arbiters of public and literary taste. Such an editor is the equivalent of a 'rent boy' within the literary industry. It is provincialism taken to its snobbish extreme, easily associated with quasi-European centres like Melbourne, for instance.

Australia, geographically the larger of the two countries, will dismiss the artist out of casual indifference; New Zealand, the smaller, out of unambiguous malice; the first is attributable to an expansive, yet cultural looseness, the second to a narrow and self-conscious insularity. The rotting carcass of puritanism. I had observed in an early poem, 'Welcome, To The Pace Train' in my collection, *Guardians, Not Angels* (1993) that New Zealand reminded me of 'a country shaped like a broken hand gun'. On reflection, it is a little more ragged round the edges, closer in shape to that of a half-gnawed chicken bone. For me, coming to Australia in the mid '80s was more a case of leaping 'out of the fire' into the 'frying pan'.

Our composite poet (and he is, necessarily, a chameleon) might have diverged slightly in career paths though he is governed by much the same motivation; and it must be remembered that poets share much the same mildly psychotic condition: 'don't trust your fellow poet and better him or her at every given opportunity'. Petty jealousies are exacerbated in part because there is very little money in the way of grants and residencies with stipends, or not enough monies to go around, and even fewer publishing opportunities open to poets; they are like dogs tearing themselves apart over the same old mouldy bone, to paraphrase the American novelist, Richard Ford. Unless he is an academic, of course, something of an El Dorado to the poet.

Travel, money, power, authority are at his fingertips. Alternate options for the non-academic poet are school-teacherly positions, petty bureaucrat in a government department (drainage or engineering), an assistant editor in a small publishing house; journalism (for the mid-career poet), and copywriting (for the younger poet). And of course, ubiquitous creative writing institutions, adjuncts of the university English Department—all empire building exercises.

If he has had dealings with the visual arts, as critic, he may chance an appointment at a 'Conservatorium of Hipster Art' and happily cease to write altogether. Composite poet number one. This means that, after an absence of a decade or so, he can then burst back upon the literary scene with a new book (and remember, our man is a consummate chameleon), and depart the Conservatorium like the Pharisee rending his garments on the steps of the temple, imploring his God (and the book buying public) to forgive him his adulation of false idols and the promulgation of sophistries which fooled an entire, now aging, generation.

He proceeds then to claim allegiance with the classical traditions, but who? Juvenal and his *Satires*, Catullus, the Odes of Horace (no, done to death by all and sundry), Virgil's *Georgics* or Theocritus *Idylls*. Hardly, he lives in a country altogether smothered in sheep (as are both Australia and New Zealand, or were; the latter now being trampled to death by cattle), and this would leave him feeling bloated and quite claustrophobic. Something with a rational edge is called for to temper those unaddressed issues of family, and hitherto disregarded filial sensitivities in previous works. He settles on a combination of four Roman poets of the Augustan Age: Propertius and his 'choleric intensity', Ovid and his 'sanguine coupling', Virgil and his 'phlegmatic musings', and Horace, with his 'melancholic equipoise'. For here we have, as Joseph Brodsky so neatly put it, the standard representations of the 'four known humours'.

Unfortunately, the collection, titled *Cantos for Connoisseurs*, proves to be at once flat and prosaic, sickly sweet, and in his attempt at *gravitas* and sincerity, mere block sentiment. His knowledge of traditional forms essentially only goes back to Ezra Pound or Charles Olson! Yet like many poets of his generation, he had simply picked up on 'attitude', a synonym for what is *dernier cri* and not the discipline which informed it; his work, unsurprisingly, exhibits a cardboard, two-dimensional perspective. A brand-new dishonesty.

The book is trumpeted a success amongst the dinner-party set (he includes a few mock ancient recipes *vis a vis* poems, only too well aware that cookery books are best sellers) of Remuera and Parnell in Auckland, Khandallah and Oriental Bay in Wellington; in Sydney, a hit in the Eastern suburbs and especially, Vaucluse and Double Bay; in Melbourne, a gracious acceptance in Toorak and South Yarra. O happy days! Welcome the return of the profligate son from the corporate wilderness. Let us lift our glasses of *curaçao* and sigh in collective, groovy relief. The fashion for sincerity and reinventing one's self takes off like wild fire amongst the high rollers and the CBD art brokers and investors.

He's also mildly sympathetic to his 'other', the less frantically received composite poet number two, the one who as a confirmed outsider lives by choice in a downbeat suburb, who might run a second-hand bookshop in an old hippy neighbourhood—maybe selling a little dope on the side to make ends meet, working as a garbo, or doing a postie run in an Alsatian-infested housing estate—or if seriously into employment (married, for instance, with a few dependants), driving a cab at night with a monkey wrench under the seat. It is toward composite *poet number two* that our man turns to first when he launches his book, and with whom he will do a select number of readings to endorse his anomic 'street cred' and new new-found popularity. Is he not, after all, still that same self-styled, establishment-destroying Aeneas his publicity machine made him out to be in the early days of his career?

Whatever the answer, funding belongs to those at the top end of the pecking order, and as a result, there is never enough to go around at any one time in this yearly lottery. As to International Literary and Arts festivals, these are the Elysium Fields of the Booker Prize Award Winners and the Queens Medal for Poetry recipients, and for those few academic poets and others—who are duly appointed, or those who are kept as token representatives of the craft (as a tax write off) by the mainstream university publishing houses—who can wangle their way through nomination committees to make up the numbers. Poetry governed by Machiavellian principles of duplicity, and the muse in such quarters is long dead and buried.

I close with a brief word on anthologists. These overseers of literary governance sit at the head of the publishing table, and might be seen as Master Carvers, serving up select cuts of prime verse from the herds of poet graduates grown and produced for the bland palate of popular consumption, and taken from the overstocked paddocks of creative writing schools, affiliated in the first instance with the English Departments of our universities, accountable for the pollution of the poetic waterways and rivers of the literary landscape with an excessive run off of lesser poetic talent. This identifies the anthologised poet as the sanctioned and marketable brand, and by implication, poetry 'prime cut'. A majority endorsement by the literary establishment; a self-appointed shareholding of academic investors, editors and publishers, intent upon exclusivity and hidden agenda as literary law makers, all the while claiming that the selection process is non-partisan, democratic, and absolutely transparent.

This is achieved by strategically culling out from the herd a handful of up and coming would-be poets (anthologies of neglected ethnicities is a winner) not yet associated with the official publishing houses of poetry (university presses in New Zealand), seen as not presenting any foreseeable threat to the established order of things, because either they do not possess the clout, or on acceptance into the ranks of the anthologised by the aforementioned 'Grand Carvers', are tacitly expected to keep their critical mouths shut. That is, if indeed they are to progress further in their publishing careers with funding and writers' residency pay offs. These methods of 'passive intimidation' are the same tactics employed by political dictatorships in any era, benign or otherwise. Toe the party line or perish. One awaits the advent of the 'Poets' Spring' with some interest.

Song Of The Immigrant

The early '50s. Salute our newly arrived man in Australia, though just a little too late for the Snowy River Scheme. If we were beginning a short story, we might describe him like this: 'his pants fell to regulation refugee length, his ankles showing pale and grey, which gave him a discarded, scarecrow look, an *ersatz* suit buttoned tight across the sternum.' Or again, it might be a family photograph. When that immigrant first landed, did he immediately fall in love with 'this sunburnt country'—what did he see or rather, what did he imagine that he saw? Rectangular buildings, many and squat, even the skyscrapers (when he got to see them), for perspective distorts fragility, looked like larger structures of the same rectangular and regular-sided form. No baroque or rococo architecture here (isn't this what all big cities were like?), no piazzas—only square, open car-parking spaces, mostly empty, as though waiting for history to fill them up.

Space and opportunity greeted him. Stretches of unworked hillside unrolled before his eyes like banknotes. Our man is many men, a composite figure and we shall call him, 'Babbo,' one who grew up in traditional poverty. He could be from any one of a number of small villages in the mountainous provinces of Barbagia of Seulo and Gennargentu in Central Sardinia, or Campidano in the south western region. The family estate (small), a few impoverished rocky acres, a handful of ancient olive trees, which he will vow to hold onto, though eventually, will sell off in his old age. So what he sees then is not so much a new land of unlimited agrarian potential (partially perhaps); what he sees, in effect, is his own land, the village and countryside of his birth, transformed (terra cotta to brick), fecund, endlessly more productive by the sweat of his brow. In his mind, he will be respected and honoured in his own village, even if the spirit of that village is encoded in such names as: Bundaberg, Innisfail, Caboolture, and the tropical hinterland of Queensland.

Babbo takes up cane cutting in those early, hard years, not the harvesting of olives. He is learning what it is to be Australian: pragmatic and 'blokey' like his newfound mates—to shout a round or two at the outback veranda pub and to rip the 'scabs' off beer bottles with his teeth. (The veranda: that enduring feminine principle of Australian architecture.) He is accepted on this basis and left alone. Babbo would save his earnings while the rest of his 'Anglo' mates pissed it away. He is learning to conceal his contempt under a clownish eccentricity—to break his back, and his teeth, to secure his tenure and survival in 'this wide brown land'. Babbo and his young wife (she is from the north-eastern province of Gallura) plan for the future and a move to one of the southern states. Our man in Australia, who saw it not through rose-tinted spectacles nor a theodolite for that matter, but through a banknote held up to the midday sun. Aleatory fortunes ahoy! Ah, but to choose the right moment, throw the dice for NSW, and the '60s!

First stop Griffith, country NSW. Babbo spent the better part of two years working the tobacco farms in the district before heading for Sydney and its environs. In the city he found himself an assortment of menial employment; street sweeping for the Sydney municipalities and crane driving at Mascot, Sydney airport. Around this time he bought himself an old wooden cottage on a triple-block at Enfield, sufficient to grow a few flowers for market; a case of *rus in urbe.* The early '60s. So began the long and arduous penny-pinching trek toward the unassailable heights of wealth; O to be a millionaire—a single-minded pursuit to which every other consideration, family and modest comfort, was subordinated.

Babbo in the best peasant tradition was loath to spend money, except in the interests of his burgeoning flower-growing business. Centuries of grubbing around on unyielding rocky soil with a mattock had taught his kind this, 'generations have trod thee down' subservience inculcated in the privations of daily necessity. To spend money is to make a sacrifice. This does not enter into the equation. It was impossible for Babbo to entertain such a thought. If he were offered a scheme whereby he could add an additional (say) $15,000 to his capital base and, no matter how long it took, further add to his fortunes, then he would not hesitate even if this involved further personal hardship to himself and his family. His tenacity cannot be overestimated. Every activity presupposes an inherent process of bargaining. Bunch-by-bunch of flowers, week-by-week, his fortunes steadily grew.

Of course, his lifestyle, such as it was, remained that of traditional village peasant—how else could it be? This desire to communicate with his neighbour operated at a minimum within the bare, and civil, restraints of proximity. Eventually, he would impose these self-same conditions upon his 'second' wife or rather, partner. But she, too, was accustomed to the monotony of hardship and expected no more—after all, she gained provisional security in this mutual arrangement; and, if she could outlive Babbo (she could wait until the mountains moved), his fortune, or at least half of it, would go to her two daughters by a previous marriage. She could take further hardship, as easy as falling off a German tank!—whatever it took. So what else is life?

She has seen as a child the German soldiers enter her village and desecrate her family hearth—oh, she knew patience all right! Hatred and denial drove her. And focused, critical cunning. Babbo's second 'wife', a bulky, big-boned Slovenian whose first husband had maltreated her severely: an alcoholic bricklayer who would regularly beat her, who had finally left this woman stranded high and dry with limited resources. She slummocked through fifteen years of single motherhood, bolstering her bigotry and embittered *Weltenschauung* through a number of the more fascistic radio talkback hosts warping the city airwaves. The John Laws Syndrome. She, with two daughters to support on her own—she instilled into her children the self-negating virtues of suburbia, and drummed into them the imperative of securing a man, with money. Patience! Babbo and his Slovenian cohort were, in effect, ideally suited to one another in the best of utilitarian worlds. He went out into the garden and worked. She washed and cooked—and waited.

Babbo's first wife (the then traditional 'arranged marriage'), an innocent girl from the mountains of Sardinia, didn't want to work the farm 24 hours a day. Born with an innocent soul, much like her daughter, rather—she wanted to rejoice in her new found freedoms, the heady atmosphere of an adventurous young Australia in the '60s: simple things, shopping, a few new bright dresses, being taken to a dance in the weekend at the Italian club, maybe? Babbo wouldn't budge an inch. Slowly, by degree, her colours dulled and she faded, become more depressed and non-communicative. Imperceptibly, her sanity became enclosed, and she retreated into a world of her own. A world of fantasy; manic-depression and anger where the distinction between some life-affirming dream and negative recall inevitably blurred, and so her spirit broke; the dignity of dream lay in a smoky haze, shattered, and she could not gauge that distinction; a destroyed person, a destroyed people, what's the difference? Babbo could do nothing for her and she refused all medical help. The stubbornness of the Sardinian character coming into play.

So it was that his intractable attitude, subservient to money and hoarding, ultimately drove her into insanity. She would end up, years later, hugely overweight, toothless; blithely out of touch with everyday reality. A 'bag-woman'. Her home a housing-commission, one bedroom unit in a brick wasteland out in the endless, western suburbs near Punchbowl. For company, she had her occasional epiphany—sudden, and brightly falling dreams of childhood in mountainous Gallura. Outlook: condition black. She bore him one daughter only—a deep and protective core of sanity at the centre of her being; the one small, tidy room she kept lit in the back of her mind for her daughter. Her goal was to die in the knowledge that her daughter was safe and secure in her own life, a life that would over-compensate for the security neither had.

So Babbo took on another life partner, but only because he was in need of someone to wash his soiled work clothes and to feed him. He was looking for a workhorse who would stand by him without question; yet he anticipated complaint. A harridan. And he found one—there were numbers to choose from, and here we must remember that feminism, being largely a white, bourgeois, and privileged phenomenon, did not in any way affect these immigrant women or their disadvantaged lives; the media appeal was absent—yes, contracted a partner from the principal multi-cultural or 'ethnic' centres in the far western districts, the Italian, Club Marconi. But long before any of this came to pass, Babbo had found a house in Enfield with a small patch of ground to cultivate in a time when Sydney still knew the clatter of trams. Every day by tram with his 'carry-box' of flowers to the old *Paddy's Market*, every day for years, making his few pennies by the bunch, 'firsts' and 'seconds' though he mainly made his money on 'seconds'. A dollar here, a dollar there.

The day came when he had enough capital to move out of the city (which he detested) to a larger property. He chose 'the hills district' north-west of Sydney at Galston. Babbo bought five acres and began farming flowers in earnest, five acres of virgin native bush in the Hornsby District that had to be cleared, despite objections from the several hippy communes which had sprung up in the district in those days, or from his pottery making, 'whole earth catalogue' neighbours. He cleared the land right down to the last Waratah, and he cleared it right down to the last square inch that his deeds of title legally allowed. His was the 'scorched earth policy' and the most effective agents which allowed him to utilize every square foot of his land were the biocides (more correctly, defoliants) 'Phosdrin' and 'arsenic'. While one portion of his land so treated lay fallow, another would be under active cultivation through a system of continuous rotation. Babbo made his fortune growing: chrysanthemums, carnations, calendula, roses (most varieties), gypsophila, everlasting daisies, candytuft, sunflowers, stock, statice, cornflowers. Late night 'bunching' and early to market, from 4am to 7am, three days a week. A fist full of dollars.

In the early '70s, he sells up and again relocates. The old trams are long gone (he has owned a truck for some years), and Paddy's Market has moved to Flemington. Babbo buys another five acres out at Arcadia and begins the whole process of land clearing all over again; stripping the native bush, laying traps for neighbourhood animals unlucky enough to have strayed onto his property, plus the generous application of 'Phosdrin' and 'arsenic' to destroy the insects. Arsenic by now has been banned as a highly toxic substance, but this makes little difference to Babbo's time-honoured farming practices and he continues, surreptitiously, to use it. He is a man set in his traditional, diurnal ways (with a little help from his poisons), and he has no intention of changing, not for anyone! What do they know about hard work, eh? Australians are a lazy lot by nature; they drink, they boast about what they are going to do, they do nothing!

These 'Anglos' believe their own lies as truth and that is why nothing gets done. No traditions, that is why! Life has got to be hard otherwise it's not worth it. What else can you do? *'Australiani sono poltroni'*, which for him signifies, 'Australians are lazy!'

Our man in Australia will hold to these views throughout his long, monochromatic, peasant existence. He is, without apology, an arch-conservative and progressively right wing in exact proportion to his accumulating wealth, which is his only yardstick to personal achievement. Babbo is 'blue-ribbon' and a staunch Liberal Party supporter in this brave new world, all the way to the bank, though, in his case, a foreign bank. He is the property of no man; he came here with nothing but a suitcase. He made something; and he thinks, 'So what if my story is told a thousand times, who cares if people laugh, what I have done is me, it is original, and that is because I have done it and felt it. Laugh if you must! you are nothing to me'. What is style? Style is polished anonymity. What Babbo had wasn't style but, given his assured métier, the next best thing; denial, that is, single-minded dismissal of other people's sensitivities in the pursuit and execution of his objectives; a razor-sharp survival instinct which promised success as its own reward (though translated into hard currency), denial as motivation, a peasant farmer with corporate attitude. When Babbo bought into Arcadia, it was already a going concern, an established orchard farm: fig, orange, peach, plum, nectarine, etc.; the land had been 'civilized'. His previous property at Galston was an entirely other, 'barbaric' proposition. The transition from comparative domestic ease of Enfield to Galston coincided with the deterioration in his marriage, and the ensuing divorce (unofficial), during the progressive move from relative security and comfort, to pioneering hardship. Before the 'divorce' Babbo irrevocably 'down sized' his Sardinian wife to rank of drudge. Yet the new world and its sudden freedoms drove her into isolate madness. Hers is not the successful immigrant's story.

The native bush and scrub on the property at Galston in those early days grew so thick you couldn't walk through it; mature blue and ghost gums, and an impenetrable understorey—his property a habitat for wallabies and all diversity of smaller creatures, from possums, bats, rabbits, to an army of funnel-web and red-back spiders, black and brown snakes, red-bellies, and the harmless green tree snake. Everything that grew, moved, flew or crawled was heaped upon burning pyres until the entire five acres lay stripped bare and smoking as if some marauding Roman legion had passed that way in an orgy of plunder and devastation. A land ready for tillage, excoriated. So too had his original wife's personality been 'levelled'. No resplendent Eden here, just an end game: Babbo, the power of one. 'This land is your land, this land is my land, from the Gulf of Carpentaria to the Great Australian Bight, from the Riverina to The Mallee ... this land was made for the likes of you and me, mate!'

Babbo has owned his 'car-space' or *slab of concrete* where he sold produce at the Flemington market for about twenty years; perhaps the oldest flower grower still active in the business? His car-space, when he comes to sell it, will fetch upwards of $80,000. He has made his fortune (mainly from 'seconds'), and is close to the end of his working life, though gnarled and strong like an old olive tree, as he closes in on his 80th year. But to stop! to retire! Such a prospect produces rising waves of panic and sleepless nights; even the regular evening (and morning) shot of scotch doesn't seem to help, and his blood pressure rises like his profit margin. To stop perchance to spend? There is no alternative for Babbo, it is not within the peasant code, for what else can he do but work, it is the whole 'transplanted' Sardinian *raison d'être.*

He will go on as long as he is able and probably drop dead in a paddock which is fine by him. Even in retirement he will tend his farm and return it to natives and gums. The completion of a life, 360 degrees back to the original, arboreal state. The overriding fear is that if he stops work he is finished, dead. The system he has had in place over the years must be maintained. Sufficient capital on record to run the business, for which he keeps $100,000 or so in the local bank, is regularly topped up. Otherwise, monies are buried in tightly sealed glass jars all over his property. At the end of each fiscal year he takes out large sums undetected and certainly unknown to the Inland Revenue Department. His first stop without fail is always *Roma*. A simple and most effective system of transfer—he hides money belts about the capacious person of his Slovenian workhorse 'wife'. This practice has been going on for decades, regular as the seasons.

In this way, Babbo is able to lodge small amounts of monies under different names in a dozen or so accounts belonging to non-existent relatives. Some investment goes into property and his home village in Sardinia, but the greater part is lodged at international banks in Roma on healthy, long-term interest rates. Given his cash flow, he is not entitled to an Australian pension. His Arcadia property is now worth around half a million at this time, yet there is no money in flower growing any longer, and Babbo is advancing now into his early eighties, toward the multiple bypass operation that awaits him; yet he believes himself relentlessly fit. He remains taciturn, deeply suspicious of his fellow man. He is as miserly as ever. 'Let them fight amongst themselves for the spoils *after* I am gone,' he reasons, 'but for now I will do precisely as I have always done as long as I am able. The rest is not my concern.'

Babbo will, when the time comes, unshakeably honour Sardinian peasant tradition and sign assets over to his one daughter who also shares her mother's innocent soul, though tempered with peasant cunning. He will have his Australian pension. In his dotage his daughter may yet be required to care for him. He reasons: 'She can deal with claims and counter-claims. She can deal with the legal wrangles'. Meanwhile, dear reader, spare a thought for his original wife, the lost and innocent one finally ignored by Babbo and her own relatives alike. She will dream of stone bridges, valleys. 'Below on the right stretched the concave valley, tapestried with cultivation.'[1] Something glowering, or should that be lowering? Shrouded, certainly. Many times she has conjured up her curse.

AMONGST VINE LEAVES [2]

for Pina Ricciu

She is young, your mother amongst vine leaves—
head thrown back in a gesture of sensual impatience
for the harvest festival, maybe, her face belonging
to sunlight that falls low over the hill where she stands
amongst the vine leaves on a Sardinian hillside,
close by her village—dreams as clear and bright as

the air which envelops her. She feels she ought to be
elsewhere, amongst laughter and song, and all the
young men of the village circling her in slow dance—
as in a tryst she would make with herself in the
bedroom mirror—the scented breath of night, cool
and secretive, she dreams of her lover who will carry

her away to far off places of fashion and glitter
promised by American movies, long silvery streets seen
from skyscrapers, New York accents, the sun warm
upon her bare arms, she stands forever in the vineyard
in that black and white photo, leaves autumn dry, ready
to drift and scatter about her feet, at harvest time.

If Babbo, either by blood or choice, did not truly belong to Australia, what settler in any historical time frame did? When does history and ownership begin? Who are the legislators of place and belonging? Long before bigotry and prejudice kicked in (if ever there existed a pre-racist phase in the development of Homo sapiens), these propositions flooded on the currents; those migratory questions in the blood of man, if you will.

Let us suppose the existence of a conscience as blank and flat as the interior of Australia, a people without any historical conduit, devoid of introspection or subjective reckoning. Where a country is without history the only course open to it is to build, and building as we are all aware, involves first the removal of pre-existing structures, first nation peoples and cultures; large volumes of earthworks (building sites, trenches), a material ideally suited to erasure and burial. For a people who possess neither conscience nor history, language becomes the tool of rationalization, a device expedient in maintaining the necessary conditions of denial or emptiness. What is not realized of course, is that most mistakes mature into present guilt. What evolves is a culture of forgetting, founded not in measured historical tradition, but in a centrifugal dynamism, a speedy lifestyle in other words. Momentary retention is the name of the game, what was once termed the 'thirty-second grab' mentality, which these days is pretty much down to 'five' seconds. A *culture of amnesia* taken to its logical extreme within the precincts of its mercantile centre, Sydney; and Sydneysiders possess an endless capacity to promulgate and believe in their own mendacity. In short, they believe their own bullshit.

If there is one distinctive feature or characteristic of this people, it is one of non-confidence (parading as youthful confidence), not forgetting non-history (parading as economic rationalism). Youth, too, as a prototype, may generally be regarded as purveyors of pretentiousness, shape-shifting, and the mercurial-mannered disposition toward an external world—*out there*. The much-vaunted brashness of youth is little more than an inherent reality-check, a mechanism designed to facilitate self-doubt, questioning, change. Youth is indefinable aside from the hyperbolic mannerisms claimed by the advertising industries who regard this demographic as their own private investment portfolio. In national terms, that change is recognised as *projected economic growth*, yearly treasury forecasts and the lurid glare of fiscal entitlements. Welcome the emergence of a new tribal grouping, not only the (now defunct) 'dot com' brigade, but the 'bankophiles', to coin a term.

Prehistoric man may have built bonfires on promontories

as beacons to guide migratory ancestors from beyond the horizontal cloud. Today, in a comparable atavistic gesture, we build 'holiday-resorts' and signal to our fellow investors that the soul's magic has ceased to be a threat, and is now dead. Here the predisposition is toward the factitious, rather than the fictitious mind. We first built churches at the beginning of the medieval era in memory of the already fading forests that we were then despoiling—hill folding upon hill in 'mast heads'. Standard church architecture is built around the design of the cross (or cross roads), yet at one pagan level the layout pays homage to the forest canopy and the interlacing of branches over ancient grottoes, as the 19th century English poet, George Darley, illustrates in his long symbolist poem, *Nepenthe:*

> Shadowy aisles of pillared trees
> Now my errant fancy please,
> Dim cathedral walks like these;
> Nave by numerous transepts crost,
> Each in his own long darkness lost,
> Cloister and chancel, thick embossed
> Their roofs with pendant foliage, thro'
> Whose fretted branchwork richly pours
> The sun, in golden order due,
> His bright mosaic on the floors.

Ley-lines? 'there's a rumour in the bush as the optic-fibre goes around', the spinning, tourbillion sun, signs and portents, good snake-oil obsessions, the vanishing-point of the super-highway *vis a vis* cyberspace clicking-on to create a brand new 'inscape' (an endless scroll down menu), and an environment plenty more habitable than the cindered interior of Australia. Salute the mid-morning glare of the Techno-Mythic Age. Most of the ancient mythologies, that is, the Greco-Roman polytheism, no longer exist as a belief system (acid rain and oil spillage played its part), a classicism re-routed into a multiplicity of sub-academic disciplines. Christian monotheism (aside from its latter day incarnation as TV 'Game Shows'), has become increasingly unsubstantiated and somewhat opaque, an unworkable proposition on a *walk-through-the-mall-of-life* basis; eastern religions—especially a nuclear-capable Islam, gathering its skirt into a knot of fanaticism—hard-pressed and up against the adamantine demands of western materialism.

In the western democracies, the individual is forced into a position, pointedly, of needing to believe in, at least, something which invariably proves false (a marriage, a job, relationships, a lottery or even in the existence-period itself), thus the overvaluing of *choice* as a commodity—and like most unfulfilled expectations, is left with a residue of guilt and subsequent loss. 'A Big Thirst, in fact, I think I've got it now!' blares the beer commercial, filling up our screens with the hard yakka, sheep and four-wheel-drive blokey-loving bustle under a red and muscle-bound sun. This has more to do with slapping an intractable landscape into shape than with the cool fountains of Apollonian reason and any slaking of thirst.

If there were two Uluru rocks, you can bet your euro-dollar one would be intagliated with the patrician faces of founding fathers and politicians—accessible via monorail, of course! with a plaque boasting 'Our fathers of the Desert': Leichhardt, Sturt, Yagan, Ruddock (Commissar of Desert Compounds), King Wally Lewis., et al. *Homage to God as Stockman*; optional extras, corporate cowboys and media barons solidly merchandized. 'Take one home as a paperweight. Your very own pet rock.' Not quite sacred-site calibre but, nevertheless, a fine beginning toward a utilitarian mythology. A flat land in search of elevation, a dry continent seeking out the cultural sweetmeats as we stomp off into the next chiliad, digital footprints kicking in the door of the solar system and feeling, in the depths of our mainframe, that we may have passed this way before. The following is taken from my poetry collection, *Either Side The Horizon* (2005):

48. OCCUPATIONS

Advance: O Let us boast a standard gauge
one rail one nation; applaud a Republic on track,
a history laid to rest optically; a white picket
fence for every home; a bar-code for every
gene; the Blackfella Hall of Fame: *Australia*.

[1] *Sea and Sardinia*, D.H. Lawrence, Penguin Books, England/New York, 1945.

[2] *LUXEMBOURG*, Stephen Oliver, Greywacke Press, Canberra, 2018.

Welcome To Karst Country

I

I landed with a thump in Te Kuiti, a small rural township in the King Country, North Island, NZ, late 2006 from Australia, having spent twenty years in 'that wide brown land', and found an old rickety wooden house (complete with Klondyke pot-bellied stove), on a hill overlooking the valley and township. So it was I realized my dream of finding a humble dwelling with a sweeping prospect where I could be left to my own devices to write, chop firewood, and relish the quietude. I occupied myself in various free-lance capacities around town, giving voice instruction to the kids of farmers' wives, the only folk who had any disposable income; but not only young kids, there were one or two secondary school boys who required some assistance with reading and literacy. I advertised in the local rag, the *Waitomo News*, offering, 'singing & voice lessons' given voice lessons alone would not have made much sense to kids who spent most of their time watching music shows on TV.

I secured a weekly forty-five minute gig assisting with news reading, on-air delivery and production at a local community radio station. In addition, I scored the occasional one-off job, writing and voicing copy for a local retail outlet, cash in hand. Such employment was easier to secure in small towns given no infrastructure exists for such skills. I was an outlier, after all. Latterly, over a period of a couple of years, with a hiatus between October 2010 and September 2011, I wrote a weekly column for the *Waikato Times*—the provincial daily that covered the King Country adjoining the Waikato province to the north.

My final column appeared at the close of November 2012. These columns, though largely satirical in nature, and occasionally provocative, covered a far broader spectrum than simply lampooning this small rural community. You might say as a columnist I used the opportunity to springboard off into an imaginative, inner world from an otherwise isolated rural setting. However that may be, it soon dawned on me that my weekly offerings over time had divided the township into two distinct and opposing camps; those who saw the humour, and those who vehemently did not, or refused to. I have a natural inclination toward sardonic satire, as anyone who has read my poetry collection, *GONE Satirical Poems: New & Selected* (2016) will have observed. As a columnist, writing a couple of hundred words weekly (usually at one sitting) was one way to alleviate that sense of growing isolation from the larger world, the one I had recently left behind. Various of my columns over a two-year period incensed (though more theatrics than anything sinister) a certain contingent of hide-bound locals, but this I was not immediately aware of. I only saw humour overlaying a rural community that otherwise held few surprises. The day-to-day round of dairy farming, and a small town getting on with its diurnal, endlessly repetitive routine. I could not allow the dull sameness of it all to stifle me in claustrophobia with a muffled cry in my head of 'No Escape'.

I soon learnt that my efforts to wake the town from its smug lethargy were not well received by any number of folk down at the Waitomo Club. This gave the members something to grind their teeth on for want of anything better to do. Nothing changes, it just mutates. The Calvinistic beast rears up yet again—will this benighted country never be rid of it, this multi-headed, Cerberus of the soul! In one of the columns that lit the fuse, I gleefully recommended that a dam be built to 'drown the town' and turn the place into Lake Te Kuiti, complete with recreational activities like scuba diving on the drowned Waitomo Council building. Lakeside properties and water skiing activities were part and parcel of this scheme. Totally absurd, of course. But this town lived under the heel of a council who insisted upon raising rates to the second highest in the country. TK was in debt to the tune of millions of dollars for unpaid infrastructure projects; extensive road works they could not pay for. The debt accumulated and continued to do so. Outlandishly high rates meant that merchants would close as quickly as they opened.

Welcome to Karst Country, and the limestone hills are alive with the sound of gushing, pure spring water! Aside from a few citizens having free access it—why no one had set up the *Te Kuiti Fresh Spring Water Company* was a mystery to me. A natural resource waiting to be utilized for the benefit of the district. Such an undertaking, if carefully managed, could only alleviate much of the council debt (or so I thought) and by implication, encourage investment, and the lowering of sky-rocketing rates crippling the community. Yet, to this day, nothing has been done to facilitate such a life-saving, debt-reducing initiative that could only loosen the Waitomo Council's stranglehold on the good folk of TK.

I cast a wide enough net beyond the boundaries of the north King Country, and it is in this spirit that I offer two of these previously published ruminations for your entertainment in this penultimate essay, in the hope that you may find as much amusement in the reading as I did in the writing of them. I eventually left the King Country (my time was well and truly up), thankfully without being tarred and feathered, at the close of 2013, and headed north to Hamilton city in the Waikato where I currently reside at the time of my writing this. I have retained the original titles and text as conceived, along with the publication date. I should note that my original titles were not adopted by the *Waikato Times*. Editors invariably favour the more sensationalist headline as blunt statement, even if there is no evidence to justify it. Here is one of the supposedly provocative columns that stirred up the township under its original title, 'The Parade of the Big Bottom or The Lard Arse Boys', publication date, February 6, 2012:

'We are all familiar with the scrofulous plaster effigy of an obscure saint or Virgin Mary luridly bedecked in flowers with the garish painted face, wobblingly carted around the cobbled and narrow streets of some medieval, mountainous village in Italy say, and with great ceremony, deposited at the cathedral entrance in the village square, presided over by a rotund priest who then proceeds to liberally douse the ornate litter in holy water. Peasant culture is a picturesque affair. Many of these ritualistic observances originated in Neolithic times and were enacted to propitiate or pay homage to resident deities who presided over the agricultural calendar. Spring planting and autumn harvest. Birth and marriage. Life and death.

In Lower Silesia, a curious procession takes place at harvest time that has some relation to an as yet uncelebrated activity, or perhaps that should be 'inactivity' which takes place year in and year out around the Waitomo district, but more on that later. Lower Silesia is a particularly historical region of Poland and fertile agricultural area. At harvest time, the church bells are rung intermittently at midnight on September 25th every year. This announces the return of the hag. The commemoration continues for three days. It is known as "Swieto Tlustej Dupy" or "Swieto Grubodupych Chlopakow" which translates as "The Festival of the Fat-Arse or Lard Arse Boys."

How this curious event came about no one is quite sure, as its origins are buried in antiquity. The story roughly goes something like this—back in the 9th century in Lower Silesia an old hag approached one of the more eligible and handsome boys in the village and begged him for a kiss. The boy refused, and the old hag then cursed him. She was in fact, a mischievous spirit that could change into a beautiful young girl but only on the condition that a handsome youth kissed her. As a result of the old hag's curse the boy's bottom suddenly grew huge, to such an extent that he could not fit through the doorway of his house, and so he become confined to sit forlornly in front of the fireplace, destined never to marry.

So then, at the close of September in the village of Szklarska Poreba, Lower Silesia, a handsome youth is carried on a litter through the winding streets and three times around the main cathedral in the town square. He wears an oversized bustle. All the young girls arrayed in traditional costume, each wearing a beautifully hand-woven headscarf in purples and yellows, gold and emerald hues, gambol after the boy. Each girl, however, wears the mask of an ugly old hag. The girls in turn, as the litter passes by carrying the handsome youth, shout out twice to him with much giggling and shrieks, "Pocaluj stare babsko! Pocaluj stare babsko!" which means, "Kiss the old hag!" The handsome youth replies in kind with much theatrical disdain, "Pocaluj mnie w dupe!" that translates as, "Kiss my arse!" He then bends over and wiggles his "bustle" at the girls who erupt in paroxysms of gleeful laughter. This is soon followed by an alfresco banquet in the town square on trestle tables laden with meats and golden corn on the cob and much local wine. A very colourful harvest festival indeed.

We have possibly, something similar within the Waitomo district, especially in the smaller townships and rural communities. The candidates for a festival like that held in Lower Silesia, are known as the "Fat Arse Boys" or "The Lard-Arse Boys." We shall call them FAB for short and there are literally hundreds of them! FAB rarely if ever leaves the house and is looked after by his aging (Old Hag) mother.

FAB spends his entire existence waiting for the "Old Hag" to "die" so that he inherits the family house without having to lift a finger to earn it. The mother (Old Hag figure) is at once his protector and his curse. His sole function in life is to sit on his backside all day long for years, cannibalizing the fridge and spending hours in front of television or swilling back beer. Before long he is middle aged. Yet the mother-old-hag-figure refuses to drop off the twig. He grows more irascible with each laboriously passing year. His backside grows ever larger as the seasons drearily come and go. He has in fact transformed into a couch potato sloth. Why not promote this phenomenon—drag it into the open. A celebration of local custom. Once nominated, prop "Fat Arse Boy" up in the back of a stock truck with a fridge full of beer. Get his mother (if still alive and/or sane) to drive him around the district. Local girls, dressed in "Mary Had A Little Lamb" costumes, would be given the task of taunting and jeering. How FAB might respond is anyone's guess, but that's all part of the fun! A sausage-sizzle and grouse day out for the family. With stagnant population growth in the Waitomo, the rural sector needs a good cheering up. Make FAB Day a Public Holiday.'

II

A small rural community functions within its own rhythm, maintained through the circuitry generated by tradesmen who do the rounds, the electricians, carpenters, roofers, bricklayers, along with council workers attending to the daily needs of households and retailers on main street who keep the town ticking over. In many ways TK felt like a self-contained island afloat, existing solely within its own psychic and geographic bubble. A small town is a microcosm of the world at large with its family and day-to-day preoccupations, gossip and petty rivalries. There were, of course, the local oddities: the guy who dressed in skirts and plaited his hair into pigtails, thinking that he was Shirley Temple—one could easily suppose from too many acid trips in the '60s. Or the dude with the cowboy swagger and the slow roll of the shoulders, who dreamed he was some sort of country music hero, a reincarnation of Waylon Jennings maybe, yet was never seen to play a guitar though he often carried one strung loosely over his shoulder, eternally on tour with his show-stopping performance and endless applause echoing on a loop tape inside his head. Yet he never said a word in public. The hero with no name. Every small town is incomplete without its village idiot. And of course, the poet on the hill who often as not filled up the bottle bin with discarded wine bottles emptied once a week by the Waitomo garbage collectors. Nearby neighbours would fiercely whisper amongst themselves, 'He filled it up!'

The place ran on an underground network of rumour and make believe. You, as an outlier by definition, fed into it whether you liked it or not. If they didn't have something on you they would make it up. Generally, neighbours for the most part were civil enough, with one or two exceptions. One of the more disgruntled and vindictive of these, however, who unfortunately lived close by (his brother belonged to the 'FAB' cult) had 'BOAR' in bold, black letters displayed on his number plate (feral locals after feral boars), yet I always thought that he had misspelt it. I was glad of the thickening barrier of native foliage, trees and shrubs I had planted over five years or so, which would soon enough enclose me within an impenetrable wall of protective greenery. Living at the top of the hill on a corner property meant that every passing neighbour driving up and down would wave out to you in that time-honoured country tradition. Hand waving from passing vehicles is big in rural communities. One was required to similarly respond, except in the event of a funeral cortège winding its way slowly up the hill, bumper to bumper, the graveyard situated 2km further on past my place. Such salutations were integral to small town culture.

Eventually, within my green compound I was spared that obligation. Night time on my viewing deck, gazing across the valley and town below (fog rolled up the valley in the autumn and winter months), to the darkening hills beyond, the night sky, the glaring full moon and deep silence, were to me articles of faith. My deck was one of the best viewing platforms I ever had either side of the Tasman. Sydney, on the other hand, offered you pokey apartment balconies. City living and holed up in the back blocks were dimensions—worlds apart. The following two poems are taken from my collections, *HARMONIC* (2008), [1] and *LUXEMBOURG* (2018) respectively:

LONE SHUNTER

The lit, landed dish that is Te Kuiti
back flips momentarily before my eyes

into the bowl-like configuration of
Wellington harbour—those running lights,

yellow along Old Petone Road; Rimutakas
nothing yet where that bulk blackness holds.

Here, the 'lone shunter' wolfs through
the centre of town
flashing flamenco signal lights the last wagon behind.

In a small, Eastern European enclave
a laden cart over cobblestone
presupposes thunder.

I am here, a Trotsky in Te Kuiti,
the first time a black sky seen in years.

The Milky Way adrift, as smoke from
some distant campfire; krill-like, a god's wet dream.

There are women who press upon your breath
like master organ players, to make or break.

I am here, isolate,
Te Kuiti. Omphalos. Limestone country.
These hills that dip and trough could

leave you swamped, the sky a swagger.

Harrier hawk switches to remote half way between paddock
and halfway house, spiralling, radial, ever reliable stage prop.

Wind that tumbles north through trees
bringing the sound of rushing water over troubled contours.

As if in that stillness from the night before
                    the morepork had orchestrated this hour.

I am here, overseeing morning fog,
twenty years shunted to a siding the other side of the Tasman.
                    That city. *That bullwhip*. Sydney.

STILL LIFE WITH BOULDERS

Oparure Road, Waitomo

Not quite stubble, more the plucked flesh of fowl,
after the maize harvest, cut to the grain, close cropped
paddocks. An April sun draws shadows across the land,

velvety black, thick as sump oil, the air glass bright,
though filtered as if the light voltage had dimmed, but
nothing as definite as that, except for the sliding

partitions that are invisible, so that the plucked flesh
has become crew cut paddock, and barely a minute gone.
The scene slipping by seemingly so ancient every second

caught up in an eternity of stillness, and the light that
lacquers the surface of everything, shiny as an iridescent
backed beetle on line-after-line of maize stubble,

in the slow and wondrous tilt of the earth, barely audible
yet felt—each valley holds its own set of mediaeval ruins,
as if one fortified town had fallen one after the other,

reduced to foundations of stacked limestone, half buried,
boulders strewn over hillsides, loosed from some
trebuchet; violence long since returned to the underworld.

It was here in the King Country that I finally returned to the writing and completion of my epic poem, *Intercolonial*, the verse recension of this memoir, as one counterpoints the other. The poem itself I had barely begun to write, save for a handful of stanzas (life boat or coracle I would return to), put aside but never abandoned so many years before, when I switched to the writing of these essays. My very own prose *dindshenchas*, all of which were completed, except for these two closing essays, in Sydney. I completed my long narrative poem, *Intercolonial*, in TK at the close of 2012, which coincided with my shift to Hamilton. I left behind me an impenetrable enclosure of greenery. As to the quiet and anonymous existence in a small town I had anticipated and looked forward to, it did not quite work out that way. I had lit the self-righteous fuse of rectitude and counter-reaction amongst a certain conservative contingent, even prompting the then town mayor, a wealthy young dairy farmer (given to wearing expensive black leather, shiny square-toed cowboy boots), to write a letter of protest to the local rag (*Waitomo News*) and, as I soon discovered, the editor of which wrote to the *Waikato Times* demanding I be fired forthwith. Outrageous stuff by any measure. The puritan ethic rears its ugly head once again!

Curiously, the council members comprised a band of South Africans, escapees from the Apartheid era. They kept a low profile, assiduously working at their appointed tasks, clandestine as ghosts, behind the scenes. Yet no one dared speak of their influence upon the council, nor against them. The local mind set being—'be thankful for what they give us, against the "creeping filth" we are subjected to, the low life and riff raff. All things being equal, we can't complain'. Thank God for small mercies, one can only suppose. Meanwhile, the rates continued to rise every quarter, and rentals on main street continued to go bust. Isolation served as 'psychic' martial law in this and many other small rural communities burdened with precarious infrastructure and limited employment opportunities beyond shelf-stacking at the local supermarket, or working at the town abattoir. Such is the state of affairs, common as dishwater (or should that be, polluted streams the colour of rust) throughout this archipelago, which translates as claustrophobia and the 'collective mind' held to ransom. Once more, self-doubt dictates the terms of paranoia, whereas the only 'escape', one imagines, is to head for a metaphoric beach in one's daydreams, which in reality lies two hours distant from any point of the compass in this country. But then, there is always the Southern Alps and Samuel Butler's 'Erewhon'. Nowhere is somewhere, after all. It is either that, or the silences of the deep interior and narrow gravel roads toward a place like 'The Forgotten World Highway' (State Highway 43), where one might find some semblance of peace free at last to descend into a myopic madness of one's own choosing. The argument is circular—there is no escape.

Other South African escapees who had chosen to call TK their home worked for the Lines Company, and others still for local tree cutting outfits around the district. I ran into one of the so called 'pruners' who had the attitude of what I imagined was an ex-cop from the Apartheid regime, but I could have been wrong; perhaps he was just a standover guy. Least, that was the feeling I got when he leaned through my backdoor, arms bracing the doorframe, head lowered like a bull, and queried in an interrogative and curt manner if he could take a few lemons off my Meyer lemon tree. Sure, that was fine by me. He then proceeded to greedily stuff the plastic bag I gave him for that purpose, stripping off the best lemons he could find, circling the tree slowly with what seemed like contained menace, grabbing at the largest and ripest lemons. How many barbecues do ex-South African thug cops have in a week? I wondered. I suppose one could say it was an insignificant episode, and I guess it was, but I saw through the mask, and saw him for what he was. A braggart, a bully, and an arch opportunist. That Meyer lemon tree was sacred to me—it kept my liver intact!

Property was cheap enough back then though it has risen considerably with the migration of Aucklanders moving south into the provinces, given the dream of the quarter acre section is long dead and buried with insanely high property prices—not only in Auckland as the most populated of any city in the country, but Wellington, too, on a par with Auckland for crazy real estate prices; a trend that continues unabated right throughout the 'land of the long white shroud'. A curious state of affairs when you consider that the population of NZ is that of Melbourne—five million souls! Anyone thinking of setting up a small business in main street TK soon found themselves unable to sustain a viable concern owing to the outrageously high rates imposed upon them by a dictatorial council. Nevertheless, aside from these ground-level domestic grumblings, within my world on the hill there were many small epiphanies. This one alone made my sojourn in TK worthwhile. Corner lamp post at the entrance to the short, gravelly driveway onto my place. Night time. A festival of fat, gum emperor-moths eclipsing the yellow lamp light. One morepork on the wire, perfectly still; then, as if in a silent film, made its move, wings flung wide, legs and claws extended. A moth in its beak and back on the telegraph wire in a moment, the whole exercise performed as if it were a mime, in dead silence—not one sound of feathers in flight. I had never witnessed such a precise balletic, dreamlike performance.

To project oneself into an imaginative world may be as much escape as imprisonment; but in either case it is the dissolution of selfhood into the thing observed through a suspension of self-awareness or the consciousness of self. An earlier, fanciful column allowed me to escape into the South Pacific, after a fashion, in response to a peculiar incident I experienced on a trip to Auckland, and subsequent encounter with an artist (of two dimensional, overpriced canvases), which proved to be, as the night wore on, both chaotic and disastrous. This sardonic parody might be interpreted as some sort of exorcism—another mode of escape. Here is the column under its original title, 'A Cautionary Tale from The South Pacific and How a New Art Movement Was Born', publication date: September 24, 2010:

'There is a new visual art movement sweeping the country and it is called, *Tsunamism*. It was "discovered" by a gentleman called Rajah To'afa Bernstein III, a person of mixed ancestry and obscure origins. He certainly came from a humble background. Raj (for short) spent his childhood growing up on an unnamed atoll in the nor' western latitudes of the South Pacific, in a sparsely populated archipelago known as The Budgeries.

His father owned and operated a small trading post and ran a battered schooner between the islands collecting the oil of the Pango tree, a species unique to this cluster of atolls. The oil served as a lubricant especially for watch springs. To the indigenes the application of the "oil of Pango" remained a mystery as time, in these azure waters, stood still.

Tsunamism. Raj "discovered" this visual art form accidentally—often the way with great discoveries. In his case, literally. He had been imbibing large quantities of the local liquor, *Masticor*, made from the fermented flesh of an indigenous bird unique to the region, the now endangered Scrum Hen. The beverage is used symbolically in ritualistic ceremony, drunk from hubcaps, and passed around the group.

This brew, if consumed in large quantities (a hubcap full will do it), acts as an intoxicating hallucinogenic. Belligerence may also be one side effect. And many a local imbiber all too often has woken up with a head thumping like a tractor engine, sadly bruised from the night before. It is unfortunately, a pervasive social problem. Other effects associated with this highly toxic traditional drink are delusional paranoia and psychosis.

Raj stumbled home late one night in a condition we can only describe as "trashed" and, lurching about in his backyard in an attempt to find the front door, knocked over assorted cans of oils and paints from the boathouse. It was only on the following morning that revelation came upon him.

He had trodden in various open containers of paint and oil set aside that night as the family schooner was up on the slip for repairs. A never-ending task. Wood panels for the cabin replacement he found splashed in a mosaic of cresting brilliant, wave like colours and engine oil perspectives in compositions of sheer primal dynamism.

On each of the three panels was planted a paint-spattered footprint. This became his signature, his hallmark. On that bleary morning in the distant archipelago known as The Budgeries, the Nuevo Oceanic Art Movement that came to be known as Tsunamism was born.

It was not long before Rajah To'afa Bernstein III found himself discovered and transported to Auckland along with his wife and ten children. With his first exhibition he became an overnight sensation. The critics and public alike were ecstatic in their reception of this new art form: Tsunamism.

The works got larger. The canvases measuring in some instances 10 x 15 metres. Monumental compositions of high cresting waves of colour textured like tree bark overhanging, in a brilliant threat of destruction, the western centres of high culture like New York, London, Berlin—and Auckland.

Raj became the toast of the town, the darling of the Ponsonby café latte set. The *cause célèbre* at the high end of the art market, his fame reaching beyond these shores to Sydney and Melbourne—his prices commanding upwards of $350,000 for a large canvas at Christie's or Sotheby's.

His fame is the stuff of legend. Tsunamism became celebrated throughout the southern hemisphere for its distinctive "wave cresting technique", its *chthonic volcanism of the subconscious.* Raj brought prestige to The Budgeries, a hitherto stone age culture from a flyspeck atoll in the South Pacific. A place known only to a few early disreputable traders, hapless missionaries, and a handful of German ethnographers. A footnote in history.

Unfortunately, Raj having ascended to such dizzying cultural heights, fell victim to his favourite brew, *Masticor.* His compositions became increasingly discordant and implosive. A form of "cannibalism" took hold. He would compose monumental black and red compositions of flame like cascading waves—and then in a frenzy of Masticor induced alcoholic violence—take to them with a machete. On his final night he was heard to scream, "Nazis! Hitler lovers!"

They found him in his barricaded studio the next morning drowned in his own paints. The coroner stated, "Death by Misadventure". The studio was stacked with hundreds of hubcaps. The place reeked far worse than any tinny house and the fumes of Masticor were said to be overpowering. The studio was subsequently condemned and demolished. Yet on the black market—those hubcaps today fetch a very tidy sum.'

But I am not the only poet to have addressed the eccentricities of TK. In my column published in the *Waikato Times*, February 27, 2012, I quoted from two poems; the first: 'The Gunfighter' a short poem by Alistair Te Ariki Campbell, O'Sullivan, V. (Ed.), *An anthology of twentieth century New Zealand poetry*, Wellington, Oxford University Press, 1979. The second a poem titled 'Bushed' by James K. Baxter. (Weir, J.K. (Ed.), *Collected Poems, James K. Baxter*, Wellington, Oxford University Press, 1979. Two stanzas from Campbell's poem serve to set the tone:

> You will see him any day in Te Kuiti
> or Cannons Creek,
> immaculate in black
> and triggered like a panther on the prowl.
>
> *****
>
> Now he stands alone
> in the pool of his own shadow,

his wrists flexible as a dancing girl's,
his palms hovering like butterflies
over the blazing butts of his six-guns.

The prose poem 'Electrician' taken from my collection, *LUXEMBOURG* (2018) strikes a more realistic note, and our 'hero' might (to contemporize the image) be seen more in the light of the ever vigilant border guard, methodical, patrolling and protecting the parameters of the town on his daily rounds, unhurriedly attending to the needs of business and town folk alike.

ELECTRICIAN

The electrician lives in a villa of brown clinker brick with aluminium window frames high on a hill in a new subdivision. Smoky tinted glass. The young wife is seen outside on washing days. Daily, she arranges ornate flowers in white ceramic vases behind those windows. A glory of colour that cannot be seen from the outside. She keeps house. From the lounge ceiling hangs one massive crystal chandelier. They live high on the hill with other villas which look the same or that represent variations of sameness. The electrician drives to jobs all over the district six days a week in his van burnished bright with signage.

His wife who knows where he is at any given moment empowers him. She has his lunch prepared daily at 12:30 PM sharp. He stares through the smoky glass windows and says nothing or says very little. Nothing more than is necessary. Why invite indecision? The countryside seen through his windows rolls away in soft brown tones throughout the seasons.

In the middle distance, below on the flatlands, the sewage treatment pond reflects early morning light. Lake Tutae to the locals. One row of poplars, as if scrawled in italic, serve as backdrop. Even at this distance it looks like a man-made lake. Further out still, a little more to the west of where he now sits, a limestone plant, steam pumping from its stack, glows whitely at this early morning hour.

> At the bottom of the exclusive, hilly sub-division a short distance into town, the supermarket, barking brand names, bustles with the comings and goings of the townsfolk. The electrician dreams of pylons standing guard over his family and over his domain. They hum to him confidentially. Everything that switches on or off is within his jurisdiction. His sworn duty is to maintain the flow of electricity to every house and family in the district. The chandelier in his lounge burns crystal bright late into the night. Every morning he rides out to meet the call and rescue the town from zombie death.

'tutae' is the Māori word for excrement.

Te Kuiti, Gateway To The South, and so night falls on the King Country. From Fagan's Hill, the town is spread below us in a fairyland of glittering lights, changing all the time—green, amber, red, red and amber, back to green, and so we say farewell to this pleasant rural backwater, as the signal lights at the railway crossing flash a tropical green, and the night train shunts through the middle of town, gently sounding its horn, while the residents draw the curtains, and settle down for the night—one by one the shimmering TV monitors fade to black, and the townsfolk slumber and sleep.

[1] *Harmonic*, Stephen Oliver, Interactive Publications, Brisbane, 2008.

An Endless Hall Of Mirrors

'Then the Jews said to Judas: How shall we arrest him (Jesus), for he does not have a single shape but his appearance changes. Sometimes he is ruddy, sometimes he is white, sometimes he is red, sometimes he is wheat coloured, sometimes he is pallid like ascetics, sometimes he is a youth, sometimes an old man ....'—*Pseudo-Cyril of Jerusalem on the Life and the Passion of Christ [Apocrypha: 1,200 old Coptic text]*

The tradition of Plato's Academy lasted 800 years. The early Christians contributed to the destruction of the Greek and Hellenistic tradition and culture. But before that, the Romans persecuted the early Christians, and the Christians kicked back later, viciously against the pagans. Look what happened to Hypatia, the first woman mathematician, philosopher, who taught according to the precepts of the Platonic school. Killed by the Christians, dismembered, her remains dragged before a Christian edifice and burnt. The Christians scraped the ancient Greek vellum texts and wrote prayers over them. Palimpsests that obliterated memory. So much lost. One contradiction overlays another in the archaeology of human endeavour in an effort to comprehend deeper spiritual premonitions. One invasion superseding another with rapidity. Immediate transplants do not work. Take a desert plant and put it into a temperate climate and it will not take, or if it does, mutates, and subsumes the local flora. It is a case of cultural evolution on speed. The mind subsumes and calcifies under an accretion of forgetfulness.

So then, we are dealing with memory in all its guises as the reader will have observed throughout this memoir—it is a deep theme that flows throughout, and occasionally surfaces and migrates into one's consciousness, then returns once again to the subconscious depths from whence it came, yet is ever present. Memory as I understand it, functions in a circular or spiral configuration that emerges from the subconscious into the conscious mind, and what it leaves behind in its wake is what we recognize as historical record—the detritus of our actions, in other words. The collective mind is an amphitheatre that echoes and reverberates within the historical pantheon from the beginnings of time. It is coterminous with the emergence of human consciousness through reflection—a state of hyper-awareness Teilhard de Chardin neatly encapsulated as, 'animals know, but man knows that he knows'.

Memory is an endless hall of mirrors, a virtual, video feedback of recall, a silent mimicry and slow dance of incident dissolving in the twilight, extending back into the unconscious but illuminated by the conscious mind and brought to the surface, images detached, something like a hologram, a ghosting image. These images are not only what we have experienced, but may also be projections from an ancestral past or person beyond time and space, into an eternal moment, deflected from the consciousness of an ancestor attuned to that wave length, whose perception of you is coexistent with your consciousness. A thought-transfer from past consciousness to a non-existent future that yet exists in the ancestor's awareness of you, and you of him; in that one captured instant—deflected back down the endless hall of mirrors through your unconscious mind. A hologram passing through and back as thought-image.

Both you and he co-exist within a simultaneity of time and space, yet are somehow independent of it; hologrammatic—part dream (the deeper unconscious), part vision (the illuminated, conscious mind). For one suspended moment in or out of time, you are fully aware of that presence from both ends of the continuum. In that sudden and revelatory moment you visualize each other, coexistent in each other's consciousness, fully cognizant of each other, which as quickly fades back down through the hall of mirrors, to take its place as reflection caught within ancient memory, endlessly. A transmission of existence, which T.S. Eliot similarly indicated in the oft quoted opening lines from Burnt Norton, the first of his Four Quartets, stating that 'Time present and time past/ Are both perhaps present in time future/ And time future contained in time past./ If all time is eternally present/ All time is unredeemable.' Though I argue here that *time is redeemable.*

In the epistemological dialogue, *Theaetetus*, where Plato assumes the persona of Socrates, he addresses the key question of memory and perception as knowledge, and uses the analogy of 'wax tablets' for the mind (or) soul. These tablets can either be hard or soft, large or small, but just as wax receives the imprint of a signet ring, for example, so too are our impressions, thoughts, perceptions imprinted upon the wax tablet of the mind; if the wax is too soft, memory fades sooner, and if hard, memory is extended. So that whatever cannot be imprinted on the wax tablet cannot be remembered. There is also the observation that perceptions and memory imprints may be transposed, and incorrect memory given to an unrelated perception. This may result in the emergence of myth. Generally speaking, Plato is examining the qualities and application of loss and preservation of knowledge, memory and perception. However that may be, I see the mind as metaphor and image as recall. I attempt to capture this sense of simultaneity as quickly as it fades in the closing section of my epic poem, *Intercolonial* (2013), which I quote here in part as we come full circle. The scene opens on the seat of Kings at Tara, and the high king, Cormac Mac Airt, in the second century AD, is sharpening his sword blade against a standing stone as he projects his thoughts into the future, and visualizes Thomas McCormack centuries hence, while McCormack, in his coexistent vision, at that very moment, sees his ancestor sharpening his blade against the standing stone, that rasping sound heard in the slowing screws of the *S.S. Ringaroma*, as the ship throws its engines into reverse, to berth at Port Chalmers, Dunedin back in 1877:

The Nith Stream fell away from Nemnack's sparkling well,
disappeared briefly into a narrow glen only to emerge and join the
Gabhra River on the broad plain below, stretching to the
horizon. In the rise and fall of air currents, he heard the creak

of waterwheel—the slow, reassuring rasp of millstones that
ground out wheatmeal, as his sword blade passed back and forth,
rhythmically along the stone's edge, a thin, shearing sound
over stream and rath, the sky shiny silver, mill-race, mill-pond—

the steady revolution of waterwheel—as his sword blade
sang against the stone for brightness, and McCormack stepping
on the gangplank of the *Ringarooma* to disembark at Port
Chalmers, glimpsed in his mind's eye the Irish monarch before

he set his heel firmly upon solid ground for the first time;
the hour lambent, the ship's screws slowed, the engine reversed.
Metal slid against metal, steady as that sword blade passing
across the edge of the standing stone on the Hill of Tara.

He dreams his foundry, warehouse, workshops, lathes,
the huge pulleys 20 feet in diameter lifting pig iron over cupola
holding two ton of melted metal; forges, emery wheels,
and the blast brazing furnaces, the steam and trip hammers ....

'I am the black North wind, and the speckled and dark winds;
I am the purple East wind, and the yellow and red winds of gentle
meetings; I am the white South wind, and the blue-grey,
and strong green winds; I am the pale West wind and the dark

brown and grey winds, wild and heavy; I am the winds
of the four cardinal points and the eight fettered winds. I am the
twelve coloured winds, a map to trace the sun's path.
All of them are braided and curbed, each fluid in harmony.

I am the lake that bursts forth upon the broad plain for light.
I am the buckler for strength and the bronze spear cast.
I am the right hand circuit-making High King, taker of hostages.'
Words sprung from the blade sang in his ears as he stepped.

Immrama (voluntary sea voyages) otherwise known as Irish Voyage Literature from the middle ages, relates the fantastical adventures and encounters of our hero and his company of men setting out in a coracle (old spelling, *curragh*—modern spelling, *currach*), into the western sea in search of the Blessed Isles, also known as the Land of Promise or the Happy Isles. All of these tales follow much the same narrative, a nautical journey for extended periods of time, and in some cases for years, into an imaginary world beyond the bounds of the western sea, where time is either suspended or ceases to exist. Herein lies the dream world of hope and expectation, essentially for a better life, and given the Christian gloss, a more fervently devout one, as much a desperation born out of poverty as anything else. Examples of these imaginary encounters from *The Voyage of Máel Dúin* (this tale, though incomplete, first appeared in the 'Book Of The Dun Cow', the oldest extant Irish manuscript, dating to around 1100) are: *The Island of the Monstrous Ants, The Island of Bloodthirsty Quadrupeds, The Isle of Red-Hot Animals, The Island of the Burning River, The Isle of Weeping, The Isle of the Four Precious Walls, The Isle of Speaking Birds*, and so on (see below).

This was very much the age of myth, whereby the line between what might be considered the world of reality and the world of the imagination was very finely drawn, and that line (vibrated like the base note of a cello) was often blurred, merged, or ceased to exist altogether. The passing of time did not consciously feature within the same defined chronological certitude with which we experience it today. Back then, vision through phantasmagoria, the Fata Morgana at the vanishing point, beyond the horizonal perspective of the ancient Irish, predominated. This viewpoint was enhanced by a primordial belief system within the collective consciousness that often as not went hand-in-hand with extreme, tribal violence; arguably, experienced as 'unreality' or transcendent states of mind. These two heightened expressions of a people's conflicting psyche, vision and violence, were intertwined and inextricable. Such fantastical voyages, real and imaginary, upon the western sea are contained in four extant tracts written down in the Middle Ages around a thousand years ago, though extrapolated from much earlier, oral accounts—not all of them complete. These accounts are as follows: *The Voyage of Bran Son of Febal* (the earliest, recorded in the 7th century), *The Voyage of the Húi Corra, The Voyage of Snedgus and Mac Riagla* (recorded between the 10th and 12th centuries), and *The Voyage of Máel Dúin*. To these might be added *The Voyage of Brendan* (*Navigatio Sancti Brendani Abbatis*), which also belongs to the *immrama* tradition, recorded around the 10th century. Though Brendan's voyage is wholly Christian, it yet retained much of the pagan, mythological ethos of the original well spring that belonged to the earlier *immrama*.

Nonetheless, and in most cases, there are both prose and verse renditions of the same journeys. One can still see through into the original pagan mindset, just as they perceived the colours in the winds of prophecy and, therefore, felt those reverberations of ancient memory at work, alive and refulgent—peering down into the Well of Forgetfulness. A closer look at *The Voyage of Máel Dúin* (perhaps the better known of the central four), translated by P.W. Joyce in his *On The Old Celtic Romances* (1879)[1] pages 112-176, and addressing a few of the delightful encounters contained therein, will take us into the transcendent world of the ancient, Old Irish story-tellers. These tales are very old indeed. P.W. Joyce states in his preface the following: 'This voyage would appear from internal evidence to have been made in the beginning of the eighth century (O'Cuny says about the year 700); for I think it likely that Maildun did actually go on a voyage, which was afterwards made the framework of the story. On my translation of this tale, Lord Tennyson founded his poem "The Voyage of Maeldune".'

Herewith, I quote from a few of the projected, envisioned

engagements or confrontations on the various islands encountered on Máel Dúin's voyage, when he first set forth in a large, triple-hide coracle (curragh) with his sixty chosen men (a voyage that would take 'of three years and seven months', we are told), to seek out the plunderers from a fleet who killed his father, Allil Ocar Aga, the chieftain of his tribe. That is the introductory storyteller's pretext for the magical encounters that would soon follow. The first encounter opens thus under the heading: Chap. 11. *The First Island. Tidings of the Plunderers.* 'They sailed a day and a night, as well as the whole of the next day, till darkness came on again; and at midnight they saw two small bare islands, with two great houses on them near the shore.' This was the den of the plunderers who had killed Máel Dúin's father. They did not make shore to enact vengeance, for ' … the wind arose, and a great tempest broke upon them. And they were driven violently before the storm, all that night and a part of the next day, into the great and boundless ocean; so that they saw neither the islands they had left nor any other land. And they knew not wither they were going.' And so our voyage begins. Curiously, these self-contained, individual island encounters, each under a separate chapter heading, read to me very much like antique prose poems. Individual chapters I have chosen are, respectively—*The Island of the Monstrous Ants*, *A Monster*, and, *The Silver Pillar of the Sea.*

Chap. III: *The Island of the Monstrous Ants*

'For three days and three nights they saw no land. On the morning of the fourth day, while it was yet dark, they heard a sound to the north-east; and Germane said—

"This is the voice of the waves breaking on the shore."

As soon as it was light they saw the land and made toward it. While they were casting lots to know who should go and explore the country, they saw great flocks of ants coming down to the beach, each of them as large as a foal. The people judged by their numbers, and by their eager and hungry look, that they were bent on eating both ship and crew; so they turned their vessel round and sailed quickly away.

> Their multitudes countless, prodigious their size;
> Were never such ants seen or heard of before.
> They struggled and tumbled and plunged for the prize,
> And fiercely the famine-fire blazed from their eyes,
> As they ground with their teeth red sand of the shore!'

Chap. V. *A Monster*

' … and on the fourth day discovered a large sandy island, on which, when they came near, they saw a huge, fearful animal standing on the beach and looking at them very attentively. He was somewhat like a horse in shape; but his legs were like the legs of a dog; and he had great sharp claws of a blue colour.

Maildun, having viewed this monster for some time, liked not his look; and telling his companions to watch him closely, for that he seemed bent on mischief, he bade the oarsman row very slowly toward land.

The monster seemed much delighted when the ship drew nigh the shore, and gambolled and pranced about with joy on the beach, before the eyes of the voyagers; for he intended to eat the whole of them the moment they landed.

"He seems not at all sorry to see us coming," said Maildun; "but we must avoid him and put back from shore."

This was done. And when the animal observed them drawing off, he ran down in a great rage to the very water's edge, and digging up large, round pebbles with his sharp claws, he began to fling them at the vessel; but the crew soon got beyond his reach, and sailed into the open sea.

A horrible monster with blazing eyes
In shape like a horse and tremendous in size
  Awaiting the curragh, they saw;
With big bony jaws
And murderous claws,
  That filled them with terror and awe:
How gleeful he dances,
And bellows and prances:
  As near to the island they draw;
Expecting a feast—
The bloodthirsty beast—
  With his teeth like edge of a saw:
Then he ran to the shore,
With a deafening roar,
  Intending to swallow them raw:
But the crew, with a shout,
Put their vessel about,
  And escaped from his ravenous maw!'

Chap. XXVI. *The Silver Pillar of the Sea*

'The next thing they found ... was an immense silver pillar standing in the sea. It had eight sides, each of which was the width of an oar-stroke of the curragh, so that its whole circumference was eight oar-strokes. It rose out of the sea without any land or earth about it, nothing but the boundless ocean; and they could not see its base deep down in the water, neither were they able to see the top on account of its vast height.

A silver net hung from the top down to the very water, extending far out at one side of the pillar; and the meshes were so large that the curragh in full sail went through one of them. When they were passing through it, Diuran struck the mesh with the edge of his spear, and with the blow cut a large piece of it.

"Do not destroy the net," said Maildun; "for what we see is the work of great men."

"What I have done," answered Diuran, "is for the honour of my God, and in order that the story of our adventures may be more readily believed; and I shall lay this silver as an offering on the altar of Armagh, if I ever reach Erin."

That piece of silver weighed two ounces and a half, as it was reckoned afterwards by the people of the church of Armagh.

After this they heard someone speaking on the top of the pillar, in a loud, clear, glad voice; but they knew neither what he said, nor in what language he spoke.'

In the closing chapter XXXV, *Maildun meets his enemy, and arrives Home*, Maildun and his crew heading back to Erin, sight the first island they had encountered on their departure many years before, that harboured his enemies and the murderer of his father; but they did not land in the first instance, and so avenge his father's murder, as they were subsequently blown out to sea by a tremendous storm, from which point their adventures began. Maildun and his crew, now recognizing the island, row to shore, and Maildun then approaches the great house of his enemies. There is no vengeance, however, as he hears at the door the head of the household say to his companions, 'Maildun has been for a long time suffering great afflictions and hardships; and if he were to come now, though we were enemies once, I should certainly give him a welcome and a kind reception'. Maildun then knocks and he and his men are received and feted. The chapter concludes thus, 'And after they had remained here for some days, Maildun returned to his own country. And Diuran Lekard took the five half ounces of silver he had cut down from the great net at the Silver Pillar, and laid it, according to his promise, on the high altar of Armagh.'

The following section is taken from *Intercolonial* (2013). My great-grandfather dreams aboard the *S.S. Ringarooma* crossing the Tasman Sea from Melbourne to Port Chalmers,

Dunedin. Within the tradition of *immrama*, and the chapters from *The Voyage of Maeldune* quoted above, the dreamscape that concludes this memoir, might be appropriately titled: *The Voyage of Thomas McCormack:*

McCormack, swung in the hammock of the sea, dreams:
'wave roar'; an elevated, floating platform on four
giant, yellow towers. In diameter, greater than boles of giant
eucalypt or columns of Egyptian temples—latticework

of steel armatures—high enough for a ship to pass
safely under. A thousand lights clustered the black, rectangular
fortress. To McCormack, it appeared an industrial city,
massive and metalled as a wetback stove rose fifty stories

above waves, a yellow dragon-flame plumed a gantry.
Cloud-hide pegged out at the corners horizoned—McCormack,
shipbound between the wind and tide (tossed by both)
in sleep that troubled deeply, across glacial moraine and rock

fall; to an Icelandic sunset—*holmgang* of cloud fastened in
hazelled lightning bolt. 'Blacksmiths forging iron, hurling molten
blocks onto the sea in the ship's wake,' he concluded.
Before him his forbear, *Kormac the Skald*, striding to contest;

yet his unforgiving lady, *Steingard*, proved his undoing—
though in every heroic deed he upheld honour hard tested by
dawn raids over the Atlantic crests to Alba and Ireland—
where he fell, locked in mortal combat, against a giant Scot.

His face the colour of dead moonlight—under dark hair,
eyes black as stones. 'He lived before letters *destroyed the Art
of Memory*,' says McCormack, 'songs faithful as sea-tides—
his broadsword cried in battle, blood-wand reddened for booty.'

The Viking longboat drifts away on the tide as though
departing one dream and passing into another, solid as shadow,
silhouette. The boat is companion to half-light and the
afterlife—men ghosting the shoreline, indeterminate shapes.

Still as statues they watch. One column of flame rises up to
the stars from the burning pyre, a flawed sunset across
northern latitudes. The sea black, velvet. Light reflects dully off
iron shields. One by one the men turn about and depart.

To the east, an island appeared, rotated in the wake of
the ship, at its centre, an iron compound with four watch towers;
behind barbed-wire fencing, a few bedraggled figures
hung in despair—all wore orange tunics and white skull caps,

all were chained at the wrists and feet, some gasped as
stranded fish, others (lips sewn shut) sat bowed, or kneeled.
At night, lanterns swung light beams into every corner;
shadowy jackals patrolled the *Island of the Asylum Seekers.*

In his ear all the while, continuous—the 'wave voice'
telling of blue storms, hinting at sea-clouds shadowing under
(pelagian depths) soundings of the original sea with the
Ringarooma plying lat. 25°/50° south, long. 145°/180° east.

Echo-sounding dream chambers bounce back and forth:
'Three things to guard against in sleep,' says McCormack,
'daring the mind leap off over the brink of an abyss,
kicking at imaginary ghosts, waking at the dead man's hour.'

He dreams: *Mundus Subterraneous:* from the earth's
molten core, caverns of fire and water, ocean and volcano,
through a network of underground channels feeding one
into another and circulating deep within the earth's interior.

He dreams a toxic dump widening in the pacific gyre,
a garbage patch the size of Abyssinia, bile ejected from the
gaping maw of some thrice-retching Charybdis, churned
bags and bottles, things broken small, opaque as nail clippings.

A place deprived of oxygen, an ocean desert devoid of
fish & fowl stretched far as eye could see, contagion shunned
by every sailor, for the dreck of the world accumulated here,
swept from the industrial wastelands of a brand new age.

A floating mass that seemed to reach out infinitely into
sea and sky, become indistinguishable, translucent as jellyfish,
an ocean heaving as 'marine lung' heavily lifted and slumped,
as McCormack in his ship's bunk rolled through the night.

He dreams a tornado, watery shaped, the ocean's navel,
obsidian black and sleek, funnelled, descending into the Pacific at
depth with an amplified roar like that of the ship's furnace;
the vessel itself twisting round and round the froth-white collar.

A diorama of distorted, ghostly figures within his cabin
flitted on wall and ceiling, cast shadow-nets over McCormack's
dreamscape, to capture past worlds or those yet to come,
while the bedside lamp glowed luminescent as the lanternfish.

[1] *On The Old Celtic Romances*, translated from the Gaelic by P.W. Joyce, Dublin, The Educational Co. of Ireland Limited, 80 Talbot Street/ London, Longmans Green, And Company, 39 Paternoster Row, 1879.

www.ingramcontent.com/pod-product-compliance
Lightning Source LLC
Chambersburg PA
CBHW070054120726
47909CB00002B/387